D0443116

Handbook for the College Admissions Profession

Recent Titles in
The Greenwood Educators' Reference Collection

HANDBOOK FOR THE COLLEGE ADMISSIONS PROFESSION

Claire C. Swann
Senior Editor

Stanley E. Henderson
Editor

Published in Association with the
American Association of Collegiate Registrars
and Admissions Officers, Washington, D.C.

The Greenwood Educators' Reference Collection

GREENWOOD PRESS
Westport, Connecticut • London

Library of Congress Cataloging-in-Publication Data

Handbook for the college admissions profession / Claire C. Swann,
   senior editor ; Stanley E. Henderson, editor.
       p. cm.—(The Greenwood educators' reference collection,
   ISSN 1056-2192)
    "Published in association with the American Association of
   Collegiate Registrars and Admissions Officers, Washington, D.C."
    Includes bibliographical references and index.
    ISBN 0-313-29113-6 (alk. paper)
    1. College admission officers—United States—Handbooks, manuals,
   etc. 2. Universities and colleges—United States—Admission—
   Handbooks, manuals, etc. I. Swann, Claire. II. Henderson,
   Stanley E. III. American Association of Collegiate Registrars and
   Admissions Officers. IV. Series.
   LB2351.6.H36   1998
   378.1'61—dc21   97-14468

British Library Cataloguing in Publication Data is available.

Copyright © 1998 by The American Association of Collegiate Registrars and
Admissions Officers

All rights reserved. No portion of this book may be
reproduced, by any process or technique, without the
express written consent of the publisher.

Library of Congress Catalog Card Number: 97-14468
ISBN: 0-313-29113-6
ISSN: 1056-2192

First published in 1998

Greenwood Press, 88 Post Road West, Westport, CT 06881
An imprint of Greenwood Publishing Group, Inc.

Printed in the United States of America

The paper used in this book complies with the
Permanent Paper Standard issued by the National
Information Standards Organization (Z39.48-1984).

10 9 8 7 6 5 4 3 2 1

Contents

Tables and Figures

Preface

The *Handbook for the College Admissions Profession* is written for the consumption of new admissions officers, new enrollment managers, new college presidents, and new boards of advisement, counsel, and trustees, as well as for students and professors of higher education. The handbook can also be valuable for experienced professionals in this young field of college admissions and enrollment planning and management.

This new "hand-text" book is laid out in six parts with stand-alone chapters designed to give the reader the full flavor of the professionals' experiences in higher education. Each author has been given license to make judgments about the everyday trials and tribulations, pleasures, and rewards of this unique business. Appendices, tables and figures, a comprehensive glossary, and a bibliography have been included to make this reference a helpful tool in the strategic planning process.

The authors and editors dedicate this book to the many prospective students, administrators, and other friends who may derive help and satisfaction from learning more about the admissions field. The book is also dedicated to all other admissions professionals, who have contributed so much in energy and talent in the efforts to making a difference.

Introduction

Part I: Perspectives and History. Understanding the admissions profession requires an understanding of the pressures and changes in modern higher education. As the eyes and ears of the institution, admissions officers take the pulse of society and interact not only with students, but also with parents, high school and community college personnel, the media, the political world, alumni, donors, and the general public. Knowing the issues in society provides the necessary lens through which admissions officers can filter the information they collect as the institutions' primary representatives to the world outside the ivy-covered halls on campus.

The chapter on current educational reform positions admissions officers appropriately as professionals with contributions to make both to solve educational issues and to affect the educational environment. Anyone in admissions can benefit from an understanding of this dual role. The perspective on admissions chapter lays a framework for both advisors and presidents to follow in developing the reasoned and reasonable working relationship that will let admissions officers do their work without undue interference while they meet institutional goals. The historical review gives an admissions perspective to the development of American higher education. For 350 years, institutions have been grappling with issues of student numbers and student quality—the very issues that bedevil admissions offices today. Part I, thus, sets the stage for the admissions profession.

Part II: The Admissions Officer. Part II describes the role, functions, and opportunities of the admissions professional. Traced here is the evolution of the admissions officer's role in an organization that formerly belonged to the nation's registrars. Chronicled also are the changes and added functions of the admissions officer as the institution changed along with enrollment explosions and declines. Structural placement of the admissions office, as well as the educational preparation and competencies required for both the beginner and the experienced admissions worker who aspires to an advanced level on the team, are included in this part.

Opportunities for professional development through membership in national organizations are described by an executive director of one such group. A noted high school counselor partners with a college dean of admissions to depict the sensitivities to and for students that constitute a part of the ethical fabric of all professionals who serve students.

Part III: Understanding Enrollment Management. Perhaps no other administrative development in the last 25 years has had as much impact on the admissions profession as has the rise of strategic enrollment management. The concept of a cradle-to-grave approach to enrollment has taken admissions out of the isolation of a front-loading office and made it a key anchor in the strategic-planning process. Gone are the days when admissions would "recruit 'em and leave 'em on the doorstep." Now registration processes and retention activities, academic support, and academic advising are as important to admissions as admissions has always been to those areas.

Part IV: Admissions Tools. The inclusion of admissions in enrollment management provides a structure that requires additional strategic thinking and planning. This strategic approach takes admissions away from the days of "roadrunners" who handed out catalogues to an environment with increasingly sophisticated tools. As modern technology has developed in the closing decades of the twentieth century, the tools of the trade have enabled professionals to work alone or to form or join expert collaboratives to offer—oftentimes at high prices—efficient service tools. Readers will find research instruments that afford credibility and evaluation for the institution's design, mapping strategies for developing the institution's marketing and recruiting strategies, computing plans, and information on current policies and procedures.

Part V: Admissions Programs. The inclusion of admissions in the enrollment management context has brought a more strategic approach to planning. The broader issues of multiculturalism and globalization in society are more easily understood and reflected in admissions work because admissions in the enrollment management context is part of a seamless web. Understanding and building bridges to other offices and constituencies on and off campus are essential for tomorrow's successes.

Multiculturalism is one of today's operative words, and program specifics are reflected here, as are programming techniques for the global diversities of the world's campuses. Also found here are descriptions of modern technologies that allow for the programming of new telephone- and VCR-based recruiting techniques to bring about needed change.

Part VI: Perspectives on the Twenty-First Century. Just as the context in which the admission officer works is essential to understanding the profession, a view to the future is necessary to provide a roadmap for professional development. The students of the twenty-first century will be so diverse in terms of ethnicity, age, and background that the nation's educational systems will have to develop new delivery and evaluative systems to ensure access. That, in turn, will demand that admissions officers respond with innovation and adaptation. Tolerance of ambiguity and flexibility in developing programs and services are essential traits of admissions officers in the next century. A projected view of new students and new ways of meeting their needs provides a springboard for admissions professionals preparing themselves and their institutions for the future.

Part I

Perspectives and History

Part I sets the stage, giving the general historic background and setting for admissions work. Responsible admissions professionals need to know the issues and how admissions—perhaps more than any other student services area—has to know what happens on campus.

1

Perspectives on Educational Reform

Donald Stewart

As the primary linking mechanism between the K–12 and higher education sectors, the college admissions process plays a central role in American education. This important bridging role has also given those involved with this process an almost unmatched, broad perspective on the partnership that makes up American education. Firmly planted in both the K–12 and higher education sectors, where they work to connect academic standards and assessment and placement and maintain ongoing relationships with many parts of the educational enterprise (students, student families, financial aid officers, teachers, academics, and guidance counselors), these admissions officers are called upon to serve in many roles as they help shape and implement the "great sorting process" of directing students to institutions of higher education.

This important role and wide perspective carry with them great responsibility and challenges, to which the profession has traditionally responded with effective action. However, the greatest test may lie ahead. In the last decade of the twentieth century, severe social and economic problems have pressured our system of education and its many component parts to change in fundamental ways. It is no exaggeration to say that over the next several years, educators may witness radical changes in what they do, how they do it, and who decides how they do it. How the reform process is handled and how end results are sought will continue to be hotly contested issues. As these debates rage within government, education, business, and other publics, those with expertise in the process of transitioning from high school to college bring unique and important perspectives that have much to add to the final outcome.

Yet the issues of change are complex and, therefore, raise the questions, "How do we join the reform movement?" and "Who is our foe?" Those with primary responsibility for the transition from high school to college cannot separate themselves from the larger process of examination and the larger issues facing education. What happens in admissions depends on the whole educational enterprise. Therefore, as the vision of a strong and vibrant admissions process develops, educators need to start with, and be involved in, the creation of a strong and vibrant future for all parts of our schools and institutions of higher education. Given our needs and our potential contribution, educators must do no less.

The development of a comprehensive, coherent, and representative vision for all of education—and workable visions in a multicultural democracy must have these qualities—means that those in the admissions area need to think through responses to fundamental and complicated social and public policy matters. Three related questions not only are crucial to the future but also combine to create a foundation for comprehensive educational reform.

- How do we achieve quality and equality? Our system of education needs to ensure that all students are given an equal and effective opportunity to achieve high academic standards. We need to face the fundamental question of how to achieve a system of this kind. What kinds and shapes of academic standards, assessment, curriculum, teacher training, educational institutions, and linkages are needed?

- Who decides on strategies and goals and defines success? While a decentralized system of education exists at both the K–12 and higher education levels, the process has many shareholders (educators, parents, business, government, etc.). As educators determine where to go, how to get there, and whether they have arrived, many voices are being raised. What are the roles of each of these voices, and how can they be brought together to create consensus?

- Who pays? At both the K–12 and higher education levels, educators must ensure that what they seek can be either continued or else created and then maintained. This raises real and sensitive issues of costs. Who pays, how much, and when? How do we develop systems of payment that will allow us to have what we want and need?

Developing responses to these questions will not be simple. Differences in philosophy must be reconciled, nettlesome matters of implementation resolved, and natural tensions comfortably settled. However, educators traditionally have resolved complex problems by steadfastly relying on the guiding principle that successful solutions take into account the many differing needs and perspectives of our diverse educational community. Through consensus building and partnerships we have met the challenges in the past, and through consensus building and partnerships we will be able to overcome present and future challenges. But educators must take the lead in this process to bring together the involved parties and strengthen structures through which problems can be defined, solutions devised, and mechanisms developed to implement and measure solutions. If we do not take the initiative in this process, others will impose solutions that will not preserve what high schools value and institutions of higher education want and need.

By building new partnerships and reinvigorating old ones, admissions professionals have a central role to play in education reform. Through professional membership organizations, such as The College Board, admissions officers have developed consensus on issues such as assessment, standards, curriculum, and the allocation of financial aid. But they now need to expand these traditional partnerships to include other educators. Using the admissions process as a starting point, academics in college and high school need to be brought more closely together to talk about standards and how they can be measured. The various parts of the system of higher education need to understand and appreciate each other's purpose and function. Admissions and financial aid officers need to communicate more effectively to develop coordinated and inclusive entrance strategies.

Those who manage and belong to membership organizations know it is time to create the forums necessary to encourage dialogue that will lead to action. The College Board has worked hard over the last several years to create a place where traditional members can be better heard, can be brought into contact with others in the education system, and can create a continuum to move from ideas to action.

It is now time for those most concerned at both the secondary and higher education levels to come together and begin to shape the form and substance of that [student preparation] process for the decades ahead. If we are unresponsive to these [changing] circumstances, who will respond and what will their responses be? (Stewart, *College Admissions Policies in the 1990s: A Look Toward the Future*, 1992)

Since the publication of that document, the issues of student preparation have increased in importance and are receiving more attention. Participants in the admissions process have a responsibility to enter the debate—and an opportunity to lead it. We need to grab this chance and shape, not only the future of admissions, but also the future of education.

REFERENCE

Stewart, Donald M. 1992. *College admissions policies in the 1990s: A look toward the future*. New York: The College Board.

2

Perspectives on Admissions

John Casteen

Admissions officers sometimes complain that their presidents do not know what they do, while presidents learn quickly enough that most people assume admissions officers do not know what presidents' duties entail. The complaints are at least partly true. But they miss the point that there is a wealth of similarity between the two jobs and a natural link between them. The pressures of this era of restructuring have made the jobs even more interdependent than they may have been in gentler times.

Most presidents have little reason to know more than a smattering about the daily management of admissions or financial aid, academic advising, and any number of other activities that contribute to the college or university's success or failure. Presidents trust the professionals who preside over these functions to let them know what matters without drawing them into the daily machinations of departments in which regular presidential involvement would surely interfere with effectiveness. Infrequent presidential involvement is not a bad thing. Sound colleges and universities generally conduct their business through collegial interactions, not through orders passed down a chain of command. Leaders in universities talk and listen to one another a good bit. If presidents are smart, they seek out people with perspectives unlike their own and frankly listen to experts, including admissions officers, on matters that lie outside their immediate areas of concern. Presidents try to define policies to move the institution toward goals that emerge from this process of constant conferral, but they rely on persons who know each unit of the university to tell them what matters, what contributes, and what detracts. Most of them follow the rule that if a thing is not broken, it does not need fixing.

Within their colleges and universities, presidents function through partnerships with provosts, vice presidents of sundry kinds, deans, directors, faculty leaders, and others. To succeed, presidents rely heavily on these officials, both to know their own functions and to communicate to the president what needs to be known in a manner that is accurate, fair, concise, and timely. Presidents expect others to make management decisions in their areas of responsibility and to confer when appropriate. And presidents work outside their universities in collaboration with other presidents, key alumni, professional staffers, and others. The effective president is not the Lone Ranger.

Perhaps, once upon a time, admissions work consisted largely of publishing applications and catalogues, visiting high schools in the fall, and then choosing the best and the brightest students. However, presidents who assume that this is still the nature of admissions work are in serious trouble. The admissions staff will be found wherever the president works, both inside and outside the university. Every good admissions officer comes into the president's field of vision because she or he engages in an endless dialogue with external constituencies— secondary school personnel, students, families, legislators, interested alumni, and others—on subjects that are fundamental to the president's job. Each of the constituencies influences the president's chance of succeeding. None is quite so accessible to the president as the admissions officer, especially if the university is sufficiently old, good, or well established as to be of interest and concern to those away from its campus.

Changes in the last 15 years or so make interdependence an essential element of the relationship today. Many educators began their careers in an era when everyone believed that colleges and universities faced endless growth. Since 1978, when the number of high school graduates fell in many states, enrollments in virtually all colleges have leveled off; indeed, they have declined. Marketing has become essential to many colleges' survival, and admissions officers have had to become experts in marketing. This change has drawn admissions officers into institutional activities other than conventional admissions work. Presidents look nowadays to admissions officers for advice on new academic programs, on athletics, on the design and operation of dormitories, on fund-raising, and on many other matters because these professionals know the prospective student market so well. In each instance, the president expects the admissions officer to know the communities that send the students, to help predict students' preferences, and to work as part of the team that designs the college or university of the next year or the next decade. Working with the institutional researchers, the admissions officers are demographers. Working with the deans of students and housing officers, they are sociologists and communitarians. And working with the academic dean and, perhaps, the head of the faculty senate, in the best of times they become the visionary, and in the worst of times, the cutter and trimmer of programs that have lost their appeal to students.

Since the recession that began the 1990s, admissions officers have participated in another kind of institutional adjustment as colleges and universities have adopted the language—and, on a very limited scale, the methods—of the corporate restructurers. Essentially, the concept is that colleges and universities must generate more with less—that is, more enrollees, graduates, and public service with less money and fewer buildings and employees. However, the analogy between corporate restructuring and collegiate restructuring is tentative at best. Corporations restructure when they cannot sell a sufficient quantity of their products to earn acceptable profits. Colleges, too, sometimes cut costs for this reason, but they have always done so. This kind of cost cutting is old hat in an activity in which sources of revenue and students have been as thinly stretched as they were in American colleges during the Great Depression and again during the 1980s. The restructuring of colleges in this era is often a matter of governmental mandate. Seeking dollars to spend on prisons or Medicaid and feeling the pressure of revenue shortfalls, legislators have cut appropriations without direct regard for enrollments and have told colleges to restructure (i.e., to cut staff) in order to operate within their budgets.

The admissions officer's role in restructuring amounts to an intensification of her or his role in planning for enrollment declines, but with the difference that the goal is to enroll essentially constant numbers of students while shifting them from one program (intended to be reduced or dropped) to another (intended to be built up). The marketing job is thus really two jobs: first, sell the college; then, sell the major or program. In the first instance, the admissions officer leads. In the second, the dean or academic advisor leads, while the admissions officer helps by preparing students for the message that comes later.

The 1992 amendments to the federal Higher Education Act have further complicated the admissions officer's role in at least two essential regards. First, the change to federal direct lending forces colleges and universities to advertise their offerings differently. Rather like an automobile dealer selling Ford Credit leases right on the showroom floor, admissions officers are beginning to be more than objective describers of financial services. In the future, they will have to be sellers of the financial plan as well.

Second, higher education's relationship with both federal and state governments was changed in the 1992 Amendments: government regulates what it previously coordinated or, in some instances, governed. The SPRE (State Postsecondary Education Review Entities) regulations on eligibility for the federal Title IV monies that support most student financial aid included provisions for data gathering, reporting, and disclosure that exceed anything previously seen in this country. Admissions officers were not alone in their opposition to the SPREs, especially because of the SPREs' potential effects on monetary allocations. Deans, institutional researchers, and others were involved as well. But admissions officers were key because the regulations called for considerable institutional liability should graduation rates and other measures not reach acceptable levels. The consequence was a new urgency to admit not only the right number of students, but also the right students—those who can succeed. All this preparedness has been exacerbated by the 104th Congress, which eliminated the SPRE provision in its 1995 budget resolution.

Conducting research that validates admissions decisions, analyzes the successes achieved by matriculants over the long haul, and documents the truthfulness of claims made for the college has become a central, inescapable institutional obligation. In each instance, the president depends on the admissions officer to carry out new duties in such a way as to protect the college and its students from new liabilities. Finally, presidents rely on admissions officers to assemble from various schools, families, and other places the persons who fill their collegiate communities. Students enroll individually. Admissions professionals meet them individually on campus or in class. Students progress individually through their studies and eventually move along to their individual destinies. At the outset, the admissions officer hears and understands their personal goals or ambitions, helps them choose, and provides the access that makes the system work. A good admissions officer spends a lot of time helping students figure out what they can do.

By way of this personal work with students, admissions officers shape our collegiate communities. In this generation, they are asked to assemble student bodies that approximate in their human qualities the largest society from which they come. Older students, minority students, women enrolled in programs that formerly were restricted to men, and many other nontraditional students attest to admissions officers' successes in redefining academic communities. The colleges and universities' motives have been many: to maintain enrollments in times when traditional students are in short supply; to comply with legal or moral mandates; to open up the ivory tower. Each motive helps define the emerging centrality of admissions officers in the core leadership of healthy institutions.

Perhaps, in the end, this is the point: presidents and admissions officers share obligations that involve futures—students' futures, their institutions' futures, and society's future. Both are accountable for the performance of these obligations; and today the accountability has grown more precise and visible than it has ever been before. Both have opportunities to enable or empower people, especially students. The scope of responsibility or opportunity of the president and the admissions director differ in obvious ways. Their common purpose cannot differ if the goal is to free women and men of the costs of ignorance and exclusion. Each needs the other.

3

A Historical View of an Admissions Dilemma: Seeking Quantity or Quality in the Student Body

Stanley E. Henderson

The decade of the 1990s has given new visibility and accountability to the admissions officer in most institutions. Charged with the responsibility for filling the class—for keeping together an institution's financial body and soul—the admissions office is a lightning rod for institutional emotions. Lionized when enrollments hit the target, admissions directors may find themselves the goat when the numbers fail to materialize as projected. Donald Stewart, president of the College Board, suggests that:

the pressure put upon admissions personnel to meet enrollment goals often puts them in a position of working against the best interests of the college. The situation has been likened to that of a football or basketball coach who is supposed to produce a winning team, regardless. (Stewart 1992)

Without a winning record every year, the admissions "coaches" may find themselves out of a job as quickly as their gridiron counterparts.

Stewart's suggestion that the desire for enrollments might work against the best interests of an institution introduces another pressure point for the admissions officer in today's higher education: quality. The pressure to produce—or else—does not just concern student numbers. There is also a push to make college and university classes beat their competition in terms of average Scholastic Aptitude Test (SAT) and American College Testing (ACT) scores, rank in class, and average grade point average (GPA) of their entering classes. This emphasis on quality seems many times to be coequal with the drive for numbers. The admissions director whose class does not meet the quality standards of a competitive president or a demanding faculty can also be in trouble. Institutions tampering with class profiles to enhance their rankings in the guidebooks have caused a minor cause célèbre in the press.

Alice Rivlin aptly described the dual tension of quantity and quality when she wrote about access and standards in health care: "We worry about access for a while, and then we discover that the system to which we have given people access leaves a great deal to be desired . . . and then we go on a quality kick" (College Entrance Examination Board 1987). This is, indeed, the history of the admissions profession in America.

In fact, from an admissions perspective, higher education has always been involved in a debate about the quantity and quality of students. The (often uncoordinated) rise and fall of numbers and standards have marked college admissions from the very earliest days of higher education in this country. The challenge of maintaining a class size large enough to safeguard financial solvency while maintaining a class profile high enough to be able to comprehend the faculty's instruction has preoccupied colleges and universities since long before actual offices of admissions appeared. Enrollments cycled through feast and famine, and standards followed the same roller coaster ride. As colleges faced the uncertainties of their times, they became imminently resourceful in turning aside adversity. "At the beginning, higher education in America would be governed less by accident than by certain purpose, less by impulse than by design" (Rudolph 1962). Enrollment management was a practical necessity before it became a theoretical basis for organizing recruitment and retention.

EARLY DAYS: A PARITY OF QUANTITY AND QUALITY

In the earliest days of higher education in America, the quantity and quality of students coexisted in a happy degree of harmony. The colonial colleges were a natural outgrowth of settling in the New World. A seventeenth-century chronicler of New England wrote that after shelter, a place of worship, and a governance structure, "one of the next things we longed for, and looked after, was to advance Learning and perpetuate it to Posterity" (Rudolph 1962). "And then," Rudolph writes, "it would seem, almost as a matter of course, there was Harvard" (Rudolph 1962). The colonial colleges had a ready-made student population. Designed with the dual purpose of providing for an educated clergy and an educated body politic from which public servants could be drawn, the colleges were immediately attractive because they helped to civilize the frontier. "Of course a religious commonwealth required an educated clergy, but it also needed leaders disciplined by knowledge and learning, it needed followers disciplined by leaders, it needed order" (Rudolph 1962). A contemporary account of the public support Harvard enjoyed comes from Lucy Downing writing to her brother, the Puritan luminary John Winthrop, "I beleev a college would put noe small life into the plantation" (Rudolph 1962).

However, the stasis of quantity and quality that came from the perceived need for an educated citizenry and the initially unanimous certainty that the standard of a classical education was the vehicle to provide that education could not last in the unique environment that developed in America. In spite of the initial welcome and support for the colonial colleges, the frontier spirit that was also developing as an American trademark worked against higher education. Particularly, as the American frontier became another source of education—a practical, individualistic curriculum that taught one to make his own way by talent and deed—colleges came to be seen by such observers as the young Benjamin Franklin as places where rich men sent their sons ''to learn little more than to carry themselves handsomely, and enter a Room genteely'' (Rudolph 1962).

The early colleges' curricular standards did not appeal to colonists with a practical bent. These adventurous early frontiersmen were intent on collecting the material rewards so abundantly available in the raw colonies. Yet Latin and Greek—not very helpful in taming the frontier—were the gateways to a quality college education. ''So fundamental were these two languages and two literatures that until 1745—one hundred and eleven years after the founding of Harvard—they were the only subjects in which applicants for admission to a colonial college were expected to fulfill entrance requirements'' (Rudolph 1962). While these requirements fit the original classical view of what the literate population should have, they did not fit the popular opinion of the faster-growing frontier population. A market was untapped, but the colleges would rise to the occasion.

The changing demographics of the colonial and early national populations and declining popularity of the colonial colleges prompted the first changes in admissions requirements. In 1745 Yale made arithmetic an entrance requirement (Rudolph 1962), but not until William and Mary added French as a requirement, in 1793 (Rudolph 1962), did modern languages enter the college preparatory curriculum. By 1826 James Marsh at the University of Vermont was proposing that students who did not intend to take a classical degree—perhaps the children of the frontier spirit had a more practical bent?—should be admitted without demonstrating preparation in Latin and Greek. The march to the broadening of admissions standards to fill college classrooms was on.

THE EARLY NINETEENTH CENTURY: QUALITY IN RETREAT

The competitive and entrepreneurial spirit of the American public profoundly influenced the enrollments and standards of American higher education in the early nineteenth century. On the one hand, there was a tension between the democratically inclined general public and the more aristocratic higher education community, as reflected by John H. Lathrop of Missouri, writing in 1841, ''The taste for a regular course of University instruction is in a good measure to be generated'' (Rudolph 1962). On the other hand, the competitive spirit could also spur college building, as a delegate to the California constitutional convention, arguing for a state university in 1849, asked: ''Why should we send our sons

to Europe to finish their education?'' (Rudolph 1962). The increasing size of
the new nation, a home missionary movement that sought to ensure the presence
of Christianity in the wilderness, and a natural tendency to recreate on the frontier what was familiar from the frontiersmen's East Coast roots all added to the
growth of colleges in the United States in the first half of the nineteenth century.
The American colonies had nine colleges as they entered the Revolutionary War;
250 were in place at the start of the Civil War. However, untold more had
started and faded. Rudolph estimates that as many as 700 colleges had tried and
failed before the Civil War (Rudolph 1962).

A major portion of the collegiate growth came from the support of religious
denominations. Congregationalists, Lutherans, German and Dutch Reformed,
Presbyterians, and, later, Baptists, Methodists, and Catholics all turned to the
founding of colleges wherever their flocks moved in the westward migration.
The drive for denominational colleges seemed tied to something of a ''me-too''
syndrome—everybody else was doing it—and only the one true denomination
(whether it be Congregationalists, Presbyterians, or Methodists) could do the
job of educating its brethren. This was particularly significant in bringing the
Methodists to the college-building tradition, as this 1832 report shows:

When we examine the state of the literary institutions of our country, we find a majority
of them are in the hands of other denominations, so that our people are unwilling (and
we think properly so) to send their sons to those institutions. Therefore we think it very
desirable to have an institution under our own control from which we can exclude all
doctrines we deem dangerous; though at the same time we do not wish to make it so
sectarian as to exclude or in the smallest degree repel the sons of our fellow citizens
from the same. (Rudolph 1962)

These sentiments were, in Rudolph's words, ''pregnant with colleges'' (Rudolph 1962). This philosophy also shows a sensibility to the need to plan for
enough students to ensure the colleges' survival. The denominational college
growth did not involve only jingoistic sectarianism. The Methodist report of
1832 laid out a ready-made, ''pure'' applicant pool—the sons of Methodists all
over the country, who would look for a good Methodist college to attend. However, the report also suggested an insurance policy for healthy enrollments: the
expectation that the new colleges would not be so exclusively sectarian that
other denominations could not be attracted. This balancing act also was pregnant
with possibilities related to standards and quality.

Obviously, the supporting denomination would, in part, determine quality by
excluding the ''dangerous doctrines,'' but standards would also be influenced
by other than denominational factors. The Methodists were one of the last denominations to enter the college-building game. Rudolph posits that it was in
response to their increasingly middle-class status. Their successes in commerce,
industry, and agriculture led them, in part, to look for the trappings of success
owned by those in the professions. Starting a Methodist college could give them
status and also allow them to control what was taught there (Rudolph 1962).

The Methodists, Baptists, and other denominations were decidedly skeptical of the intellectualism of existing colleges. There was something faintly, or even overtly, heretical in the approach of the leading institutions. The president of Williams College suggested that his students remember the people of Boston in their chapel prayers because of the influence of godless Harvard over them (Rudolph 1962). This bad influence must be guarded against by ensuring a pure curriculum. Part of this purity came from doctrine, but part of it was purely anti-intellectual.

Some of the most aggressive college builders, including the Methodists and the Baptists, embodied the pioneer spirit in their denominations. The pious self-made man was far more impressive than just an educated man. If the plan laid out in the Methodist report of 1832 was to be realized, the colleges it would incubate could not take learning very seriously (Rudolph 1962). In 1837, Philip Lindsley, president of the University of Nashville, was writing, "Massachusetts is perhaps the only State which continues to bestow spontaneous honours and unsought offices upon superior talent, learning, and integrity" (Rudolph 1962). In Lindsley's eyes, the rough-and-tumble world of Tennessee was the real world, and his institution could not prosper if it continued to define quality and standards as the classicists at Harvard did. It was inevitable then that the colleges spawned in the early half of the nineteenth century would "adopt either some shield of protective coloration or some sincere indifference to learning" (Rudolph 1962).

The national ambivalence toward higher education was not overcome by the denominational plans to care for their own flocks and to extend themselves to those of others. Too often the denominations fell to bickering over who was the purest doctrinally, and the enrollments too often failed to materialize. What was more successful was curricular change. In the 1820s, institutions such as Vermont and Union were developing a parallel course of study to compete with the classical education of Greek and Latin that had dominated American higher education for its first 200 years. More modern courses in languages, science, and political economy were included, courses considered to be more in keeping with what the public wanted. Ample evidence existed that this was a surer road to success in enrollment than the path of denominationalism. In 1829 merely 20 years after its adoption of the parallel course of study, Union ranked number three in size among American colleges, and 10 years later, only Yale enrolled more students. Union's "success in attracting students, a success which most American colleges were being denied, must have contributed to the gradual adoption of the parallel course idea elsewhere" (Rudolph 1962). Elsewhere, the pressure to abandon the classical curriculum was growing, leading Miami University of Ohio to develop a certificate program, which their literature promised would make education "the common property of the mass of the human family" (Rudolph 1962).

The early part of the nineteenth century clearly showed that those institutions that listened to the public could develop programs that would attract students. The theory of "Build it and they will come" was not a recipe for success.

However, the resulting incorporation of a broader range of students and the perceived anti-intellectualism in the curriculum was not greeted with unanimous support. The man who was set to become president of the University of Michigan in 1850 lamented, "We have cheapened education so as to place it within the reach of everyone" (Rudolph 1962). Some 50 years later, enrollment and curricular changes would be so complete that the remaining classicists would accuse the reformers of visiting the "greatest educational crime of the century against American youth—depriving him of his classical heritage" (Rudolph 1962). In the ongoing battle between quantity and quality, the classicists, at least, would argue that quantity had routed quality.

THE ELECTIVE PRINCIPLE AND THE PEOPLE'S COLLEGES: QUANTITY VICTORIOUS

"During most of the 19th Century," Joshua Fishman wrote,

American colleges needed neither a philosophy of admission nor a procedure of selection. . . . Colleges did not complain that they could never be quite sure just what it was that applicants had studied in secondary schools nor just what their grades implied with respect to level of proficiency. (Fishman 1958)

In Fishman's view, this "low order of intensity" regarding problems of admission and selection was the result of the relative homogeneity of students in preparatory schools and colleges. As long as the students of the aristocracy continued to study the classical curriculum both in preparatory school and in college, standards were controlled in the hunt for numbers. The survival of the fittest meant finding the right students, not just any students. However, by the second half of the nineteenth century, the broadening of the curriculum, which had begun as a trickle in response to a changing student pool, would become a sea of change in American higher education. With it came different students, then a variety of standards, and then the standardization of standards.

The land grant colleges and state universities that rose in the latter half of the nineteenth century faced enrollment pressures like those faced by the denominational colleges but for different reasons. The Morrill Act of 1862 set up a new branch of American higher education, one imbued with the notion of a collegiate education for everyone at public expense (Rudolph 1962). However, the target markets for the new practical schools—the sons and daughters of farmers and merchants who would study agriculture and industry—were not particularly interested in such study (Brubacher and Rudy 1976). The new colleges designed for the entrepreneurs of the Victorian Age (the new embodiment of the colonial frontier spirit) found their target markets uninterested or outright hostile, just as the frontiersmen of the colonial days had been. To convince the people to enroll at the people's colleges, these pioneer educational institutions tried inducements that would accelerate the lowering of standards.

Shortly after its founding, the University of Arkansas offered a $25 scholarship to the agriculture student who made the best five pounds of butter. However, Ohio State found easier and cheaper ways to enhance its enrollment yield, adding 20 students in 1877 by dropping algebra from its entrance requirements. By 1885 the Arkansas legislature, at least, had seen the light and ordered the university to abandon the scholarship inducement and lower admission standards. In 1888 applicants to South Dakota State College had to show only one year of schooling beyond the eighth grade to gain entrance. Not until 1914 would Connecticut Agricultural College require high school graduation as an admissions requirement (Rudolph 1962).

Veysey (1965) suggests that the development of the Western universities in the United States flowed from the balance of three significant themes: academic excellence, broad accessibility, and social distinction (Veysey 1965). There is some evidence that this balancing act between the quantity and quality of students even extended to some of the nineteenth-century universities that had evolved from the original colonial colleges. A Columbia University spokesperson, near the end of the century, wrote, "Numbers do not mean everything, but if they are not swelled by the maintenance of low standards, they mean much" (Rudolph 1962). And Harvard's Charles William Eliot opined that "quality being secured, the larger the quantity the better." However, Eliot gave, perhaps, a more insightful clue to the importance of numbers when he said, "I find I am not content unless Harvard grows each year." The University of Nebraska's chancellor, James H. Canfield, was far more blatant in his quest for numbers: "My entire political creed, my entire political activity, can be summed up in a single sentence: a thousand students in the State University in 1895; 2,000 in 1900" (Rudolph 1962).

John Bascom, president of the University of Wisconsin, attempted to cast the numbers game in the garb of access when he wrote:

Our state universities must spring out of the soil, the roots in the earth commensurate with the branches in the air. When one and another section, one and another class, feel that they have no part in the university, the university itself will suffer as a reservoir of knowledge. When the fibers of growth begin to withdraw themselves from the world in which they are planted, the yellow leaf will soon follow. (Rudolph 1962)

However, Andrew S. Draper of the University of Illinois seemed more pragmatic in addressing the access issue, not in altruistic terms, but in the pragmatic language of survival: "The universities that would thrive must put away all exclusiveness and dedicate themselves to universal public service. They must not try to keep people out; they must help all who are worthy to get in" (Rudolph 1962).

A new breed of academic leadership was influencing the path of admissions in the latter half of the nineteenth century. Highly competitive, these new presidents were also exceptionally sensitive to public sentiment. "Wedded to their institutions, academic executives did whatever they believed necessary to assure a favorable posture for their establishments; . . . [this] competitive urge may well have underlain the thinking of those who pondered enrollment figures in the late 60s and 70s'' (Rudolph 1962).

The competitive drive for public support, as expressed in enrollments, led to the earliest recruitment tactics. Johns Hopkins ''came into existence unasked for and uncared for; and so must first create a demand and then supply it'' (Rudolph 1962). Showing the public how good they were so that they could attract more students became an obsession with the competitive academic executives. Cornell boasted that its scenery ''far above Cayuga's waters'' was worth five full professors at other institutions. The University of Chicago countered with a listing of faculty publications in an impressive 182-page tome. Yale's graduate bulletin prompted Chicago's William Rainey Harper to develop one also lest Chicago fall behind in the race for students. Stanford's David Starr Jordan lamented that ''the competition for numbers . . . often leads to discrepancies between the actual requirements and those laid down in the published catalog'' (Rudolph 1962). As more students of modest means, ''anxious to advance,'' joined the undergraduate ranks (traditionally drawn from the wealthy), colleges and universities hurried to attract them with a flurry of articles in the 1890s on the practical nature of college. ''The Practical Value of a College Education,'' ''Does College Education Pay?'' and ''College Men First among Successful Citizens'' were all aimed at the business-minded new students (Rudolph 1962). ''As a result of such desperate concern to remain on top, large numbers of students were sometimes wooed at the expense of academic standards'' (Rudolph 1962).

The acquiescence to numbers was also hastened by the introduction of the elective principle at Harvard. Eliot, over a several-year period beginning with his inauguration in 1869, systematically removed required curricula from Harvard students' education, allowing students to choose which courses they would take. This quickly spread to admission requirements as well.

As the colleges began to abandon their prescribed curricula in the latter quarter of the nineteenth century, the American high school movement was developing. Serving more heterogeneous student bodies than colleges, these new secondary schools offered more choice in their curricula in order to meet the varied interests and needs of their students. Because the high schools provided an increasingly ready-made pool of prospects for college enrollment, higher education—particularly the new land grant colleges and state universities of the Midwest and the West—was particularly sensitive to students and what they were studying. Because the high schools were friendlier to more modern curricula, the colleges were soon accepting subjects such as American history, physical geography, natural philosophy, physiology, English, and modern languages for admission. By 1910 the University of California was accepting 30 different subjects for admission (Rudolph 1962). Rudolph suggests that the embrace of the elective principle by American colleges gave them the opportunity to gain popular support at a time when higher education was increasingly isolated and in danger of becoming an anachronism (Rudolph 1962). Quantity had redefined quality.

THE RISE OF ADMINISTRATION: QUALITY STANDARDIZED

College enrollments soared as the state universities tapped into new markets, but the defenders of standards were mounting a new assault against the weakening of quality. This time, however, the passion for quality was expressed, not so much in terms of standards, as in a system of standardization. With the elective principle in full flower by the 1880s, it was becoming difficult for students looking at college to know how to prepare, and it was difficult for colleges to know in what ways students were prepared. To some higher education leaders this was the unhappy result of an obsession with access; greater quantity could not help but undermine quality. William T. Foster, president of Reed College, could not accept the access arguments of Bascom and Draper and instead railed against "this democratic leniency toward the unfit," adding that indeed, "our democracy errs still farther in favoring self-supporting students at the expense of intellectual standards" (Veysey 1958).

Some schools with a surplus of students could be content with tending to standards as well as numbers. When Cornell University opened in 1869 with the princely number of 400 students, President Andrew D. White had "experienced that incredible luxury for an American institution of higher learning of actually rejecting 50 applicants for admission." The rejection seems warranted on the basis of geography exam answers at least: these were young men who had named "Portugal the capital of Spain, Borneo the capital of Prussia, India a part of Africa, Egypt a province of Russia" (Rudolph 1962). The rigor hardly hurt Cornell's enrollment. Its third freshman class in 1871 was the largest in the history of American higher education (Rudolph 1962). However, Cornell may have been a happy example of one institution's discovery of a successful solution to the admissions dilemma of balancing quantity and quality. Cornell rode the early crests of both Eliot's work with the elective principle at Harvard and the land grant movement. Access was a keystone for founder Ezra Cornell as he embraced the elective principle and also secured a land grant from the New York legislature. His philosophy of a university "where any person can find instruction in any study" may have positioned the new institution so positively with regard to numbers that quality could still be upheld.

Even though the burgeoning high school movement in the United States in the latter part of the nineteenth and early years of the twentieth centuries helped to satiate higher education's fascination with numbers by providing a steady supply of students, the real push for more standardization in college preparation was also fueled by the rise of this same high school movement. First, the universities in the Midwest began to use the high schools to prequalify students. In 1870 the University of Michigan began admitting students from high schools

that the university determined did an acceptable job of offering college preparatory instruction. This prequalifying of applicants firmly established the high
schools as preparatory institutions and relieved the university of remediation
(Rudolph 1962). By 1895, of all students in American higher education, 41
percent were high school graduates (Rudolph 1962).

However, as the high school movement grew, its already-eclectic curriculum
multiplied and more elective courses came into the college preparatory curriculum. The increasing options, even with university accreditation of schools,
made it difficult for colleges to determine the level of preparation of students
for college. In 1879, New England colleges met in Hartford to discuss standardized admission requirements in English. By 1885 colleges and universities
were pushing for the standardization of college entrance requirements. There
was a need to decide what a college was and what college preparation was
(Rudolph 1962).

Similarly, as colleges diversified their admissions course requirements, secondary schools began to push for more standardization of requirements. The
National Education Association (NEA) joined the movement toward standardization in 1892 with their Committee of Ten and the subsequent development of
a standard secondary school curriculum. After this success, an NEA Committee
of Twelve turned to the issue of college admission requirements, and in an 1899
meeting of the Association of Colleges and Secondary Schools of the Middle
Atlantic States and Maryland, the subject of an entrance examination board was
a principal topic (Rudolph 1962). In 1901 the first College Entrance Examination
Board exams were given.

The movement to standardization was not uniformly well received. A heated
exchange between President Ethelbert D. Warfield of Lafayette College and
President Eliot of Harvard illustrates the continuing tension between standards
and institutional well-being. Said Warfield:

Lafayette College does not intend to be told by any Board whom to admit and whom
not to admit. If we wish to admit the son of a benefactor or of a Trustee, or of a member
of the Faculty, and such action will benefit the institution, we are not going to be pre-
vented from taking it. (Rudolph 1962)

President Eliot responded:

The President of Lafayette College has misunderstood. . . . It will be perfectly practicable
under this plan [of a College Entrance Examination Board] for Lafayette College to say,
if it chooses, that it will admit only such students as cannot pass these examinations. No
one proposes to deprive Lafayette College of that privilege. (Rudolph 1962)

By 1910, 25 eastern colleges were using the standardized exams for admission
purposes (Rudolph 1962).

In 1908 the Carnegie Foundation sponsored a conference to create the ultimate standardization of college preparation: the definition of a unit of admission credit. One unit was to equal any one of four courses taken five days per week in secondary school, and thus was born the Carnegie unit, which for over 80 years remained the unchallenged symbol of college preparation and is still the predominant secondary school measure. It represented, said Rudolph, "the ultimate in organization, the epitome of academic accountancy, the symbol of the search for standards" (Rudolph 1962).

The search for standards in admission also led to the development of the admissions office as a separate administrative unit in higher education. As enrollments increased in the wake of the high school movement, colleges and universities responded by creating service officers to handle the needs of students and relieve the faculty from the tedium of administration required by increasingly complex organizations.

Administrative responsibility was necessarily splintered: first a secretary of the faculty, then a registrar, and then in succession a vice president, a dean, a dean of women, a chief business officer, an assistant dean, a dean of men, a director of admissions, and in time a corps of administrative assistants to the president who were in charge of anything and everything. (Rudolph 1962)

Between 1860 and 1933 the median number of administrators in American colleges and universities had grown from 4.0 to 30.5, with one boasting 137 (Rudolph 1962).

To admit and register students and to maintain their records after enrollment, colleges and universities developed the registrar as one of the first administrative officers. Initially, a faculty member was given an additional responsibility with an added salary bonus, but by the end of the nineteenth century, this had become a full-time position. "The Registrar: whose authority is supreme, whose methods are autocratic, whose ways are beyond the highest research," became increasingly powerful, as an early twentieth-century writer complained (Veysey 1965). During the 1920s, the registrar took on more and more responsibilities now recognized as admissions activities, including corresponding with prospective students, visiting high schools, sending and receiving application forms, handling scholarship and financial aid, greeting freshmen and transfer students, conducting orientation, advising, and counseling (Quann et al. 1979).

Private colleges and universities had developed admissions officers to take their institutions' stories into the field before World War I. Columbia University established its Office of Admissions in 1915. By 1937 admissions offices were prevalent enough to warrant the founding of the Association of College Admission Counselors, now the National Association for College Admission Counseling (Quann et al. 1979). Still, the major development of admissions as a profession came after World War II, and, again, quantity and quality went hand in hand. Institutions, struggling from the privations of depression and war, had insufficient faculty, facilities, and equipment to handle the influx of veterans who took advantage of the GI Bill. The new colleges developing in the postwar years would be "open door" community colleges, but most existing colleges handled, first, the GIs, and, later, the baby boomers by tightening admissions standards. In this selective admissions environment, the admissions officer took on increasing responsibility for screening applications and controlling the numbers.

In 1949 the American Association of Collegiate Registrars (founded in 1910), at its annual meeting in Columbus, Ohio, amended its constitution to add "and Admissions Officers" to the association's name (Constance 1973). The admissions officer had arrived as a coequal with the registrar, with his or her own responsibilities for "recruitment, interviewing, testing, counseling, evaluation and placement, orientation, research, and publication" (Quann 1979).

NEW STUDENTS AND NEW STANDARDS: THE
ADMISSIONS DILEMMA INTENSIFIED

The standardization of quality measures through the development of The College Board and the standardization of procedure through the growth of the administrative cadre in colleges and universities formalized college admission standards. However, the Great Depression and World War II again brought declining enrollments in America's colleges and universities; and, as a result, standards again became so much excess baggage. During the 1930s, colleges and universities again engaged in intensive recruitment practices. "The chief priority was to enroll enough cash customers to maintain solvency." Admissions requirements were "largely ignored or somehow 'adjusted' as required to satisfy the primary need, that of attracting a sufficient number of students to enroll" (Stewart 1992). The postwar enrollment crunch brought on first by returning GIs and then by the baby boom relieved the pressure for numbers and refocused the higher education community on standards and quality. The baby boom led secondary schools to look more closely at how to work with students going to college. Colleges and secondary schools formed a partnership in developing "concepts of educational guidance in general and college guidance in particular. This was the beginning of a professional approach to the process of student transition from secondary school to higher education" (Stewart 1992).

Expressing the development of this "professional approach," Fishman described admissions as "a theory of administrative action based upon knowledge of the interaction between a given college environment and various crucial characteristics of the applicant population. Selection and guidance represent the techniques and procedures through which this 'philosophy' is implemented" (Fishman 1958). But even as the standards were formalized, the postwar baby boom was redefining them. "Those concerned with the philosophical and the empirical foundations of admission and selection are aware of more than the usual amount of public and professional pressure to introduce greater clarity and effectiveness into this field" (Fishman 1958).

With increasing numbers, the admissions office was faced with a gatekeeping function of limiting enrollments to what institutions could handle. Requirements developed to bring order out of chaos in the high school movement of the late nineteenth and early twentieth centuries now became icons of selection: "Indeed [grades] are undoubtedly becoming more, rather than less, difficult to eliminate. Increasing numbers of young people are attending college, and grades based largely upon achievement examinations are a part of the traditional bureaucratic machinery for 'processing' these students" (Fishman 1958). The fact that those grades resulted from courses measured in Carnegie units made them even more a part of that "bureaucratic machinery." This philosophy of admissions officers as gatekeepers would last throughout the baby boom years.

However, as the baby boom of the 1960s and 1970s turned into the baby bust of the 1980s, the shrinking pool of potential college students provided another watershed in the admissions officer's eternal tension between quantity and quality. "The decline in the college-age cohort . . . places all but the most selective institutions in the position of recruiting, rather than admitting students with the possible effect of further diluting standards" (Stewart 1992). To combat declining numbers, institutions turned increasingly to business methods, initially adapting commercial direct mail strategies and techniques, then moving to telemarketing and telecommunications methods (see Chapter 16). Targeting market segments of high-ability students, students of color, specific academic majors, children of alumni, and so forth has brought new strategies and new programs to college admissions. "During the past 25 years—tentatively at first, and now aggressively—higher education has embraced traditional marketing definitions and techniques to try to affect the basic determinants of student choice" (Stewart 1992).

So great has been the change that:

Admissions practitioners of the late 1960s and early 1970s would probably recognize only the general admission objectives and some of the admission folkways that have persisted to the present. Much that is done now on the admissions landscape would be foreign territory to many of them. (Stewart 1992)

However, significantly, the basic tenets of admission remain the same in Stewart's view: enroll a class that meets the institution's budgetary and resource requirements as well as its quality and diversity goals (Stewart 1992). The twin themes of the admissions dilemma remain the same: quantity and quality. While the baby bust has brought new techniques to bear in the battle for numbers in American higher education, the decline in the traditional age cohort has also given a practical urgency to the message of those who advocated a broader way of viewing college admissions. In 1991 Pascarella and Terenzini wrote:

If admissions decisions are based solely on applicants' academic credentials and their promise for successful grade performance, important opportunities to enroll students with special talents or gifts that would enrich the academic or interpersonal climate of the school may be lost. . . . There is mounting evidence that traditional admissions criteria [test scores and grades] are not the best predictors of college performance and retention for all students. (Pascarella and Terenzini 1991)

The K–12 educational reform movement of the 1990s has given operational meaning to Pascarella and Terenzini's observations. The legislatively mandated use of portfolios and performance-based educational assessment in elementary and secondary schools has brought higher education admissions to the brink of another seismic event. College and university admissions standards are under increasing attack, as the Oregon State Board of Higher Education noted in 1994:

The existing system, based on Carnegie units, course title, grade point average, and class standing (combined with SAT and other measures), does not result in the uniform selection of students who perform at minimally acceptable levels in key performance areas such as math and writing. (Conley 1994)

The educational reforms proposed and, in some places, actually legislated, will bring students with totally different credentials for admission selection. For example, Oregon's Certificates of Initial and Advanced Mastery are to be based on student-demonstrated performance of specified skills and knowledge. They reject the notion of seat time and credits as organizers of, or proxies for, learning. Students who pass through the Oregon schools will be assessed on their demonstrated knowledge and will come to think of learning in such terms. Furthermore, transcripts are unlikely to look as they do today. Course titles will have less meaning. More interdisciplinary learning seems likely as students work on projects that span more than one discipline. The length of classes may vary tremendously, thereby affecting the number of Carnegie units assigned to each, which in turn affects student accumulation of the required number of credits. More opportunities for students to "challenge" courses or demonstrate proficiency in ways other than course attendance seem likely (Conley 1994).

Much of the pressure for the K–12 reform movement has come from the public's frustration with the quality of student achievement in the schools; shrinking resources, which demand more efficient use of tax dollars; and the resulting intrusion by the political process. Initial resistance from higher education to reforms that threatened traditional standards in the admissions process has been tempered by the public's criticism of collegiate attrition rates and the time-to-graduation rates for those who do persist. The implementation of new statewide university standards based on Carnegie units was aggressively attacked by K–12 education groups in Michigan. Only demonstrated flexibility in applying the new standards to students from schools with innovative curricula placated the opposition (Western Michigan University correspondence).

Today, in the mid-1990s, the adversarial relationship has given way to more collaborative efforts. The University of Minnesota and the University of Georgia

System have developed Postsecondary Options programs to allow high school students to accelerate their baccalaureate program by taking college courses in high school. This dual enrollment approach is being used in a number of states, often under legislative mandate. The University of Wisconsin System is working with four pilot school districts to implement an outcomes-based admissions system. And the American Association of Collegiate Registrars and Admissions Officers has charged a Task Force on Performance-Based Education to examine practices in the country and make recommendations on the impact of, and responses to, these practices.

SUMMARY

The admissions office and its staff are relatively new on the administrative lists of American higher education. However, admissions as a concept has been around from the very beginning. Likewise, the forces that shape and buffet the admissions office today were present at the founding of Harvard. In every period of higher education history, academic institutions—whether struggling colonial colleges before the Revolution, denominational institutions in early nationhood, or the emerging universities of the twentieth century—have wrestled with the twin prongs of the admissions dilemma: the quantity and quality of students.

And in every period there has been someone in the role of admissions director. Sometimes it was the clergy of a particular sect, sometimes the institutional president, sometimes the registrar. In every case the person playing the role filled by the admissions director today has been involved in determining the requirements for institutional survival, reading the mood of the public, ascertaining the size of the applicant pool, and creating a product. Whether to educate the clergy; attract the self-made frontiersmen; entice the sons of merchants and farmers; or welcome the high school graduates, the GIs, or the baby boomers— the admissions function has shaped the quantity and quality of institutions, and borne the burden of balancing the two.

Often quantity—or the lack thereof—has defined the limits of quality. Indeed, the analysis of this chapter would suggest that quality indices are often dictated by the vagaries of enrollment pressures. However, defenders of quality have often seen changing standards as a lessening of quality. In fact, the quantity prong of the admissions dilemma has been instrumental in shaping the face— and the quality—of American higher education. From the cynical view, the democratization of American higher education may be seen as a way to fill libraries, lecture halls, and laboratories, and there is much evidence that economic survival served more to dictate who would go to college than who was prepared to do so.

However, the sometimes insatiable need for enrollments has always been met by creative and resourceful methods of widening the applicant pool to maintain enrollments. "When there are not enough students, find more," is the simplest, and oldest, motto of admissions. Thus, the children of workmen and farmers, women, the returning GIs, students of color, and adults have found educational opportunities opened to them in times when institutional products and facilities were underutilized. Just as the diversity of students may be said to have come from the creativity of admissions people through time, so has the diversity of the curriculum been the result of a marketing mentality that read the needs of new students and created a product to meet those needs. The quality, then, of higher education is determined by how well the institutions diversify their curricular and service offerings to attract the students they must have to fill their halls. Quality, in the long run, is the necessary outcome of quantity, even as it may be the victim of quantity in the short run. That is, in the final analysis, the proper balance between the quantity and quality dichotomy of the admissions dilemma.

REFERENCES

Brubacher, John S., and Willis Rudy. 1976. *Higher education in transition: A history of American colleges and universities, 1636–1976.* New York: Harper and Row.

The College Board. 1987. *Educational access and achievement in America.* New York: The College Board.

————. 1992. *The great sorting: A report on The College Board's admission study colloquium.* New York: The College Board.

Conley, David T. 1994. *Proficiency-based admission standards study (PASS).* Eugene, OR: Oregon State System of Higher Education, Office of Academic Affairs.

Constance, Clifford L. 1973. *Historical review of the association.* Washington, DC: American Association of Collegiate Registrars and Admissions Officers.

Fishman, Joshua A. 1958. Some social psychological theory for selecting and guiding college students. In Nevitt Sanford, ed., *The American college: A psychological and social interpretation of higher learning,* New York: John Wiley and Sons.

Pascarella, Ernest T., and Patrick T. Terenzini. 1991. Implications of the research for policy and practice. In *How colleges affect students.* San Francisco: Jossey-Bass.

Quann, C. James et al. 1979. *Admissions, academic records and registrar services: A handbook of policies and procedures.* San Francisco: Jossey-Bass.

Rudolph, Frederick. 1962. *The American college and university.* New York: Vintage Books.

Stewart, Donald M. 1992. *College admission policies in the 1990s: A look toward the future.* New York: The College Board.

Veysey, Laurence. 1965. *The emergence of the American university.* Chicago: University of Chicago Press.

Webster, Harold, Mervin Freedman, and Paul Heist. 1958. Personality changes in college students. In Nevitt Sanford, ed., *The American college: A psychological and social interpretation of higher learning.* New York: John Wiley and Sons.

Part II

The Admissions Officer

Part II describes the admissions professional's role, functions, and opportunities for career development.

4

Admissions Officer: A Profession and a Career

Claire C. Swann

THE HISTORY OF ADMISSIONS AS A PROFESSION

Chapter 3 treated the history of admissions in higher education. The *Historical Review of the Association* (Constance 1973) notes that in April 1949, at the 35th annual conference, the American Association of Collegiate Registrars (AACR) by constitutional amendment changed its name to the American Association of Collegiate Registrars and Admissions Officers (AACRAO). Even earlier, in 1914 and 1920, conference notes referred to college preparatory curriculums, and pretesting and transcript formats.

The 107 members attending the 10th annual meeting of AACR in 1920 at the Washington, DC, New Ebbitt Hotel recommended that a basic entrance form for high school graduates be developed with the National Association of Secondary School Principals (NASSP). This collaborative step may have been facilitated by a move in 1914 by registrars to allow transcripts to be sent to schools in the case of designated students. The face of the form would be uniform, and the back would be available for institutional variations. AACR members at that meeting also voted that intelligence tests be given in high school for prospective college students. By 1924, proceedings of the business meeting recorded that a five-member committee had been approved to study and report the use of intelligence tests in admissions processes. One could postulate that committee members examined the literature and interviewed a number of their college professors, who were experts in the fields of general counseling and tests and measurement. Some of these giants included Alfred Binet and Sigmund Freud. Later giant contributors included Ruth Strange, E. G. Williamson, Gilbert Wrenn, Arthur Traxler, and Carl Rogers. Perhaps these forebears foresaw the humanistic and psychological aspects of this evolving and needed segment for the helpful passage of students from one educational level to the next.

The 214 members attending the 1927 annual AACR meeting voted to request that the College Entrance Examination Board (CEEB), now simply called The College Board, develop a test for foreign students' use of the English language. CEEB was commended at the 1930 meeting for having developed the Test of English as a Foreign Language (TOEFL), which the AACR convention had requested. It was not until 1950, however, that AACRAO became a member of the College Board.

Reviewing the historic base allows today's professionals to realize how many pieces or related areas fit into the present job description. Through the decades, as the admissions profession has developed and changed, institutional settings have also changed. In the 1950s, admissions officers and any staff they had were, first and foremost, processors of the paperwork for prospective students. Registrars considered themselves stewards for only the enrolled students, and the teaching faculty were responsible for classroom scheduling and distributing the grades earned by students. The admitting officers became the convener of necessary paper record files (including test results, though few colleges required entrance tests in the 1950s) before the enrollment of the chosen class of first-year, professional, and graduate students.

In the 1960s, with the emphasis that Sputnik played in encouraging young people to enter college, admissions officers began to play a role in high school relations. Secondary school counselors and administrators had more space than time to present the packages of postsecondary options to their students. Consequently, college admissions officers began making presentations to high school prospects, often during the school day and, if academic or class schedules did not allow, at nighttime programs, where parents could participate in the sessions and, thus, in the college decision making.

One of the primary messages carried by admissions officers to college prospects and their families was the invitation to visit the representative's campus. Already researchers and surveyors, including Alexander Astin of the University of California, Los Angeles, longtime director of the Higher Education Research Institute at UCLA, were designing questionnaires and finding that the campus visit was the single most important reason high school seniors chose their college. Thus, the visit soon became the single most effective recruitment tool. Astin's annual survey of 200,000 college freshmen has become a popular measuring stick of college patterns and trends which admissions and other student personnel officers regularly study. The campus visit in the 1990s remains the most important reason for student selection of a college and a primary factor around which visitation calendars are built.

In spite of the fact that visiting families often witnessed the presence of liberal students and an air of the antiestablishment on campus, college admissions officers in the late 1960s began devising systematic calendars of campus visitation. And in the 1970s, college faculties became involved in welcoming visitors.

Admissions officers began involving their entire campuses in visitation programs and found deans of students, housing, and financial aid offices especially helpful. It was during this period that admissions officers were often designated orientation directors and retention officers—though it did not take long to convince presidents and other institutional leaders that retention is everyone's responsibility—and, at best, an ombudsman on the academic leader's staff or an institutional researcher conducting surveys and charting longitudinal attrition data to help with retention.

Forced to be efficient interpreters of the college community to visitors, admissions personnel found themselves cast in the role of counselor. While visiting high school communities, the admissions officers were called upon to interpret the college environment they represented. Counseling the prospective customer was (and still is) perhaps one of the most salient descriptors of the profession because, certainly, the admissions officer did not want to be guilty of trying to sell the student the institution. Less than a happy match of the student to the college could result in a bad experience. Serving as counselors to the families helped admissions officers refrain from becoming too personally involved or disappointed when a family chose another college. In addition, the family could not personally accost that admissions individual if the student did not qualify for admission in a selective college admissions situation. Because no one else on the college campus performed this task, often the admissions officers felt solely responsible for delivering this negative message. This unique counseling function may be one reason so many friendships in the professional associations evolve and continue throughout the admissions officers' lives (see Chapter 7).

Because so many college spaces have been available for high school graduates since the late 1950s, a relatively high percentage of students pursue postsecondary study, in numbers certainly higher than in most European countries. For this reason, U.S. students have more than 3,000 institutions from which to select places for their postsecondary years. Only about 5 percent of the colleges are selective (i.e., offer freshman class spaces to fewer than 50 percent of their applicants). However, since this is the case, admissions professionals have also become public relations officers. To cast their employing institutions in the best possible light to the many constituents is incumbent upon the admissions officer at all times. One of the mottoes by which the admissions officer lives is, Keep it positive! "How is your psychology department?" a naive senior asks. "Very good, and let me tell you why," responds the eager public relations person working as an admissions officer. As this public relations role gathered steam, the marketing and imaging requirement grew and ballooned if the institution needed to grow. Imaging took on new meaning as segments of people—formerly unknown to campuses as college prospects—were now approached. For nontraditional populations and international prospects, recruitment programs were designed that could be delivered by trained (or not-so-trained, but willing) alumni of the institution. Naturally, the business of managing these enrollment projects also grew.

In the 1980s, new labels were bestowed upon some admissions officers who were called upon to critically manage a precarious balance resulting from careful analysis and projections of the numbers of students expected to enroll. Among these new titles were enrollment planner, enrollment manager, and enrollment director. Some enrollment officers were placed in chairs closer to vice presidents or presidents and had few or no staff. (Enrollment management is discussed later in this chapter.)

THE ADMISSIONS OFFICER

The purpose and mission of the admissions officer (and office) has been, and always will be, determined by the institution. A number of the profession's forebears have said that admissions directors serve at the pleasure of their presidents. (The admissions directors who cannot accept the president's goals and objectives should pack their proverbial bags!) The field's giants—from Thrasher to Hossler and other contributors to the field and from Astin to Zimsky—tout the significance of the cyclical role of the admissions office led by a strong person who is mindful of this required cyclical requirement. But this person must have the confidence and support of the institution's leader to accomplish the institution's goals. (See Chapter 5 for the qualities of the competent professional at progressive levels.)

The ladder of success climbed by the admissions professional has many rungs, pitfalls, and sacrifices, and yet it also has strange rewards encountered by few others at the institution. These professionals come to appreciate the collective joys of parents whose offspring are happy with their college decisions and, thus, their orientation to the institution. The business is exciting to admissions staff because they know that unwritten institutional success is riding upon their shoulders and the goals they achieve each year. It is incumbent, therefore, upon admissions directors who are to be successful in the enrollment mission to hire the brightest and most capable assistants available and give these workers the responsibility and authority to create effective programs within their assigned territories and duties.

Personality characteristics that make for probable success in the admissions profession—whether employed in a large or small, public or private institution—are listed here. While there is no standard group of personal characteristics embodied in the skills and competencies (see Chapter 5), the following traits make for a smooth acquisition of basic skills that are required in the business and for probable (but never automatic) advancement within the ranks.

- ability to analyze quickly and make solid decisions
- ability to maintain balance or centeredness (i.e., staying physically and mentally healthy)
- dedication to purpose and mission; being flexible but confident

- endless energy for erratic hours, changing schedules
- friendly attitude with proclivity for automatic outreach and willingness to take the first step in conversations and in large groups, always employing kindness, sincerity, and honesty
- an innate capacity for public relations
- keen self-discipline and mastery of motivating techniques
- reliable sense of responsibility, undergirded with an obvious tendency toward unselfishness

Interested prospects often ask what college majors would best prepare them to perform well in the admissions setting. Again, there is neither an established standard nor an always reliable answer. Because the job involves working with people constantly and perpetually analyzing and treating data, psychology, sociology, mathematics, and statistics may be the most helpful and related studies. Other popular undergraduate majors are public relations, liberal arts disciplines, business administration, journalism, and education.

In some institutions the competition for admissions jobs is keen and graduate degrees give prospects an advantage. Most popular graduate degrees include administration, business, personnel, psychology, counseling, education, student personnel services in higher education, and journalism. The admissions officer with an interest in employment in the classroom is probably wise to earn at least two degrees in the preferred academic areas. The candidate who is prepared to teach may be strong in training other staff, students, and alumni; and the one who is prepared to teach is almost assuredly skilled in public speaking and taking leadership roles in such areas with little or no assistance.

SKILLS ACQUIRED

Because there exist few basic models for the training of admissions officers, the most reliable readiness occurs from the thorough knowledge by the candidate of the institution where he or she will be employed. Therefore, hiring one's own graduates is generally a good practice in the field of admissions. Early training soon after employment should include interviews and getting to know all the campus offices affiliated with the admissions function. Entering the profession with salient interviewing skills is a desirable characteristic. If this characteristic is not present in the most qualified candidate, the skill should be honed quickly because of the constancy of visitors to the admissions office and other publics to whom the employer needs the institutional message delivered. The best learning mode is probably the daily practice of observing colleagues by sitting in on their sessions for the first several weeks of employment. Working steadily on interview skills enables one to gradually build an assertiveness and an assurance that prepares the admissions officer to competently address groups, regardless of the size of the audience. Many institutions now have areas or rooms where visitors congregate to hear presentations by one or more admissions personnel and view audiovisual resources. Having a daily service of this type requires the admissions professional staff to stay in a state of "performance" readiness.

Report writing is another skill that must be acquired early or that the candidate may bring to the job. Every professional documents his or her work on projects and events, which later will form the basis for the staff's annual report for the administrator or president. The director or employer must routinely require this report from the employee from the outset of employment. This skill becomes a productive one that serves the individual and the team well. The director becomes the editor and synthesizer. The annual reports become a tool to which all staff are proud contributors and owners. The pieces also become a valuable archive of the current year's productivity and the future's goals and objectives, that is, the strategic plan. In a continuing and an unobtrusive way, this professional office is a virtual setting of skills demonstrating admissions readiness to meet the institution's present and future needs and directions.

To summarize, an admissions professional team is composed of individuals who complement the institution they serve and each other so that the staff's total functions are performed successfully. In general, roles performed skillfully by a group of people well suited to each other and the institution make satisfied employers and happy employees. The director of admissions then has two extremely important roles which, if performed satisfactorily each year, make the director's job rewarding. These two roles include overseeing an adequate budget that ensures rewarding employees for their tasks and underwriting effective programs to ensure the enrollment of the desired mix of new students. The second role for the director is filling staff vacancies. The work of a productive and efficient staff indirectly recruits for itself because of the respected reputation it gains. Consequently, the director's prospective personnel file always has one or two good applicants who want to join the staff and who can be contacted when vacancies occur.

Rewards for the individual admissions officer are numerous and varied, though they may not be financial in nature. Working in education is not reputed to be financially rewarding. However, merit and cost-of-living raises routinely occur, and the entry-level professional is rarely aware of the ways in which the decisions on pay advances are made.

Generally, the professional admissions officer carried a rigorous travel schedule, with expenses being covered by the office's budget. Many consider, therefore, these travel responsibilities as opportunities for discovering other peoples and places that may affect consequent decisions about additional travel and/ or future places to live. For swift advancement or sizable salary increases, many career admissions professionals incorrectly think they need to change jobs and institutions. Moving should always be scrutinized carefully, considering even the most minute pros and cons. Often, promotions and pay advances come to those who elect to stay at the first or second institution and accrue seniority. It is assumed by employers that a vast storehouse of knowledge is acquired along with seniority, which is not the case. Professionals who spend only three to five years in the admissions business acquire useful skills and tools that transfer to other business, public relations, and educational areas.

The lifelong privilege of acquiring a cadre of friends who share interests, talents, and annual schedules must be counted. Admissions officers with the responsibility for educational outreach generally share that duty with no one else on their campuses. This factor automatically throws them in with like peoples from other colleges and universities. "Longtimers" in the profession have been known to remark that presidents would be surprised to see the truest of friendships among people who compete so vigorously with each other for the enrollment of many of the same students. Because admissions officers generally have membership in three or four professional associations, that opportunity affords an official forum to exchange a formal know-how and field experiences (see Chapter 7).

ROLES

Completing given tasks to successfully meet annual goals is the major undertaking of the office and of the individual officer. For this reason, the group's strategic plan and planning are crucial. Equally important is supervising the many and varied tasks that constitute the annual goals. When these tasks include attracting the attention of hundreds or thousands of people, attention to detail and outcomes is just as essential. Overall success can only occur if daily tasks such as directing and completing large mailing projects and simultaneously accomplishing off-campus assignments are routinely completed efficiently and effectively.

Delivering and supervising are the daily roles played by all admissions officers. The delivering aspects specifically pertain to completing each year's class of beginning students. Daily roles common throughout the profession are as follows:

- processing applications and credentials,
- analyzing the processing and reporting analysis to internal and external parties,
- distributing admissions, scholarship, and financial aid materials to the constituent schools and prospect lists; and presenting program sessions about the institution at those feeder schools,
- conducting preview programs and tours at the institution, and
- counseling visitors to appropriate referral resources within the institution (advisors and student personnel sources such as housing, financial aid, placement, and testing).

REFERENCE

Constance, Clifford L. 1973. *Historical review of the association.* Washington, DC: American Association of Collegiate Registrars and Admissions Officers.

5

Competencies and Training

Stanley E. Henderson

BACKGROUND

In 1952 the Committee for Professional Development of the American Association of Collegiate Registrars and Admissions Officers (AACRAO) developed a training program that was presented and approved at its Annual Meeting in Washington, DC. The training program assumed successful admissions officers were "persons whose intellectual qualifications [were] above the average of those required in training programs for teaching in higher education" and advocated a broad education to provide skills suitable for establishing appropriate working relationships with colleagues on the faculty and in administration. The successful admissions officer, it reported,

> should be able to speak and to write well, to organize work and supervise employees, to cooperate with faculty and administrative officers. Coupled with these abilities should be certain qualities of character—emotional stability, perseverance, decisiveness, poise, good balance, charity under criticism, patience and objectivity with people—and in adverse situations, fearlessness under pressure. (Deering 1954)

Finally, the report also advocated "an enthusiasm for completing tasks and an eagerness to undertake new ones," with an attention to "service above all other means of personal satisfaction" (Deering 1954).

The recommended training included broad academic areas from which prospective admissions officers might choose specific courses: History of Education, Higher Education, Curriculum Development, Secondary Education, Personnel Management, Office Management, Educational Measurements, Statistics, Educational Administration, Public Relations, Counseling Procedures, Student Personnel Work, and Communications Techniques (Deering 1954). In addition, two highly specialized courses were recommended. One, the Administration of the Admissions-Registrar Functions in Standard Colleges and Universities, was a course detailing organization, standard practices and procedures, policies, and ethics from the AACRAO perspective. The association's handbook, *Policies and Procedures*, along with other association literature, provided the basis for the course. For the second course, the association's *Bulletin* recommended a supervised training experience, a kind of practicum, to provide prospective professionals with hands-on experience with the admissions operation. "An important aim of this actual experience would be to cultivate and develop appreciation and understanding of the interrelationship of admissions, registrations, recording, and the issuance of transcripts" (Deering 1954).

The association also envisioned in-service training to serve a number of purposes:

1. to develop knowledge so as to increase confidence in the office

2. to develop greater efficiency in office routines

3. to develop pride in the work of the office

4. to reduce turnover

5. to fit the work of the office to the educational aims of the institution

To accomplish these purposes, the in-service program prescribed staff meetings, college coursework and summer session workshops, visits to other offices, national and regional meetings, circulating publications, an office library, and research (particularly for admissions). Sabbaticals were also encouraged so that admissions staff might take advantage of the AACRAO training program, whether the supervised seminars or other parts of the training program that might "supplement previous training" (Deering 1954).

In spite of this ambitious emphasis on training efforts, little came of the association's plans. The 1979 admissions and records handbook by Quann and associates presented a thorough analysis of the functions and responsibilities of admissions and records officers but had very little to say about the training necessary to undertake those duties. Oliver, writing in the handbook about admissions officers, observed, "Professional preparation . . . is not well defined or highly visible in American higher education" (in Quann et al. 1979). Surveys by Hauser and Lazarsfield (1964) and Vinson (1976) showed little correlation between courses taken and value received for admission positions. In fact, in Oliver's words, "Personal qualities are as important to success for an admissions officer as the subjects studied" (in Quann et al. 1979). One admissions wag suggested that the key personal ingredients included: "The Shoulders of Babe the Blue Ox, . . . the Oratorical Ability of Demosthenes, . . . the Numerical Facility of the Wizard of Avis, . . . the Optimism of a Presidential Press Secretary,

... the Patience of Job, ... the Prescience of Jeanne Dixon, ... [and] the Pizzaz of P. T. Barnum'' (Treadwell 1977).

Oliver noted that the Vinson study of admissions officers found that a sizable minority (23 percent) felt they had a job rather than a profession. That group identified the absence of formal training requirements as the chief obstacle to admissions workers being seen as professionals (in Quann et al. 1979).

PROFESSIONAL DEVELOPMENT IN THE 1990s

The nine years after the publication of the handbook saw dramatic changes in American higher education. These changes required a sharpening of old skills or the acquisition of new ones. The National Association of College Admission Counselors (NACAC, now known as the National Association for College Admission Counseling) took a leadership role, offering workshops and institutes for school and college admissions counselors and helping students plan and successfully make the transition from high school to college. In 1988, the NACAC Commission for the Advancement of Professional Standards (CAPS) was created to "examine professional preparation, certification, accreditation, and related credentialing issues." In 1990 the association released its "Statement of Principles of Good Practice," "Statement on the Counseling Dimension of the Admission Process at the College/University Level," and "Statement on Precollege Guidance and Counseling and the Role of the School Counselor." In 1991 its executive board approved the "Statement on Counselor Competencies," a list of eight competencies effective school counselors would be expected to possess.

AACRAO also developed self-audit guidelines for admissions officers and continued to produce a series of publications describing foreign educational systems that included recommendations for placement of foreign students in U.S. colleges and universities (AACRAO was later joined by NAFSA: The Association for International Educators and The College Board in sponsoring these publications). In 1990 AACRAO released its competencies for admissions and records professionals. In 1991 AACRAO and NACAC released "The Admissions Profession: A Guide for Staff Development and Program Management." Other professional organizations such as The College Board and ACT also provided publications and professional training programs. In 1995, AACRAO, the College Entrance Examination Board, the Educational Testing Service (ETS), and NACAC released *Challenges in College Admissions: A Report of a Survey of Undergraduate Admissions Policies, Practices, and Procedures.*

Very few professionals will possess all of the skills outlined by either association. However, the attainment of these skills can provide the means for success and advancement in the field. As a roadmap for professionals, those entering the admissions field can more readily assess the likelihood of a fit between their skills and the competency areas of the profession. Those already in the profession now have a better means to assess their training needs by identifying those competency areas where they lack skills. And associations and others at the national and regional or state levels have a means of gearing training programs to specific competency areas for more focused and effective training. Prospective employers, too, now have a checklist for specific skills that fit specific duties, by which they can compare candidates and more easily assess their ability to succeed in a position.

The competency areas deal with basic skills or the entry-level knowledge base judged necessary to predict success in the field and advancement skills that are necessary to move up the career ladder. Resources at the end of each competency area list the avenues for skill development.

Competency Area: Personal Characteristics

Basic skills include (1) a demonstrated well-developed sense of integrity and humor, and (2) the ability to deal with ambiguity and to pay attention to detail and accuracy. *Advancement skills* include (1) a knowledge of and commitment to the ethical standards of the profession, and (2) the ability to think creatively and innovatively and to be proactive (versus reactive). *Resources* to develop these skills include appropriate readings, management courses, experience/on-the-job training, and workshops.

Competency Area: Oral Communication

Basic skills include a demonstrated ability to (1) convey information in a well-organized, logical, and succinct fashion; (2) speak positively to stimulate interest; and (3) organize information orally. *Advancement skills* include the ability to (1) speak in a formal or informal setting, (2) speak persuasively, (3) read an audience and adjust the style and content of remarks, and (4) speak well extemporaneously and on diverse topics that are institution specific (college night presentation, registration instructions) or generic (transition from high school to college, transcript fraud). *Resources* to develop these skills include public speaking courses, appropriate readings, in-service/on-the-job training, and workshops.

Competency Area: Interpersonal Communications

Basic skills include (1) a demonstrated ability to (a) listen attentively and perceptively, (b) receive and follow directives, (c) respond positively to constructive criticism and performance feedback, (d) present a positive personal appearance, and (e) handle oneself well in social settings; and (2) an awareness of cross-cultural communication needs. *Advancement skills* include (1) a demonstrated ability to (a) read nonverbal language, (b) confront in a positive manner, (c) work in a small group/team situation, and (d) utilize conflict resolution techniques; and (2) a demonstrated knowledge of (a) common work styles (those who need encouragement to perform better, those who are loners, etc.), and (b) personality types (authoritarian, dominant, submissive, etc.). *Resources* to develop these skills include interpersonal communication courses, appropriate readings, in-service training, workshops, and projects that require working with others as a team.

Competency Area: Written Communication

Basic skills include (1) a demonstrated solid grounding in English grammar; (2) the ability to (a) organize ideas on paper in a logical succinct fashion, (b) think analytically and critically, and (c) write business letters and reports; and (3) an understanding of different styles, as appropriate. *Advancement skills* include (1) a demonstrated ability to write (a) advertising copy designed to accomplish specific goals, (b) formal proposals and research articles, and (c) for professional publication; and (2) a demonstrated ability to communicate steps and procedures in written form so that others may understand and learn from them. *Resources* to develop these skills include English composition courses, technical writing courses, workshops (professional organization or commercially sponsored), and appropriate readings.

Competency Area: Employee Relations

Basic skills include a demonstrated ability to work with diverse kinds of individuals and as a team member. *Advancement skills* include (1) a demonstrated commitment to service orientation for students, faculty, staff, and the entire university community; (2) a demonstrated knowledge of (a) interviewing techniques, (b) the search process (what to look for, how to find it), (c) supervision techniques, (d) collective-bargaining strategies and techniques and affirmative action policies (institutional and/or governmental), and (e) institutional personnel policies; (3) a demonstrated ability to (a) develop job descriptions, accountabilities, and performance measures, (b) provide constructive feedback to employees, (c) handle evaluation sessions in a positive manner, (d) handle confrontation and discipline appropriately, (e) motivate and understand the use of positive recognition as a motivator, (f) foster pride and loyalty to the institution or organization, and (g) find and/or create and utilize staff development and training programs; and (4) knowledge of and ability to use team-building techniques. *Resources* to develop these skills include human resource courses, graduate programs, in-service/on-the-job training, workshops/conferences (institutional, commercial, professional), appropriate readings, and industrial psychology/organizational behavior courses.

Competency Area: Administration

Basic skills include (1) a demonstrated ability to (a) set effective, attainable goals, (b) prioritize responsibilities, (c) plan, organize, execute, and evaluate programs/projects, (d) develop objectives and strategies, (e) conduct a meeting,

(f) develop an agenda, and (g) use time effectively, and (2) a demonstrated understanding of administrative styles. *Advancement skills* include (1) a demonstrated knowledge of (a) the history and philosophy of higher education and (b) legal issues facing higher education; (2) a demonstrated ability to (a) display positive leadership, (b) motivate staff, volunteers, faculty, and administration to accomplish goals, (c) assess strengths and weaknesses of staff members, and (d) assign tasks/responsibilities accordingly; and (3) a demonstrated understanding of (a) the formal and informal political environments of the division and institution, (b) organizational theory, communication, and behavior, and (c) time and stress management techniques. *Resources* to develop these skills include graduate-level management, administration, and organizational behavior courses; MBA/Educational Administration master's or doctorate; in-service/on-the-job training; workshops, conferences, and institutes; and appropriate readings.

Competency Area: Research

Basic skills include (1) a demonstrated computational ability, (2) a demonstrated knowledge of statistics, (3) a demonstrated familiarity with existing literature in the field, as well as other research resources, and (4) demonstrated computer literacy. *Advancement skills* include (1) a demonstrated ability to (a) assess problems or needs, (b) develop research questions, (c) design a test instrument, (d) draw a sample, (e) analyze demographic and enrollment trends to forecast enrollments, (f) analyze data and draw a conclusion, and (g) interpret research results to others; and (2) a demonstrated knowledge of appropriate data and collection techniques. *Resources* to develop skills include graduate programs, research design courses, statistics courses, in-service/on-the-job training, conferences/workshops, and appropriate readings.

Competency Area: Technology

Basic skills include (1) a demonstrated knowledge of personal computer (PC) operation and application and the basic computer environment, and (2) a demonstrated ability to access and use electronic mail, Gopher, and/or the World Wide Web. *Advancement skills* include (1) a demonstrated knowledge of computer hardware; (2) basic knowledge of computer software logic and programming structure; (3) demonstrated programming ability/understanding; (4) a demonstrated ability to (a) identify database needs, (b) direct development of a database, regardless of whether the work is done in-house or through a vendor, (c) supervise development and implementation of computerized systems, (d) write requests for proposal, (e) understand and interpret technical terminology, and (f) think creatively in utilizing emerging technologies; (5) a demonstrated understanding of Electronic Data Interchange (EDI) and SPEEDE/ExPRESS; (6) a demonstrated knowledge of, and ability to select, vendors; and (7) a demonstrated understanding of and/or ability to develop on-line admissions applications, request forms, and other materials/forms. *Resources* to develop these skills include computer science classes, programming courses, appropriate readings, in-service/on-the-job training, conferences/institutes, vendor workshops, and interinstitutional networking.

Competency Area: Business Practices

Basic skills include (1) a demonstrated understanding of basic accounting principles, (2) demonstrated computational ability, and (3) demonstrated computer literacy. *Advancement skills* include (1) a demonstrated understanding of budget development and management; (2) a demonstrated ability to (a) do cost and productivity analysis of recruitment efforts, and similar tasks, (b) obtain goods and services in a cost-effective manner, and (c) write funding proposals and requests for proposal; and (3) a demonstrated knowledge of institutional business office policies and practices. *Resources* to develop these skills include an MBA program, accounting/finance courses, in-service/on-the-job training, workshops (institutional, commercial, professional), and appropriate readings.

Competency Area: Enrollment Management

Basic skills include (1) a demonstrated understanding of (a) marketing terms/ concepts, such as positioning, segmenting the market, target audiences, and primary, secondary, and tertiary markets, and (b) retention terms/concepts such as graduate rate, attrition, persistence, and at-risk students; and (2) a demonstrated ability to apply basic marketing concepts in developing recruitment strategies. *Advancement skills* include (1) a demonstrated ability to (a) foster a campus-wide commitment to enrollment management, (b) understand, interpret, and influence academic policies and practices, (c) explain and forecast enrollment trends, (d) conduct market research and develop a market plan, (e) create and communicate an institutional image, (f) determine compatibility between institutional image and identity, (g) utilize techniques for assessing image and identity (focus groups, etc.), (h) utilize marketing/retention approaches and systems to include telemarketing, direct mail, and freshman year experience, (i) develop retention studies and reports, and (j) identify key performance indicators (KPIs) to use as benchmarks for institutional progress; (2) a demonstrated understanding of (a) institutional pricing and financial aid, (b) enrollment management as a comprehensive, strategic-planning approach to determine, achieve, and maintain optimum institutional enrollment, (c) enrollment management's relationship to the academic context of the institution, and (d) interrelationships between various enrollment management units (admissions, financial aid, registrar, orientation, academic advising, support programs, career services, etc.). *Resources* to develop these skills include graduate programs, marketing courses, forecasting courses, appropriate readings, in-service/on-the-job training, and workshops, conferences, and institutes (commercial, professional).

Competency Area: Publications

Basic skills include (1) demonstrated effective proofreading and simple copyediting, (2) a demonstrated sense of proportion and design, and (3) a demonstrated ability to write effective copy. *Advancement skills* include (1) a demonstrated ability to (a) design concepts, (b) develop thematic approaches to publications (families of publications), (c) do visual imaging, (d) develop and/ or oversee advertising campaigns, (e) develop complex/technical publications (catalogues, schedules, viewbooks) as well as simpler ones (brochures, invitations, programs, forms, applications), and (f) select and work with advertising/ public relations agencies; and (2) a demonstrated knowledge of (a) ink colors, paper stock, and print styles, and (b) the concepts and use of desktop publishing. *Resources* to develop these skills include design courses, in-service/on-the-job training, workshops, conferences, and institutes (commercial, professional), and appropriate readings.

Competency Area: Counseling

Basic skills include (1) a demonstrated interest in, and ability to work well with, people; (2) a demonstrated ability to listen to, and work with, diverse groups of people; and (3) a demonstrated understanding of psychology. *Advanced skills* include (1) a demonstrated knowledge of, and ability to use, counseling techniques; (2) a demonstrated ability to meet the needs of special emphasis students (minority, handicapped, academically talented, at-risk, international, etc.); and (3) a demonstrated knowledge of student development theory and academic advising approaches. *Resources* to develop these skills include graduate programs in counseling and student personnel areas, workshops/conferences, in-service/on-the-job training, and appropriate readings.

Competency Area: Other Publics

Basic skills include (1) a demonstrated understanding of the interrelatedness of areas in higher education, on and off campus; (2) a demonstrated sensitivity to differences in philosophy and the approach of different offices to the same tasks; (3) a demonstrated knowledge of, and ability to work cooperatively with, other institutional areas/divisions (Development, Financial Aid, Legislative Affairs, Alumni Relations, Orientation, Student Activities, Academic Advising, Athletics, Business Office, Departmental offices, Deans' offices); (4) a demonstrated sensitivity to, and ability to work well with, outside publics (staff of governmental agencies, high school counselors, administrators, faculty, other higher education institutions, the general public); (5) a demonstrated ability to (a) provide a leadership role in representing admissions and records areas across campus, (b) network on and off campus; and (c) work effectively with the media; and (6) a demonstrated willingness to serve on division, institutional, and professional committees and projects. *Resources* to develop these skills include some graduate programs, in-service/on-the-job training, workshops/conferences, and appropriate readings.

REFERENCES

American Association of Collegiate Registrars and Admissions Officers (AACRAO), the College Entrance Examination Board, the Educational Testing Service (ETS), and the National Association for College Admission Counseling (NACAC). 1995. *Challenges in college admissions: A report of a survey of undergraduate admissions policies, practices, and procedures.* Washington, DC: AACRAO, The College Board, ETS, and NACAC.

Deering, Ellen, ed. 1954. *Professional training recommended for the registrar and admissions officer.* Washington, DC: American Association of Collegiate Registrars and Admissions Officers.

Hauser, J., and P. Lazarsfeld. 1964. *The admissions officer.* Washington, DC: American Association of Collegiate Registrars and Admissions Officers.

Henderson, Stanley E. 1990. Competencies for admissions and records professionals: An AACRAO guide to entry and advancement in the profession. *College & University* (Spring): 243–59.

Quann, C. James, et al. 1979. *Admissions, academic records, and registrar services: A handbook of policies and procedures.* San Francisco: Jossey-Bass.

Treadwell, D. R., Jr. 1977. In admissions, the ideal director boasts the speech of Demosthenes and the patience of Job. *Chronicle of Higher Education* 14(7): 18.

Vinson, D. E. 1976. *The admissions officer: A decade of change.* Dissertation copy 77-08, 122. Ann Arbor, MI: University Microfilms.

6

Ethics and Sensitivity to Students

Mary Lee Hoganson and Steven T. Syverson

The establishment of an ethical code of conduct to guide the recruitment of students and award of scholarships was the focus of a professional meeting of college admissions personnel as early as 1937 (NACAC 1937). As admissions matured into a profession, issues of ethics were continually at the forefront of discussions among practitioners, and concerns surrounding ethical admissions practices soon became a primary focus of professional associations.

Today, issues related to ethical behavior in admissions quickly capture the attention of the media. Superficial rankings of institutions in the popular press have led enrollment managers at some colleges and universities to value public image over the reporting of accurate information. The public has begun to question the veracity of any institution-reported data, as well as the motivation of admissions officers who purport to offer a good match between student and college. In such an environment, it is clearly time to refocus on ethics and sensitivity to students in the admissions process. The primary goal of the admissions process should be to serve students well. It follows that the ethical principles of the admissions profession evolve from admissions practices that place the interests and well-being of students as the highest priority. In recent years, demographic trends that have created exceptional competition for students have led to a greater emphasis by institutions on the marketing aspects of the admissions function. This, in turn, has created tension between institutional self-interest and student interests.

Although a student may have access to a superior college counselor, excellent resources such as guidebooks and electronic college-search materials, and perhaps even older siblings or family friends who have recently gone through the experience, most students will be engaged in this particular process only once. The learning curve is steep, and a great body of folklore suggests to students that college admissions offices control all the rules. College admissions professionals become adept at playing the admissions game with students, but they must remember to treat those students with respect, patience, and candor. The occasional student who behaves unacceptably in the college search process does not justify the admissions officer's deviation from a commitment to honesty and integrity when dealing with all students. Adolescents are acute observers of adults. The ethical practices of admissions counselors set the standards in the admissions process and will be noticed by applicants. Because college admissions professionals control the rules, they must set the standards. There is a direct relationship between the responsible behavior that can be expected from students and the propriety they observe in the conduct of admissions officers.

Students should see the college selection and application process as a primer on how good decisions are made. Applicants should see college selection as an orderly process that follows clear and logical rules and leads to one, and only one, final decision. The promotion of admissions practices that emphasize accurate, representative reporting of information on program and admissions standards and counseling toward a careful match between student and college will protect institutions from the destructive snowball effect of unchecked competition for students. Students are far less likely to make hasty decisions, which they may later recant, when they have received access to all of the information essential to making a good decision (including financial aid information) and have been given sufficient time to compare options before making a selection. This chapter addresses the role of the admissions officer as a counselor, ethical standards, accepted admissions conventions, and guidelines for maintaining a sensitivity to student issues.

THE ADMISSIONS OFFICER AS COUNSELOR

While institutions may define the roles of their admissions officers primarily in terms of recruitment and selection, many young people look to these professionals as counselors, especially since secondary school guidance counselors carry increasingly large caseloads in the schools or find their jobs have been eliminated due to budget tightening. College admissions counselors should be prepared to share accurate, important information about their institutions, admissions standards, the admissions process in general, standardized testing, and financial aid. Admissions counselors should be prepared to help students assess their abilities, interests, and goals; should suggest strategies for gathering and evaluating information about colleges; and should be familiar with reputable college information resources through which the student can research a range of options. Students should be encouraged to consider the appropriateness of academic programs, location, size, cocurricular options, housing opportunities, and affordability as they evaluate each of their college choices.

The goal of the professional admissions counselor must be a good match between institution and student. This focus will prompt the admissions officer, initially, to place student needs and considerations at the forefront—which may lead to a conflict with institutional goals, such as increasing the raw number of applicants or recruiting students for specific underenrolled programs. Over the long haul, however, a good match is clearly in the best interests of the institution as well as the student. Excellent retention and graduation rates result from careful admissions decisions, which should focus on enrolling students who will be satisfied over the length of their college experience. Admissions officers should provide accurate and up-to-date information about their own institution and avoid making comparisons with others. They should be candid and clear in describing to prospective students the objectives and philosophies underlying admissions decisions at their institutions. All students should receive an honest appraisal of the likelihood of admission. If admission is unlikely because of the student's academic credentials or preparation, the student should not be aggressively encouraged to apply. No responsible admissions officer should encourage inappropriate applications.

The public has a common misperception that all colleges have a specific set of statistical criteria (i.e., test scores, grades, rank) that define the level at which a student is deemed admissible. In many instances, the applicant's family assumes that the applicant who meets those criteria will be admitted, and, failing to reach those criteria, will be denied. In reality, however, it is rare that a set of statistical criteria provides an absolute guarantee of admission. Generally, the admissions office is responsible for shaping a freshman class in response to institutionally defined priorities. At the most highly selective colleges, the admissions office may choose not to admit numerous students who, on the surface at least, appear to be better prepared than others who are offered admission. Such an office is probably striving to admit a well-rounded, diverse class of students to comprise a group representing different perspectives and motivations and bringing with it individual strengths in many areas. Priority will likely be given to such factors as athletic or musical talent; cultural, geographic, or socioeconomic background; demonstrated leadership or journalistic skills; significant alumni connections; and the potential to benefit the institution through financial or political resources.

Finally, admissions counselors, as professionals, must look beyond their own experiences and listen carefully for the values of the student being counseled. An individual student's previous educational experience, family situation, economic circumstances, ethnicity, and religious background are just a few factors to be considered in planning a four-year education. Issues such as diversity of student body and access to an ethnic or religious community—while they may not be an issue for the admissions counselor—may be pivotal to a good match for a given student. Similarly, immigrants or first-generation Americans may bring a unique perspective to the meaning or value of education. The parents of these students may think of colleges in this country only in relation to the most famous institutions. They may not understand the financial aid system and be reluctant to apply for financial aid. The challenge, then, is to expand their thinking in relation to the wide range of opportunities, both in terms of respected institutions and financing options.

ETHICAL STANDARDS WITHIN THE PROFESSION

Currently, with the exception of practices resulting in discrimination against protected classes of students (e.g., women, the disabled, and the traditionally underrepresented) and the awarding of federal financial aid, there are few, if any, legislative or governmental efforts to regulate the college admissions process. While this leaves colleges with great freedoms, the onus of responsibility then falls to professionals in the field to carefully define, publicize, and monitor compliance with a code of ethical behavior.

Admissions professionals should be familiar with professional association documents that address ethical standards in admission and should refer to them regularly in their work. The American Association of Collegiate Registrars and Admissions Officers (AACRAO) publishes "Professional Practices and Ethical Standards," a set of principles to which members subscribe (see Appendix A at the end of this book). With regard to admission standards, that document specifies that AACRAO members shall

- Understand and respect the civil and human rights and responsibilities of all individuals and support and protect the principles of due process and confidentiality.
- Adhere to the principles of equality and nondiscrimination without regard to race, color, creed, gender, sexual orientation, age, disability, religion, or national origin.
- Communicate an accurate interpretation of [an] institution's admissions criteria, educational costs, financial aid availability, and major offerings to assist prospective students and their parents in making an informed decision.

The National Association for College Admission Counseling (NACAC) annually reviews, updates, and publishes the "Statement of Principles of Good Practice" (SPGP) (see Appendix B at the end of this book). The SPGP addresses the professional behaviors and practices expected of admissions professionals, secondary school counselors, and independent college counselors. Its provisions cover admissions promotion and recruitment, admission procedures, the use and reporting of standardized test data, financial aid, advanced-standing students, and the awarding of credit. NACAC monitors practices of both member and nonmember institutions. Oversight of compliance is coordinated by Admissions Practices committees at both the state/regional affiliate and national levels.

Monitoring professional guidelines over the past decade, NACAC has found lack of compliance is likely to occur in

- misrepresention of programs or statistics,
- unethical marketing strategies,

- abuses of the May 1 National Uniform Candidate Reply Date, which most often involve asking students to make enrollment commitments prior to receipt of all information on admission and financial aid options,

- abuses of the wait list,

- recruitment of students who have previously made a commitment to attend another institution,

- unethical practices relating to the awarding of scholarships or financial aid, and

- the consideration of financial need as a factor in admission, despite the fact that the practice has historically been considered unethical.

These abuses arise from increased competition for students and are frequently promoted by institutional decision makers outside the admissions office. The admissions officer who is well grounded in the ethical expectations of the profession will be most able to make a compelling case for ethical behavior to ensure that the interests of both students and institutions are well served.

Students' clear understanding of the variation in application deadlines and dates by which they must respond to offers of admission is enhanced when institutions limit application and response calendar plans to the following: Rolling Admissions, Regular Decision, Early Decision, and/or Early Action. Guidelines for these calendars are specified in the National Association for College Admission Counselors "Guidelines for Admission Decision Options in Higher Education" (see Appendix C at the end of this book). With the exception of students applying under an Early Decision plan, no student should be required to make an enrollment commitment or accept a scholarship prior to May 1, the National Uniform Candidate Reply Date.

NACAC publishes statements of rights and responsibilities for students and transfer students to outline the rights and responsibilities of students as specified in the SPGP (see Appendix D at the end of this book). These statements are intended for distribution to the public and those seeking admission to colleges and universities. Some institutions include copies with the application materials sent to students in order to make clear their commitment to ethical practices, as well as their expectations of students. Other NACAC documents with which admission professionals should be familiar are the "Guidelines on Recruitment and Admission of Student Athletes" and the "Guidelines for the Traditionally Underrepresented in Higher Education." Related financial aid administration standards are the "Statement of Good Practices," published by the National Association of Student Financial Aid Administrators (NASFAA), and the "Statement of Principles Guiding the Administration of Financial Aid Programs" of the College Scholarship Service Assembly of the College Board.

It is important to avoid the tendency to challenge any offensive behavior as unethical and also to clearly distinguish between issues of ethics versus those of etiquette. Although it is not within the purview of this chapter to discuss them in detail, to aid in making the distinction readers can consult resources such as the "Statement of Practices and Courtesies" (see Appendix E at the end of this book), developed by the Illinois Association of College Admission Counselors (IACAC).

ETHICAL RELATIONSHIPS WITH SECONDARY SCHOOL COUNSELORS

Admissions professionals should be meticulous in building a relationship of confidence and trust with secondary school colleagues. This means that all recommendations and any other formal or informal communication must be handled in a confidential manner. Recommendations intended for use in the admissions office should never be released to a third party without the recommender's permission. This prohibition should include, for example, athletic coaches.

School counselors will typically counsel students toward a range of appropriate college options, as opposed to promoting one particular institution as an ideal placement. They may not accept any type of compensation from a college or university for students who apply or enroll. Because school counselors should make information about postsecondary options equally available to all students, it is generally inappropriate for an admissions officer to request a school visit or information session with a prescreened group of students. It is vital that school officials not be placed in the untenable position of being asked to do the unethical. Secondary schools may not release lists of students to colleges and universities without the knowledge and permission of the students. Unless the counselor first secures the permission of the students involved, requests by colleges for lists of top students, high scorers, or scholarship candidates are generally unacceptable. Except in the case of an Early Decision application, counselors should never be asked to suggest a student's first choice of college or the ranking of college preferences.

ETHICAL ISSUES THAT LINK ADMISSIONS AND FINANCIAL AID

The pressures of attaining enrollment goals in the face of demand for burgeoning financial aid has led to an integration of the financial aid and the admissions processes. This, in turn, has raised a number of ethical concerns, which should be paramount in the minds of both admissions and financial aid professionals. Historically, there has been an expectation that applicants will be considered for admission without regard to financial need (commonly referred to as *need-blind admission*). Shrinking aid dollars from federal, state, and institutional resources have led a small number of institutions to move toward a need-conscious admissions strategy in which some portion of the applicant pool may be denied admission because of a lack of family financial resources. The admissions profession will likely continue to debate for some time to come the ethical merit of admitting all applicants solely on the basis of academic and personal criteria (versus such desired goals as securing a high yield from among admitted students or fully funding all admitted students).

In an era of stiff competition for students, merit scholarships offered by many institutions, large and small, have become commonplace. In many cases, these scholarships are not being provided by restricted endowment funds, but are funded from the same sources as the institution's need-based grants. The extent to which merit-aid awards deplete funds available for students with demonstrated financial need may raise ethical concerns relating to equity and access. Another relatively widespread, but objectionable, practice relating to merit scholarships is that of requiring students to accept the scholarship prior to May 1. The college's intent, obviously, is to solicit from students an early enrollment commitment—clearly an unethical procedure, because it may require the student to make an ill-informed college choice (i.e., one in which the student does not yet know of the admission and aid offers that will be made available by other institutions).

Competitive marketing tactics pressure institutions to adjust their aid offers to compete directly with other institutions trying to enroll the same students. This encourages the tendency of students to pit one college against another in a financial aid bidding war, a situation that serves neither students nor institutions well. Financial aid packages that are quite different in terms of the relative amount of grant and loan and based upon the desirability of particular candidates may also lead to inequities. Some institutions have been accused of bait-and-switch tactics whereby they offer excellent financial aid packages to first-year students but fail to match these original offers to returning students. All these issues speak clearly to the need for an ongoing, cooperative working relationship among the admissions office, financial aid office, and enrollment management office at every college and university.

ETHICAL REPORTING OF STATISTICS

A number of statistical indicators are commonly used to describe and compare colleges. Although none of these statistics gives much insight into the educational impact the college has on its students, these statistics have become a shorthand notation that many people use in an initial assessment of colleges. Particularly in the reviewing of selective colleges, it is widely agreed these statistics have been assigned too great a value as benchmarks for assessments of academic quality. Notable for their use by guidebooks in various ranking or rating schemes are profile data about the college's average class size, the student-faculty ratio, the proportion of applicants admitted into the college, and the standardized test scores and high school rank-in-class data for the freshman class. Other primary descriptors that are typically cited but less frequently included in ratings of academic quality include total student body size, availability of financial aid, and the geographic and ethnic distribution of freshmen.

Data often can be compiled and presented in ways that are technically accurate yet misleading to students, who should suspect omissions of data for groups of the population. For example, it is a commonly accepted principle that direct student contact with professors is likely to offer a better learning experience. The incremental value of increased faculty contact obviously varies by academic discipline, the quality of the professor, and the learning style of the student. This principle is the impetus for scrutinizing the student-faculty ratio and average class size. How best, then, are these ratios assessed and reported? Which faculty and which students should be included? The most representative statistic probably is the ratio of full-time equivalent (FTE) teaching faculty (based upon teaching load), to FTE students (based upon enrollment), which will match neither the number of faculty nor the number of students at the institution. What is an average class size? Is it an attempt to describe the typical freshman experience? If so, should it include only those courses in which freshmen typically enroll? Statistics such as student-faculty ratio and average class size relate to the type of experience a student is likely to have on the particular campus. Thus, although no specific guidelines have been articulated here, the responsible admissions officer should report data and information in a manner that will give prospective students the clearest possible insight into the environment they will encounter should they enroll.

Most pernicious, perhaps, is the use of data about application-to-admit ratios and standardized test data. Because these measures of selectivity often are the most commonly used descriptors in assessing the academic quality of institutions, admissions officers believe that these measures have the greatest potency in affecting the public image of the quality of their college. Thus, there is a great incentive to have these statistics appear as favorable as possible.

What comprises an application? Should it be only an application that is complete enough to be reviewed and potentially admit a student? Some colleges require only a brief application form and a transcript—no student-written essay and no recommendation forms from counselors or teachers. Others require multiple recommendation forms and multiple essays. Even many selective colleges will waive some of their requirements in the cases of some students who are clearly attractive candidates. Should applicants include anyone who submits an application fee, thus signifying an intention to apply? Some colleges do not require an application fee. Should applicants include only those students to whom the college sent a decision letter? This would exclude applicants who formally withdraw from consideration prior to receiving a decision letter, even though their applications are complete. It might also encourage some colleges to inappropriately send denial letters to all those candidates who never completed their applications, thereby bolstering their application count.

For similar reasons, it is seductive for an admissions office to report standardized test data in a misleading fashion. There is no external verification of any of the scores reported to the media or publishing organizations. It is relatively easy to rationalize excluding certain subsets of students (e.g., members of traditionally underrepresented groups, athletes, foreign students, alumni children) from the freshman profile data. The rationale commonly invoked is that such students have been admitted based upon characteristics other than their academic prowess, so to include them in the profile is misleading to the average student attempting to assess the likelihood of admission to the institution.

Prospective students and their counselors use data about the number of applicants and the academic profile of the freshman class primarily to assess the student's likelihood of admission (see Chapter 13). There are numerous ways in which admission officers can misuse these data. It is critical to remember that good, accurate data that are clearly representative of the college will help students apply to colleges that are the best match, and, in turn, will help colleges enroll successful, enthusiastic students.

STANDARDIZED TESTING ISSUES

The use of standardized testing was introduced into the college admissions process to allow colleges to assess students' level of preparation for college in some standard fashion, thereby decreasing the impact of differences in educational background and school-to-school variations in grading standards and academic rigor. Ironically, over time, standardized admissions testing has given rise to concerns that relate not only to the appropriate and ethical use of test scores, but also to issues of sensitivity to students. Admissions professionals should become familiar with the specific guidelines of the testing agencies that outline educationally sound practices related to college entrance testing such as *Guidelines on the Uses of College Board Test Scores and Related Data* (College Entrance Examination Board 1988) and *ACT Statement of Policies* (American College Testing 1979).

It is widely agreed that a student's academic performance during high school is the best statistical predictor of academic performance in college (Morgan 1994). The results of standardized tests, however, have become a preoccupation in the minds of the college-bound population as well as too many admissions officers. At most institutions where large numbers of applications are processed, the best test scores presented by the applicant become a part of the regression analysis equation used to predict freshman academic success. Virtually all published college ratings incorporate test scores into their analyses. As a result, standardized test scores of the freshman class have become a shorthand notation for assessing a college's academic quality and rigor—a use that was never intended. All college applicants and their families need to clearly understand that past academic performance is the single best predictor of future academic success (see Chapter 14). In recent years, a similar situation has begun to occur in some states in the assessment of the quality of high schools. At best, it is illogical to use such test results to evaluate institutions unless all students are required to sit for the exams.

It has been argued repeatedly that there is gender and ethnic bias in the tests.

Although proponents and opponents of this theory can both cite evidence confirming their opinions, it is important to note that college admission tests (notably SAT-I, ACT, and SAT-II) should not be thought of as intelligence tests. These tests are specifically designed to measure particular aspects of acquired knowledge and types of thinking. Tests utilized as college admissions criteria are designed to help assess the likelihood of success in college, not innate intelligence. Both the testing agencies and the leading professional organizations recommend that colleges report the range of scores describing the middle 50 percent of their classes, rather than average or median test scores. Not only does this help to deemphasize the significance assigned to a single set of scores in describing a college's student body, it actually gives the student much more information about the characteristics of the freshman class. Two colleges might have the same average test scores, but one might have a very homogeneous population, with the range of scores being clustered very tightly around the middle, while the other might have a very wide range in test scores.

Admissions professionals will need to exercise sensitivity in working directly with students on the subject of standardized testing issues. For some students, their standardized test scores are a real boost; for others, however, they serve as one more blow to an already shaky adolescent self-concept. In addition to reconciling their own feelings about test performance, students must deal with high parental expectations. Of particular concern are students for whom there is a large discrepancy between standardized test results and academic performance in a demanding college preparatory program. Too often these students may question the relative value of four years of focused self-discipline and hard work when three hours spent on one test seems to them to count nearly as much.

Students often talk about their scores as if they were a shoe size—unchangeable and beyond their control. They worry that they will not be able to fill the shoes laid out in median test scores displayed in catalogues and guidebooks. Even worse, they think about their scores in terms of passing or failing. It is imperative that school counselors and admissions professionals meet these misconceptions head-on. Counselors should educate themselves about the real significance and value of standardized tests, the context in which they are used and useful, as well as their clear limitations. It is important to provide students with this information as often and in as many ways as possible. Students are reassured to know that:

- college admissions decisions are almost never based on test scores in isolation and the scores often are less important than the academic record and personal accomplishments. Some colleges, however, publish minimum test requirements;

- every standardized test score represents an estimate of potential performance rather than an exact measure, as evidenced by the fact that students who test more than once regularly achieve different scores on each administration;

- test scores are generally viewed by colleges within the context of a student's educational, cultural, and socioeconomic background;

- there can indeed be, and often are, for many very bright and achieving students, large discrepancies between academic performance and standardized testing, which are attributable to a variety of factors beyond the student's control, such as language background, unfamiliarity with the test format, or anxiety in the test situation; and

- the insight into personal strengths and weaknesses gained over 12 years of daily academic experiences is far more meaningful than the results of any examination viewed in isolation.

RELATED LEGAL GUIDELINES

The admissions process falls under the federal guidelines of the Family Education Rights and Privacy Act of 1974 as Amended (FERPA; formerly known as the Buckley Amendment). These guidelines apply to any institution that receives funding administered by the U.S. Department of Education. The most pertinent provisions apply to the maintenance of admissions records and specify that enrolled students must have access to all information in their admissions file with the exception of letters of recommendation for which they have voluntarily waived their right of access. FERPA does not apply to records of students who are denied admission or are accepted but choose to attend another institution. Furthermore, rights are not given by FERPA to students enrolled in one component of an institution who seek admission to another component of the same institution (e.g., a student, admitted and enrolled in one college within a university but denied admission to another college does not have any FERPA rights in the college that denied admission) (Guidelines for Postsecondary Institutions for Implementation of the Family Educational Rights and Privacy Act of 1974 as Amended). FERPA applies to notes made by admissions officers from interviews or evaluative deliberations should they become a part of the admissions file. For this reason, many admissions committees do not make such notes a part of the permanent admissions record.

Students with learning disabilities or other physically or mentally handicapping conditions are afforded clear rights under both Section 504 of the Rehabilitation Act of 1973 and the Americans with Disabilities Act of 1990 (ADA). While Section 504 applies to institutions that receive federal financial assistance, the ADA applies to almost all institutions, regardless of whether they receive state or federal funding. Students with documented disabilities who self-identify may not be discriminated against in the admissions process and must have reasonable accommodations provided upon enrollment. These accommodations must provide students with equal opportunity to participate in a college's programs, courses, and activities. Admissions officers should be prepared to describe these accommodations as well as applicable special support services to applicants.

As they are confronted with the frequent use and discussion of confidential information, admissions officers must be ever diligent in assessing the appropriateness of their use of this information. A relatively limited number of individuals have a legitimate ''need to know'' any of the information included in either the admissions or financial aid application folders. Revealing any of this information to anyone else constitutes an invasion of the student's privacy. In their official capacities, admissions officers and high school counselors routinely deal with confidential information (e.g., transcripts, recommendations, interview notes, financial data). Because confidential information comprises a substantial portion of the information on which admissions decisions are made, there is frequent discussion of such information within the admissions office, sometimes causing admissions candidate anecdotes to become the currency of admissions officers' dialogue. The danger inherent in these conversations is that admissions officers may, casually and inappropriately, discuss confidential information in the hallway and out onto campus or other venues.

SUMMARY

Good admissions decisions are made through an amalgam of the responsible efforts of admissions professionals, secondary school counselors, and students who understand the admissions process. Indeed, from the institution's perspective, admissions work is often seen as marketing, sorting, and matching. But admissions officers who value their work as vital members of the educational community—those who will build and nourish a career in admission—see themselves as far more than recruiters and gatekeepers. They are counselors and advocates as well, and they maintain a commitment to the ethical standards that are at the very heart of the profession.

James J. Scannell, Vice President for Enrollments, Placement and Alumni Affairs at the University of Rochester, in writing about college and university financial aid policies, states that:

The financial aid profession need not and should not abandon its principles and practices because of market competition. On the contrary, reaffirming the most important principles, practices, and policies, and working hard to reach outcomes consistent with those ideals, should be the task at hand. The challenges will be many, the decisions difficult, but if that were not the case, there would be no need for principles, practices, and attendant policies. (Scannell 1992)

These words speak eloquently for the admissions profession, as well. The maturation of admissions into a profession clearly parallels the definition, evolution, and monitoring of its attendant professional standards of behavior and practice. The survival of a professional identity will depend largely upon an abiding commitment to ethical principles and practices. Many factors today conspire to erode these standards. There is a constant and growing tension between admissions strategies which are market driven and those which are student centered. Ultimately and over time, admission practices that are sensitive to the needs of students and serve students well will also serve institutions and the profession well.

REFERENCES

American Association of Collegiate Registrars and Admissions Officers (AACRAO). 1995. *Guidelines for postsecondary institutions for implementation of the Family Educational Rights and Privacy Act of 1974 as amended.* Rev. ed. Washington, DC: AACRAO.

Lowery, William R. et al. 1982. *College admissions counseling: A handbook for the professional.* San Francisco: Jossey-Bass.

Matthay, Eileen R. et al. 1991. *Counseling for college: A professional's guide to motivating, advising, and preparing students for higher education.* Princeton, NJ: Peterson's Guides.

Morgan, R. 1994. *Effects of scale choice on prediction validity.* Princeton, NJ: Educational Testing Service.

National Association for College Admission Counseling. 1995. *The admission practitioner.* Alexandria, VA: NACAC.

————. 1998. *Membership directory and association policies.* Alexandria, VA: NACAC.

National Association of College Admission Counselors (NACAC). 1937. Minutes of a meeting of college representatives at the LaSalle Hotel, Chicago, in May. Washington, DC: NACAC Archives.

Pope, Loren. 1990. *Looking beyond the Ivy League: Finding the college that's right for you.* New York: Penguin Books.

Scannell, James J. 1992. *The effect of financial aid policies on admission and enrollment.* New York: The College Entrance Examination Board.

7

The Role of Professional Associations

Wayne E. Becraft

WHAT IS AN ASSOCIATION?

An association is an organization of people who share common interests or a common purpose. An association is a vehicle for bringing together people with similar interests, concerns, and problems to share ideas and solutions; to develop standards and guidelines; and to provide publications, information, training, and encouragement to its members, both experienced and new. It is an independent, nongovernmental, usually not-for-profit organization that provides information, programs, and services to help people in a particular field of endeavor. Among the diverse interests represented by associations are trade, education, employment, social, and cultural areas.

Associations are very commonplace in the United States. The *1995 Encyclopedia of Associations* (1994) lists over 22,000 national and international associations and 64,000 state, regional, and local associations, from the AAAA Scholarship Foundation to the ZZ Top International Fan Club—and new ones are created each day. There is even an association for associations—the American Society of Association Executives (ASAE). According to a study by the Hudson Institute on behalf of ASAE, 7 in 10 Americans belong to one association and 1 in 4 belong to four or more such groups.

Associations have a formal organizational structure. In forming an association, the first step is usually the development of a constitution and set of bylaws that provide the framework and rules of operation for the association. Once the constitution and bylaws have been adopted by the membership, a new organization is born. Most associations are governed by a board of directors or executive committee elected by the membership, with specific tasks delegated to volunteer committees and task forces.

Larger associations may feel the need for an ongoing presence and a staff to carry out the work of the organization between meetings of its board and committees. Such associations typically appoint a president or executive director (depending on the organizational structure) to oversee an office and staff. Association offices vary in size depending on the number of members in the organization and the tasks assigned to the office. Tasks assigned to such offices typically include research; professional development programs, publications, and other membership services; fund-raising; governmental relations; maintenance of the membership database; management of association resources; service as a resource for the board of directors or executive committee; and implementation of special projects. Because of high interest in governmental relations and the perceived need to interact with legislators and other government officials, many associations locate their offices in the nation's capital, Washington, DC.

Individuals outside associations, and occasionally those within them, sometimes mistake the national office of an association for the association itself. There should be no mistake, however; the members are the association. The national office and staff merely carry out the duties and responsibilities assigned to them by the association, usually through the board of directors or executive committee.

ASSOCIATIONS SERVING THE ADMISSIONS FIELD

Four nonprofit associations serve the admissions community. They are the American Association of Collegiate Registrars and Admissions Officers (AACRAO), the Council for the Advancement and Support of Education (CASE), the College Board, and the National Association for College Admission Counseling (NACAC). Each organization has a unique mission and set of programs.

AACRAO

Founded in 1910, AACRAO is a nonprofit, voluntary, professional education association of degree-granting postsecondary institutions, government agencies, higher education coordinating boards, private educational organizations, and education-oriented businesses. The mission of the Association is to provide leadership in policy initiation, interpretation, and implementation in the global educational community through the identification and promotion of standards and best practices in enrollment management, information technology, instructional management, and student services. More than 2,400 institutions and 9,000 individuals make AACRAO a dynamic, member-driven association. Unique programs or services offered to members include a consultant referral service, the Office of International Education Services, Standards Council (electronic data exchange) office, and many publications and other services. AACRAO provides its newsletter, the *AACRAO Data Dispenser*, and a quarterly journal, *College &*

University, to help members focus on emerging issues, interassociation news, federal legislation, new techniques in the field, and the use of technology in higher education.

CASE

More than 2,900 colleges, universities, independent elementary and secondary schools, educationally related nonprofit organizations, and commercial firms in the United States, Canada, Mexico, and 27 other countries belong to the Council for Advancement and Support of Education (CASE). Representing their institutions in CASE are more than 14,250 professionals in institutional advancement. This field, encompassing educational fund-raising, alumni relations, student recruitment, and the management of those areas, is part of philanthropy in the United States and abroad. Many college and university presidents, school heads, deans, and other administrators are also member representatives. CASE's mission is to assess the needs of its customers and continually improve products and services to meet their needs. Programs unique to CASE are publications and videos on major, matching, and planned gift programs; volunteerism; writing for fund-raising; and student recruitment. CASE offers its magazine, *Currents*, 10 times annually.

The College Board

Founded in 1910, The College Board is a national nonprofit association that champions educational excellence for all students through the ongoing collaboration of more than 2,900 member schools, colleges, universities, education systems, and organizations. The board promotes—by means of responsive forums, research, programs, and policy development—universal access to high standards of learning, equity of opportunity, and sufficient financial support so that every student is prepared for success in college and work. Programs and services unique to The College Board are the College-Level Examination Program (CLEP), College Scholarship Service (CSS), Community Assessment Program, Office of Adult Learning Services, Preliminary Scholastic Aptitude Test/National Merit Scholarship Qualifying Test, SAT I, SAT II, Student Search Service, and numerous publications, videos, and software programs. The *College Review* and other student and member publications are provided throughout the year.

NACAC

The National Association for College Admission Counseling (NACAC), founded in 1937, is an organization of high school and college and university professionals dedicated to serving students as they explore options and make choices about pursuing postsecondary education. NACAC is committed to maintaining high standards that foster ethical and social responsibility among those involved in the college transition process. The mission of the association is to support and advance the work of counselors as they help students realize their full educational potential, with particular emphasis on the transition from secondary schools to colleges and universities, and with attention to access and equity for all students. High school and independent counselors, college and university admission and financial aid professionals, for-profit and nonprofit educational organizations, and companies and individual members comprise the 6,500 members. The monthly newsletter, the *Bulletin*, and the *Journal of College Admission*, offered quarterly, provide insights on professional issues, state and regional sharing, governance matters, and national news impacting education.

While numerous organizations and for-profit companies exist to serve the admissions community, one nonprofit organization, without members, that serves the college admissions process should be acknowledged. ACT, Inc., is a nonprofit organization dedicated to measurement and research primarily in support of individuals making decisions about their education, training, and careers. For 35 years, ACT, like The College Board, has developed assessment instruments to aid students, schools, and colleges during the college transition process and the school-to-work movement. Among its unique programs and services are the ACT Assessment; the Educational Planning and Assessment System (EXPLORE); ASSET, a placement program for two-year colleges; DISCOVER, a software program to aid decision making by providing career opportunities and occupational profiles; and its work supporting student financial aid and student participation in college athletics.

ASSOCIATIONS BENEFIT MEMBERS

Members' needs are an association's primary focus and the reason why admissions professionals choose to join or utilize its services. Associations may serve as advocates for the work of their members. Although structures may vary from organization to organization, most offer opportunities for leadership within the governance structure through executive boards; standing and advisory committees or special commissions; or state, regional, or similar affiliate organizations; or as a voting delegate. Members have an opportunity to shape the direction, vision, goals, or mission of the association by participating in the association's programs, or simply by voting on major policy initiatives. It is crucial that they take advantage of these leadership and professional development experiences.

ASSOCIATIONS PROVIDE VISIBILITY

An association provides visibility for a profession, trade, or interest area by bringing together many individuals to form a large or small organization. It is very difficult for a scattered group of individuals to obtain any sort of visibility at the local, state, or national levels. It is only by joining forces, amassing talent and resources, and identifying common interests that all can support those individuals who have the visibility and recognition essential to providing leadership in a field.

Many associations use their visibility and recognition to influence elections, legislative decisions, governmental actions, and individual decisions and actions. Generally, governmental relations efforts are directed to obtaining legislation or regulations that are favorable to the members of the association, although at times the energy may be directed to benefiting the nation, the state, or the local jurisdiction. The efforts to influence individual or organizational decisions or actions most often take the form of professional standards or guidelines that provide a legal, ethical, and orderly framework within which the members should operate. The organization, however, must be strong and visible before it can influence even its own members to follow the standards and guidelines it promulgates.

ASSOCIATIONS PROVIDE NETWORKING OPPORTUNITIES

Associations bring together colleagues from across the nation, and sometimes the world, to share knowledge and exchange ideas. This type of networking is, perhaps, the greatest benefit of membership in associations. The annual meeting that most associations host brings together members to conduct business, learn through professional development programs, and share information and ideas. These meetings also provide an opportunity for attendees to network with colleagues and, if exhibits are a part, with vendors to exchange information on a one-to-one basis.

Often associations offer other professional development programs that provide similar opportunities for personal networking. However, with today's electronic communications, it is also relatively easy to be in immediate contact with colleagues across the nation and around the world. The telephone, which introduced the era of instant communication, was for many years limited to voice communication. When fax transmission was introduced, virtually every office was able to use telephone lines to send and receive documents instantly. Today, telephone systems serve as the connecting link, not for only voice and fax, but also for electronic networks that make it possible to instantaneously exchange voice, images, videos, documents, and data from one site to another anywhere in the world. With conference calls and computer conferences beginning to replace travel to meetings, this trend is likely to continue. Associations use these technologies to connect with their members and enable them to network with each other.

ASSOCIATIONS DEVELOP STANDARDS AND GUIDELINES

Associations spend $14.5 billion on industry standard-setting activities each year, according to the American Society of Association Executives (ASAE) Hudson Institute study, which is approximately 400 times more than the federal government's expenditures for setting and enforcing product safety standards.

The collective wisdom of an association's membership provides a vast pool of knowledge and experience for the development of standards and guidelines. And associations provide a mechanism for identifying common principles and practices that form the bases for personal and professional standards and guidelines. Standards and guidelines are roughly the nongovernmental or independent-sector equivalent of laws and regulations; they regulate the industry, activity, or behavior of the membership. Standards must be followed precisely. AACRAO, for example, has been instrumental in the development of electronic data interchange (EDI) standards for the electronic transmission of applications for admission and student transcripts that must be followed precisely if applications and transcripts are to be interpreted correctly. Guidelines, however, are recommendations that individuals or organizations are encouraged to follow to promote uniformity, although associations generally have no authority to require their implementation other than their prestige.

Suggestions defining what information should be collected on the application for admission, what information should be maintained in the student database, or how students with foreign credentials are placed in U.S. institutions are guidelines that institutions may or may not choose to follow. NACAC's "Statement of Principles of Good Practice," which serves as a code of ethical standards for its members, is one example. Through an adherence to monitoring procedures and the possibility of sanctions, NACAC enforces these principles to protect the integrity of the college admission process. The College Board's "Guidelines for the Use of Standardized Tests" is another example.

ASSOCIATIONS OFFER PROFESSIONAL DEVELOPMENT OPPORTUNITIES

The ASAE study by the Hudson Institute indicates that associations annually spend $8.5 billion to offer education courses to their members and the public. In fact, associations spend more on continuing or specialized education than 49 of the 50 U.S. states. In addition to the annual meeting, which provides a forum for experienced and knowledge-specific members to share that knowledge with others through workshops and program sessions, associations also offer workshops and seminars. These programs might vary in length from a few hours to several days and be offered in one place or a variety of locations around the country. Where licensure is required, associations might require members to attend a certain number of professional development programs each year in order to continue to practice in that profession. Other associations might offer optional programs that provide a particular level of expertise that is recognized with the awarding of certificates or continuing education units. Still others offer programs for those who simply want to enhance their knowledge, with no sure reward.

Professional development programs offered through teleconferencing and through videotaped or computer-based programs are beginning to replace many in-person programs because they are less costly and more convenient, both time- and site-wise. All provide mechanisms for the professional development of association members. Professional development programs also enable associations to generate nondues revenue to support other projects and activities that are not revenue producing.

ASSOCIATIONS PROVIDE INFORMATION

By bringing together groups (e.g., committees or task forces) whose collective knowledge represents a wealth of information on a wide range of subjects, associations are able to provide publications that assist their members and other groups with whom they interact. Publications may cover standards, guidelines, policies, procedures, and other information of interest. The College Board, for example, produces a variety of publications to assist students and parents with college choices, in addition to those it produces for its members. The printed word is still the most common means of exchanging information, but publications are now also being made available in electronic form.

In addition to books, many associations produce newsletters that share information of current interest to members and help them in their jobs or area of interest. Association magazines and journals also provide opportunities for members to showcase their writing and research and at the same time benefit other members. Associations use publications, like professional development programs, to bring in nondues revenue that helps underwrite the costs of projects and activities that do not produce revenue.

Through their members and national offices, associations provide information on a wide range of topics to assist members of the association and others in the higher education community and the at-large community. Associations accomplish this through networking, professional development programs, and publications. However, information is shared in many other ways: through facsimile machines or electronic networks, through visits with other members at their campuses, at annual meetings and other professional development programs, or at the national office of the association.

ASSOCIATIONS PROVIDE SERVICES

In addition to all of the areas already discussed, associations provide other services to their members. While these often include consulting, insurance, and credit card programs, more formal services are also often provided. Each of the four associations for admissions officers referred to earlier offers specific services for its members, the higher education community, and/or the at-large community.

SUMMARY

By increasing visibility, providing networking opportunities, developing standards and guidelines, offering professional development opportunities, developing publications, and providing information and services, associations are the mechanism through which members advance their own interests. Associations are the backbone of American society, fulfilling leadership roles often relegated to the government in other countries. Associations provide the opportunity for their members to participate in the determination of their own destiny.

REFERENCE

1995 encyclopedia of associations. 1994. Detroit: Gale Research.

Part III

Understanding Enrollment Management

Part III gives the rationale for institutional inclusiveness in the new field of enrollment management.

8

Strategic Enrollment Management

Michael G. Dolence

The pressures of the 1980s and the 1990s on higher education have brought increasingly complex challenges to admissions officers. Changing demographics, budget crises, shifting public perceptions of the academy and the professorate, creeping consumerism—all have combined to put the pressure on the admissions offfice. "Numbers," say the finance staff, "Quality," cry the faculty. And the admissions officers find themselves trying to do their job faced with variables over which they have no control. Long discarded is the "roadrunner" focus in admissions where the staff members apply a shotgun approach to as many students as they can reach in frenetic travel to college nights and high schools. No longer will even the best marketing efforts of an admissions office alone provide the edge needed to meet enrollment and quality expectations. The increasing complexity of the higher education environment requires the incorporation of the admissions office into a more comprehensive conceptualization of enrollment issues called Strategic Enrollment Management.

Many campus cultures fail to understand that the institution must look at enrollment from the perspective of cradle to grave, beginning with recruitment, moving on to retention, and ending with graduation and placement. The successful institutions of the twenty-first century will have a different view of both recruitment and retention. In fact, they will see these activities as part of a seamless cloth. To be successful in this new environment, admissions officers must embrace the structural and conceptual tenets of enrollment management and become key players in its development and implementation. Unfortunately, many admissions officers feel that enrollment management diminishes their role in the institution. However, the admissions office that is embedded in the strategic enrollment management process described in this chapter will be a far more powerful player in the institution and a far more successful one.

THE SEM CONCEPT

The concepts, principles, and practices of strategic enrollment management (SEM) continue to evolve. The key attribute that sets SEM apart is the holistic, institution-wide nature of strategic enrollment management. Simply defined, strategic enrollment management is a comprehensive process designed to achieve and maintain the optimum recruitment, retention, and graduation rates of students, where optimum is defined within the academic context of the institution. When applied to a given institution, the definition can be modified or refined to address more specific attributes. For example, graduation, meaning the receipt of a degree, can be recast as attainment, meaning the achievement of a degree or nondegree objective.

While this definition of SEM is fairly straightforward, certain key words have very significant implications for an institution's future. The first keyword in the definition is *comprehensive*. To be comprehensive, the SEM program must fully involve academic affairs, student affairs, and information resources management, as well as the traditional enrollment services functions. The SEM program also must extend to operations such as physical plant, maintenance, custodial services, and landscaping. The rule is that any factor that influences a student's decision to attend or to continue enrolling is fair game for an enrollment management group to tackle.

The second key word is *designed*. The plan is created in the design phase. The critical elements of design include a well-reasoned and articulate purpose, a clear and concise intention, a broad and effective scope, and an explicit set of expectations that are designed to meet the institution's priority goals and objectives. Translated into action, the design phase requires involvement (two-way communication and action) by a wide range of individuals. In most cases the design phase is perhaps more appropriately the redesign of programs, practices, policies, and procedures aimed at optimizing enrollments.

The third and fourth key words, *achieve* and *maintain*, come as a pair. Implied is not only that benchmarks will be identified and pursued (achieved), but also that the SEM program will continue into the future as an ongoing model or paradigm. Achievement can only be substantiated and maintained if the numeric goals of the SEM program are clear. This means that careful attention needs to be paid to outlining realistic numbers and understanding the fiscal implications of making them a reality. Maintaining the numbers is often the ultimate goal of the SEM approach. Therefore, SEM is not a one time event but rather a sustained effort.

The fifth key word, *optimum*, is central to the focus of any SEM program and will be described in more detail later in this chapter. Briefly, optimum enrollment is the number of students between maximum and minimum physical capacity that enables the institution to achieve fiscal stability while maintaining optimum quality. The qualitative element of optimum is an extremely important focus of any SEM program and will also be addressed later in this chapter.

The sixth and seventh key words are *recruitment* and *retention*. Recruitment is the active process an institution undertakes to favorably influence a student's decision to attend an institution. Retention is the maintenance of a student's satisfactory progress toward her or his pedagogical objective until it is attained. Recruitment focuses on both institutional and student preenrollment decision processes; retention focuses on both institutional and student postenrollment decision processes.

THE GOALS OF SEM

The importance of SEM as an institution-wide process cannot be overemphasized. SEM crosses all functional domains within an institution. No one element can be neglected without diminishing the quality of the effort.

SEM's primary goals are:

- *To stabilize enrollments.* This may involve stopping declining enrollment, controlling enrollment growth, and/or smoothing out fluctuations in enrollment in order to stabilize finances. It may also mean working with individual departments to increase the number of majors, bringing the department to break-even enrollment numbers, or handling overenrollment pressures.

- *To link academic programs and SEM.* Too many departments and schools leave their enrollment profiles to the whims and forces of chance and change. Embedding the principles and practices of SEM in academic unit management and operations affords the opportunity to establish stable departments and improve both quality and retention. Most important is to align all of the academic planning, review, and evaluation processes, including program review, accreditation self-study, annual budget preparation, academic master planning, curriculum planning, and others.

- *To stabilize finances.* Higher education cannot fix its financial problems by working the expenditure side of the equation alone. With the costs of higher education rising consistently faster than the Consumer Price Index and the deep concern of the public over the continued escalation, serious long-term revenue planning must be undertaken. The link between enrollments and revenues is inexorable. In fact, enrollment planning and revenue planning go hand in hand.

- *To optimize resources.* This goes beyond budget. It includes containing growth in the number of employees, redirecting and refocusing employees' efforts, optimizing campus information systems, and so forth. It has been suggested that every campus in America underexploits its existing resources.

- *To improve services.* Many services are misguided, redundant, or unvalued by their recipients. SEM provides methods for dramatically improving services, including shortening response time, increasing satisfaction, and reducing overhead and paperwork.

- *To improve quality.* Quality in most institutions is poorly defined. This lack of definition hinders efforts at improvement. SEM can make quality more explicit, better defined, and more approachable than systematic methods of enhancement. Quality has three dimensions: inputs, processes, and outputs. SEM helps focus upon all three.

- *To improve access to information.* SEM cannot be implemented without an integrated information system on-line. SEM also cannot be implemented if an insufficient number of people are trained to run that on-line system. This does not mean that more people need to be hired, but it does mean that those who can be trained should be; and those who cannot be trained need to be replaced by individuals who can.
- *To reduce vulnerability to environmental forces.* Sound SEM programs continually monitor and evaluate environmental signals. This monitoring and evaluating helps mitigate the negative impact of local and regional events, and, where necessary, expands the pool of qualified prospects.
- *To evaluate strategies and tactics.* Any formal SEM program tracks initiatives against expected results to determine what works and change what does not.

SEM is not a quick fix. It is a deliberate process that requires approximately three years for full implementation and an information infrastructure to sustain it. SEM can usually be developed with existing resources and can be implemented in a wide variety of ways, which can be supported through various organizational structures. SEM calls for new levels of trust and cooperation from those involved in different aspects of the process. The success of SEM rests on sound, ongoing planning, and evaluation based on criteria established in the development phase of the program.

DEFINING OPTIMUM ENROLLMENTS

Optimum enrollment is not a single number but a derived function of many numbers that describes the most desirable state of enrollments. Optimum enrollment can be defined and measured in a variety of terms such as headcount enrollment, full-time equivalent (FTE) enrollment, class rank of incoming freshmen, the distribution of course enrollments among departments, the segmentation of enrollments by college or school, or the geographic origin of students, to name a few. This family of numbers that describes the optimum enrollment is unique to each institution. These numbers can be a function of physical capacity, fiscal capacity, academic program strategy, service strategy, or any number of other factors. Each factor brings a number of key campus issues to the SEM design process.

Optimum enrollment is the benchmark enrollment figure that indicates revenues and expenditures are in balance. Optimum enrollment is a number that falls between the maximum and minimum fiscal/physical capacity. The concept is multidimensional and includes, but is not limited to, the following components.

Optimizing headcount enrollment relates to the physical capacity of the campus. Key issues such as the size and configuration of classrooms; the amount and configuration of housing units; the number and location of parking spaces; the capacity, quality, and desirability of food services; the number and configuration of study areas; facility seating capacities; and campus information network capacity are all germane to headcount enrollment. It is easy to see in these examples that optimizing headcount fully involves, and is inseparable from, the physical facilities–planning process.

Optimum segmentation relates to the distribution of enrollment based on such distinctions as departments, colleges, and schools; undergraduate or graduate levels; or professional versus liberal arts and sciences. This is the primary purpose for developing strong SEM linkages to the academic department level.

Optimum geographic origin relates to the geographic dispersion of the institution's service area. Generally, the more narrow the geographic service area, the more vulnerable the institution is to local factors, events, and phenomena. Changing this dimension requires several years and very careful planning.

Optimizing FTE enrollment relates to productivity and fiscal capacity. These factors are often measured by course load and faculty-to-student ratio. An essential, but often overlooked, component of optimizing FTE enrollment is revenue planning. A sample revenue plan, outlined later in this chapter, illustrates the inescapable relationship between revenue and FTE. Optimizing both headcount and FTE enrollment fully involve the entire institution. This accounts for the number of institutions that initiate their strategic-planning process with an SEM focus.

Optimizing quality is of utmost importance. Despite its importance, many institutions fail to develop adequate strategies to do so. In order to begin the process of optimizing quality, the meaning of quality and how it is measured must be defined in unambiguous terms. In traditional terms, quality relates to the academic ability and rank of students; the skills, characteristics, and expertise of the faculty; and the appropriateness of the academic infrastructure (labs, computers, etc.). As it is emerging in the strategic enrollment management context, the concept of quality has three distinct components. These components can be articulated within the structure of the classic inputs-process-outputs (IPO) model.

1. The first component encompasses inputs to the institution's teaching/learning process. Inputs on the student side of SEM include such student measures as rank in high school, GPA, and SAT/ACT test score performance. On the institution side of SEM are faculty and services, including such metrics as faculty-to-student ratio, percentage of faculty with terminal degrees, average class size, and percentage of faculty who teach undergraduates.

2. The second component encompasses the teaching/learning process. Here are such metrics as student satisfaction surveys, student evaluations of faculty teaching, accreditation self-studies, and reviews.

3. The third component encompasses output measures such as time to degree, placement rate upon graduation, and success in life surveys.

The IPO quality model can be simplified to the following equation. Enrollment is equal to dollars generated in the form of tuition, fee, and/or appropriated funds revenue. Dollars equal the resources needed to maintain quality such as faculty, facilities, and staff. The combined resources available to learners, when brought to bear, equal quality.

$$\text{Enrollment} = \text{Dollars} = \text{Resources} = \text{Quality}$$

This simplified equation makes clear the linkages between enrollment, revenue, resources, and quality. It also makes clear the essential nature of SEM as an institution-wide priority. Translating the principles of SEM into management principles and decision making is not as simple as the equation, however. To facilitate the translation and foster strategic decision-making processes that optimize the equation, it is necessary to consider a family of key performance indicators.

USING KEY PERFORMANCE INDICATORS

Optimum enrollment strategies can be designed around a core of essential key performance indicators. Key performance indicators (KPIs) are measures that are monitored in order to determine the health, effectiveness, and efficiency of an organization. They are not broad, general, categorical metrics, such as quality, resources, satisfaction, efficiency, or effectiveness. KPIs are specific quantitative measures that tell stakeholders, managers, and other staff whether the college or university is accomplishing its goals while using an acceptable level of resources. KPIs are precise numbers that have one, and only one, definition throughout the organization.

The examples of KPIs outlined in Table 8.1 are considered primary because they relate to institution-level metrics. These primary KPIs are comprised of a number of secondary KPIs. For example, KPI #1, undergraduate FTE, is the sum of FTE enrollments of all departments. Departmental FTE enrollment is considered at the second level. Occasionally, an institution will rename this a contributing KPI to avoid any inadvertent interpretation of secondary as being inferior. To enable the institution to meet its undergraduate, full-time equivalent KPI target, each department must contribute at a prescribed level. When departmental FTE is coupled with #10, the Break-even-major Index, the KPIs begin to establish both the numeric enrollment targets and revenue targets for each department. In this way the selection and monitoring of primary KPIs frame departmental-level metrics and strategies. This process helps any strategy reach deeply into an institution.

The combination of primary and secondary KPIs can further be enriched by a third level of KPI. Tertiary KPIs are a family of metrics that measure tactical effectiveness. For example, an institution may propose three tactics to increase minority enrollment (KPI #5, Table 8.1). The tactics may or may not be part of the standard operating procedures of the institution. In order to determine the effectiveness of the tactics, the yield of minority students attributed to each tactic

Table 8.1

Examples of Key Performance Indicators with Definitions

Example Key Performance indicator	Example Definition*
1. Undergraduate FTE Enrollment	Number of units attempted divided by 15
2. Graduate FTE Enrollment	Number of units attempted divided by 12
3. Tuition Revenue	Tuition Revenue Collected Net of Institutional Financial Aid
4. Graduation Rate	Percentage of full-time undergraduates who graduate in 4 years
5. Minority Enrollment	Percentage of all enrolled students who are minorities
6. Placement Rate	Percentage of graduates employed or in advanced study one year after graduation
7. Student Faculty Ratio	Number of FTE students divided by the number of FTE Faculty
8. Recruitment Yield	Percentage of students offered admission who enroll
9. Retention Rate	Percentage of students who maintain satisfactory progress
10. Break-even-major Index	Total Revenue deriving from students in each major minus the attributable cost of the major department
11. Average Debt Burden	Total value of loans divided by the number of loan recipients
12. Student Satisfaction	Composite score from annual student needs and priorities survey
13. Average SAT Score	Average SAT score of incoming freshmen
14. Value of Endowment	Book value of endowment at the end of each quarter
15. Deferred Maintenance	Dollar value of maintenance backlog
*These examples are excerpted from strategic plans developed using the SPE	

would be monitored as a key performance indicator designed to facilitate tactic or program evaluation. Tertiary KPIs can also help program evaluators, designers, and managers better understand the precise components of what works and what does not.

This level of accountability has been strongly resisted in some institutions, but the increasing demand from policy makers and constituents makes it unlikely that the academy will avoid accountability for much longer.

LINKING ACADEMIC PROGRAMS AND SEM PROGRAMS

An institution's academic program is inexorably codependent with enrollment management. The quality of the academic program can only be developed and maintained in a stable enrollment environment, and stable enrollments are only possible through the sound planning, development, and management of academic programs. The alignment of institutional academic policies with SEM goals and objectives is essential to successfully structuring the SEM process.

Academic Programs and Student Choice Drive SEM

The curriculum and resultant degrees are higher education's principal product. It is, therefore, the curriculum, academic policy, and the corresponding choices students make to attend, persist, or drop out that drive the planning, implementation, and evaluation of an institution's recruitment and retention programs.

Optimizing Academic Policy

Academic policy establishes the rules guiding students' progression through the curriculum toward their degrees. Because academic policy establishes the rules, this policy is one of the most powerful tools of strategic enrollment management and must be aligned with both recruitment and retention strategies.

Balancing Demand

Demands for programs vary. Many professional programs such as nursing or engineering experience cyclical levels of demand. Others, such as business, accounting, and premed, have stable, or even increasing, growth curves over time. SEM is extremely valuable during periods of very high demand because of its keen focus on optimizing enrollments and throughput. SEM helps institutions balance the effects of changing demand by adjusting geographic recruitment areas, establishing sustainable enrollment targets, and monitoring competition, thereby facilitating the health of academic departments.

Students as Clients

Students have free choice. SEM recognizes students' freedom to choose their institutions and programs. It establishes a client relationship with students, their parents, and the recruitment/advising community. With its recruiting and retaining strategies, developing and offering essential services, launching new program initiatives, and evaluating all SEM programs are all based on decisions made from students' perspectives.

Optimizing Teaching and Learning

SEM is not simply an administrative function. Creating the best learning and teaching environment is as important to the success of a strategic enrollment management program as good marketing. Achieving optimum teaching and learning environments means balancing a complex set of factors that include academic program development, academic infrastructure development, faculty development, faculty hiring, academic policy formulation and enforcement, recruitment policies and procedures, and retention policies and procedures.

Optimizing Academic Planning

Academic program planning, planning the pedagogy, and academic product planning require particular focus.

Academic Program Planning. The focus of academic program planning (what subjects and subject areas will be taught) is to maintain an alignment between societal learning needs and the institution's Academic Master Plan. This focus requires the careful monitoring of developments in the learning environment, a careful identification of initiatives required, and the continuous development, review, and refinement of proposals to meet emerging needs and priorities.

Planning the Pedagogy. Planning the pedagogy (the processes by which the material will be taught, presented, or learned) involves the continuous design and redesign of the processes by which the subject material will be taught, presented, or learned. This continuation requires a much more intense focus on various methods of learning, the careful measure of what works for whom, and the planned infusion of effective methods into the delivery of learning.

Academic Product Planning. The academy must recognize that the curriculum it offers, the methods it uses to facilitate learning (how the curriculum will be packaged and presented to a learning marketplace with dramatically changing parameters), and the outcomes it certifies are essential products of the information (learning) age. Redefining these products to better align them with a twenty-first-century context is an important step in academic planning.

Examples of reengineered courses follow:

1. The Principles of Twenty-First-Century Socioeconomics (formerly Socioeconomics 235). The systematic examination of five classic socioeconomic events of the twentieth century and what they can tell us about the emergence of twenty-first-century socio-economic principles. The XYZ econometric modeling package will be used to predict the effects of policy proposals.
2. Computer-Simulated Genetics (formerly Genetics 250). Using the DriFlyLab simulation tools, the principles of genetics will be simulated using *Droisophiola Malanogastor* as the test species. Students will master the principles of population genetics and be introduced to the concepts of molecular genetics.
3. Simulating Urban Environments of the Future (formerly Urban Geography 250). Students will build four simulated cities of the future and run each simulation for 50, 100, 200, and 300 years. Students will prepare an analysis of each simulation.

These examples illustrate the emergence of a curriculum where the principles are taught in context and the basics are conveyed using computer-based tools.

ORGANIZING TO MANAGE ENROLLMENTS

The enrollment management domain reaches across virtually all sectors. At a minimum, admissions, financial aid, recruitment (if separate from admissions), registrar, and retention should be aggregated for planning, operational management, and accountability purposes. The inclusion of the offices of the registrar and retention show how the enrollment management domain becomes embedded in the academic affairs of the institution. Individual institutional characteristics, personalities, motivation, commitment, and understanding determine the success of a program more than where it reports. However, enrollment management has successfully been implemented under academic affairs, student affairs, and its own cabinet-level enrollment management leader.

The probability of achieving success in strategic enrollment management increases with active leadership from the executive officers of the institution (president and vice presidents) and the adoption of a formal SEM process. There are four basic organizational options with numerous variations within each: the SEM organization, the SEM Task Force, the SEM Committee, and the SEM coordinator.

The Strategic Enrollment Management Organization

Sometimes referred to as the SEM Division, this unit of the institution is headed by an executive officer of the institution who reports directly to the president. The division or unit can be constructed in a wide variety of ways. The typical division gives all SEM-related administrative functions one central focus. Policy, procedures, budgets, and other essential components are more easily coordinated and developed in cooperation with academic affairs. A task force or steering committee is used in conjunction with the division to provide policy guidance and oversight.

The SEM Task Force

The SEM Task Force is usually a representative body of key individuals from academic affairs, student services, admissions, financial aid, and the registrar's office who are charged with recommending a design for the SEM program and developing the first strategic enrollment management plan. In some institutions, the task force remains in force to provide policy oversight and evaluation of the SEM program.

The SEM Committee

The SEM Steering Committee is a line committee within the institution's governmental structure. It is charged with policy oversight; evaluation; planning; and advising on strategies, goals, and objectives of the SEM program. The committee convenes work groups to recommend and review policy, develop alternatives, facilitate cooperation and coordination, and advance the SEM program. The SEM committee serves as the communication hub with the academic senate and other governmental bodies.

The SEM Coordinator

The SEM coordinator, who may or may not have line responsibility for SEM functions, coordinates and integrates diverse enrollment management functions, services, and strategies by improving communications, coordinating cooperative

Figure 8.1
The Enrollment Management Funnel

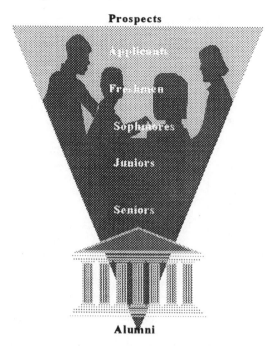

Prospects

Alumni

planning, and acting as liaison and often mediator. The position, often in place in the early stages of SEM program development, helps the institution focus more on the principles of SEM before a more structured approach is adopted.

MAPPING THE FLOW OF ENROLLMENTS

From the discussion of KPIs, it becomes evident that optimum enrollment is not a single number but a derived function of many numbers that describes the most desirable state of enrollments within an institutional context. As stated previously, optimum enrollment can be defined and measured in a variety of terms such as headcount enrollment, FTE enrollment, class rank of incoming freshmen, the distribution of course enrollments among departments, the segmentation of enrollments by college or school, or the geographic origin of students, to name a few. These numbers are not static but dynamic and ever changing as students move through the enrollment process. It is vitally important to both understand the flow process and monitor the enrollments at each step.

A classic method for mapping the flow of enrollments is by using the enrollment management funnel. The funnel illustration (see Figure 8.1) demonstrates a few of the stages an individual moves through in the enrollment process.

Table 8.2
The Four Phases of SEM

Institutional Decision (Examples not exhaustive)	SEM Phase & Key Performance Indicators	Student Decision (Examples not exhaustive)
Image, Program Service Mix, Geographic Sphere of Influence, Admissions Standards...	**Identification Phase** Number of Prospects Number of Respondents Requests for Application	The decision to examine your institution
Application Procedures, Admission Standards, Financial Aid Policy Curriculum...	**Recruitment Phase** Number of Applications Number of Accepted Number of Deposits	The decision to attend your institution
Financial Aid Policy Grading Policy Student Life Curriculum...	**Retention Phase** Number of Freshmen Number of Sophomores Number of Juniors Number of Seniors	The decision to complete their pedagogical objective at your institution
Relationship Strategy	**Sustaining Phase** Graduates Alumni	The decision to continue to support your institution

It also illustrates the rather large number of individuals who must be identified in the prospecting stage in order to make the numbers necessary at each subsequent stage of enrollment.

The funnel diagram is useful in mapping the flow of enrollments, in developing revenue projections, and in enrollment management planning because it identifies key attrition points and provides a framework to begin to map institutional policy against key enrollment management phases. The flow of enrollments must also be mapped against both institutional and student decisions. Table 8.2 frames the SEM funnel into four distinct phases: the identification phase, the recruitment phase, the retention phase and the sustaining phase. These four phases of SEM help articulate the specific decisions that both students and institutions face.

BUILDING AND USING A REVENUE MODEL

Once the flow of enrollments is mapped and the factors affecting recruitment, attrition and retention are understood, it is time to begin building a revenue model for the institution. In its simplest form, the revenue model derives income from each stage of enrollment. The model calculates forgone revenue using attrition data and can be used to feed basic budget processes, strategic planning, financial aid decisions, and a host of other key decisions. Revenue models almost always start out simple and grow significantly more complex as they are used and modified.

Table 8.3 illustrates a simple revenue model from a state institution. In this particular example, tuition revenue goals were established by the state; in-state and out-of-state tuition rates were both established by the legislature. State policy mandated that tuition revenue shortfalls result in direct and immediate budget reductions for the institution.

The first revenue model (Table 8.3) the institution used calculated revenue by term, geographic origin, and level. While instructive, this model drove demand for a more detailed model to be developed. The second version added revenue lost to attrition. The third version of the model added state appropriations revenue tied to enrollment. The fourth added nonenrollment categories.

Shortly after the fourth version of the model was developed and folded into the SEM analysis, the group began to look at expenditure policies as a function of their impact on revenue. Coupled with a modestly comprehensive retention analysis, the SEM group developed several proposals.

One of the first proposals involved an expenditure policy used in setting retention priorities during budget development. The revenue analysis helped individual schools make a case for increased expenditures on retention programs in anticipation of saving revenue by decreasing attrition. Specific revenue and student retention KPIs were selected and targets were set. A retention initiative was designed to deliver the revenue targets, and the necessary budget augmentation proposals were developed. The proposed budget amounted to between 34 percent and 56 percent of anticipated revenue gain.

Two decisions ensued. First, the decision was made to fund the budget augmentation to increase retention and conserve the revenue while maintaining appropriate quality. Second, the SEM group decided to examine the cost of recruitment and the impact of various recruitment strategies on revenue when attrition was taken into consideration. A proposal for the planned migration to higher admissions standards was developed that conserved revenues and avoided special retention expenditures. Again, specific targets were set and the planned migration was approved and enacted.

A WORD ABOUT ENROLLMENT PROJECTIONS

For years institutions have grappled with the complexities and uncertainties of projecting enrollments. Many models have been developed and projections made—and chosen models have repeatedly been a disappointment. Many factors have been cited to account for inaccuracies: enrollment projection methodologies are in their infancy, no one can predict prospect behavior, not enough infor-

Table 8.3
Sample Tuition Revenue Model

Student Classification	Fall Term	Spring Term	Summer Term	Pay at Time of Service	Annual Tuition Revenue Total
In State Undergraduate	12,000 @ $1,200= $14,400,000	11,500 @ $1,200= $11,400,000	1,000 @ $1,200= $1,200,000		$24,600,000
In State Graduate	1,000 @ $2,200= $2,200,000	1,000 @ $2,200= $2,200,000	1,000 @ $2,200= $2,200,000		$6,600,000
Out of State Undergraduate	2,000 @ $5,200= $10,400,000	2,000 @ $5,200= $10,400,000	500 @ $5,200= $2,600,000		$23,400,000
Out of State Graduate	400 @ $5,200= $2,080,000	400 @ $5,200= $2,080,000	400 @ $5,200= $2,080,000		$6,240,000
International Undergraduate	320 @ $5,200= $1,664,000	320 @ $5,200= $1,664,000	80 @ $5,200= $416,000		$3,744,000
International Graduate	80 @ $5,200= $416,000	80 @ $5,200= $416,000	80 @ $5,200= $416,000		$1,248,000
Independent Study				135 @ $1,200= $12,000,000	$162,000
Continuing Education				3,250 @ $1,200= $12,000,000	$3,900,000
Special Category				160 @ $1,200= $12,000,000	$192,000
Column Totals	$31,160,000	$30,560,000	$8,912,000	$4,254,000	$74,886,000

mation is known about student choice factors, and so on. SEM was developed in part as a response. The goal was to make enrollments more certain, predictable, and budgetable.

The fact is that virtually no one has succeeded in predicting enrollments. Many institutions hit their enrollment targets on the mark, but they do not predict or project enrollments. Instead, they turn the projection model equation around, decide on their optimum enrollment, and set yearly or term targets. Then these institutions analyze their academic policies and align these policies with their goals. They further tune their recruitment, retention, and academic policy decisions, as necessary, to meet their enrollment goals. This is done well in advance of the recruitment and enrollment cycle for which the goal has been set.

Often when reviewing this reversal of the predicting equation, a cry is heard; "Another example of quality suffering from quantity." The fear is unfounded. Where sound SEM principles have been put into practice, the result has been a significant improvement in student quality.

REVENUE VERSUS FINANCIAL AID

Financial aid plays a critical role in many institutional SEM programs. It is used to balance access, attract students with particular characteristics, maintain competitiveness, fill classes, or even attract certain majors. In an effort to cap expenditures, institutions have often used a firm and fixed budget for institutional financial aid. While the institution accomplishes the task of capping expenditures, it may well hamstring recruitment and retention efforts. Increasingly in competitive markets, this policy is seen as obsolete because it is difficult to anticipate who will accept the financial aid offer and enroll. A guessing game ensues, and offers are made based upon budgeted dollars or not made at all because of fear the financial aid budget will be exceeded. To avoid these situations, institutions are going to a percentage-of-tuition-revenue model to control financial aid. Financial aid officers are authorized to grant whatever aid is necessary to meet goals; when the final tally is made, total aid should not exceed a certain percentage of tuition revenue.

Financial Aid and Student Decision Processes

Enrollment managers have long known the importance of understanding the impact of financial aid packaging and timing on student decision processes. From this understanding there has emerged a method of developing packaging heuristics to help guide the process. The heuristics or rules are most often developed by experimentation informed through experience. Table 8.4 illustrates several behavioral phenomena through probability tracking.

In the case of this example, the probability climbs most sharply until net cost to the student reaches $5,000. Even a fully funded student has only a 53 percent probability of enrolling, and there is little performance difference between giving $7,000, $8,000, or $9,000 in aid. Given this example, an enrollment manager may cap offers for students with family income of $50,000 at $7,000. This cap would yield aid at 28 percent of revenue and bring net revenue after aid of $18,000. Tracking like this would be done for students in increments of family income of $10,000, thereby building a profile of enrollment yield against aid. Each institution must build its own performance and yield data, since information of this type is highly confidential and of significant strategic advantage.

RECRUITMENT STRATEGIES

Recruitment can be defined as the active process an institution undertakes to favorably influence a prospective student's decision to attend the institution. The recruitment phase begins with identifying prospects, that is, those students who are eligible to attend and may have some affinity for the institution. Recruitment ends and retention begins once the student enrolls.

The root of recruitment is the student's enrollment decision process, which

Table 8.4
Example of Probability Tracking, Family Income $50,000*

Cost of Attendance	Total Fed/State Grants/Loans	Institutional Financial Aid Award	Net Cost to Student	Probability of Enrollment
$25,000	$15,000	$1,000	$9,000	3%
		$2,000	$8,000	7%
		$3,000	$7,000	12%
		$4,000	$6,000	18%
		$5,000	$5,000	33%
		$6,000	$4,000	42%
		$7,000	$3,000	47%
		$8,000	$2,000	47%
		$9,000	$1,000	49%
		$10,000	$0	53%

*This table illustrates the principle only; it is not intended to provide an actual benchmark.

rests on two primary sets of variables, one centered around the student and the other around the institution. Student variables affecting the decision include the student's ability and interests, his or her socioeconomic background, the influence of key advisors, the student's aspirations and values, demographic characteristics and geographic considerations, the characteristics of the institution the student last attended, and finally, his or her expectations of college. Institutional characteristics that enter into the enrollment decision process include academic program availability and orientation, price, location, reputation, sponsorship and control, and the condition of the physical plant.

The decision to enroll results from a student's analysis of these variables and results in a perceived alignment between student needs and priorities and institutional characteristics. The student-centered variables become the prospect search criteria, while the institution-centered variables become the focus of institutional development.

The most straightforward strategy to increase prospects is to simply buy more prospect names. An institution should expect its yields to decrease, however, unless it is extremely focused when it undertakes this strategy. Strategies to increase the quantity and quality of prospects go far beyond just buying more names. While purchased names are an essential part of any prospecting strategy, they may not be the source of highest yield. Prospects who come through referrals usually have a much higher yield rate, but building an active referral network requires both time and attention. An institution can target high school guidance counselors and faculty, alumni, and other significant groups such as churches or local unions. Institutions can also focus on good press and public relations, a positive image in the community, and student participation in campus programs and activities (early entrance, participation in special programs).

UNDERSTANDING YIELD

Prospects are the number of potential clients in the marketplace. Yield is the percentage of those prospects who decide in favor of attending an institution at each stage of the enrollment decision process. The key to maximizing yield is to understand the students' reasons for deciding in favor of the institution or a competitor. It is insufficient for the recruitment staff alone to understand these factors. Virtually everyone, especially academic administrators, must pay close attention to the reasons students cite. Everyone needs to understand the yield profile of his/her institution. A hypothetical profile follows.

100% of prospects

50% of the prospects request an application

10% of those who request an application apply

75% of those who apply send a deposit

95% of those who send a deposit enroll

80% of those who enroll as freshmen become sophomores

90% of the sophomores become juniors

90% of the juniors become seniors

95% of the seniors graduate

The yield profile can be broken into two phases: recruitment (up to the first enrollment), and retention (first enrollment to graduation). The following illustrates a hypothetical yield during each phase.

During the recruitment phase, 100,000 prospects yield 50,000 requests for applications. The 50,000 requests for applications yield 5,000 applications, which in turn yield 3,750 depositors, who yield 3,563 registered students. Using this simple model, it is easy to see that there are two ways to change enrollment: increase (decrease) the number of prospects or increase (decrease) the yields. The yield profile in this example indicates that during the retention phase, 3,563 freshmen yield 2,850 sophomores; these sophomores yield 2,565 juniors; these juniors yield 2,308 seniors; and these seniors yield 2,193 graduates. Retention is usually the most effective and efficient recruitment tool.

Yield has significant fiscal implications. For example, using the same figures but changing the percentage of freshmen who become sophomores from 80 to 90 percent increases enrollment by 274. At $10,000 each in tuition fees, this amounts to more than an $8 million increase in net revenue over three years. If one adds to that the expenditures spent getting the student to enroll in the first place (purchase of name, mail cost, visit, etc.), the economic incentive is substantial and must be understood. Yield ties the flow of recruitment through retention together and therefore requires a family of SEM strategies to focus on it, from prospects through graduates.

HAVING SOMETHING TO MARKET

Marketing is the process of putting the right product before the right audience at the right price and time. Higher education programs are products, and consumers are getting increasingly more sophisticated. Marketing has its roots in product design. In higher education the product design involves curriculum and academic program development. Regardless of what one calls programs, an institution must have a product to put before prospects. Often heard among admissions and enrollment management circles is the errant faculty who insists: "We have programs. You just don't know how to recruit the students we deserve." This command begs for mass educating the curriculum gurus on the basics of market demand and competition.

When a product appeals to a well-defined, yet not necessarily small, segment of the total prospect base, that segment is called a niche. Niches in higher education's prospect base may be based on price, location, ease and convenience of attendance, specific program offerings, industry affiliation, research acumen, sensitivity to discrete populations (women returning to the workforce, professionals undergoing midlife career changes), spiritual affiliations, cultural affiliations, and the reputation of faculty, alumni, or specialized facilities.

Finding prospect groupings with common interests and characteristics is called market segmentation. Many market segments exist within the domain of any institution. Examples of market segments include those based upon quality (high selectivity drawing from a wide pool of applicants), regional (a wider range of academic ability exhibited by applicants over a narrower geographic distribution), or local demand (high affinity over a small geographic area).

Identifying market segments, describing their characteristics and extrapolating them to buying behavior is a function of market research. Market research can (1) derive strategies by finding segments of the population with a high affinity for niches peculiar to an institution in areas now underserved, (2) help the institution uncover new niche opportunities within segments of the population now served, (3) help decision makers identify niches and populations and provide insight into price sensitivity, financial aid need and performance, and long- and short-term demand.

Market research is not supplementary to the SEM function but rather an integral part of its success. It must contain a solid institutional research component and extend far beyond the domain of the institution. Demographics, lifestyles, purchasing power, buying behavior, competing institutions, commuter behavior, and a host of other research domains can be essential to the success of institu-

Table 8.5
Factors Influencing Recruitment and Retention Activities

Academic Factors	Administrative and Service Factors	Student Life Factors
Academic climate: teaching-learning process faculty-student interaction	Service climate, customer service orientation	Peer relationships
Curriculum: program focus and content	Support systems: information system etc.	Participation
Academic policy	Administrative policy	Student development

tional SEM strategies. Marketing strategies are also integral to retention. Students recruited by an institution are those the institution seeks to retain.

RETENTION STRATEGIES

Retention can be defined as the maintenance of students' satisfactory progress toward their educational objectives until the objectives are attained. Students recruited and admitted to an institution should reasonably expect programs, policies, procedures, and interventions necessary for them to successfully complete the programs to which they have been admitted. Research supports the conclusion that efforts to foster student development and promote quality also increase student persistence.

Retention, however, can be approached from a variety of perspectives (that is, from the perspective of the individual institution or the state in which the institution is located, or within the context of national policy). These perspectives bring different causes and outcomes of dropout and retention behavior into focus, whether the college or university is institution centered or student centered. Regardless of perspective, the retention process begins long before the individual student enrolls. Recruitment and retention are synergistic and are inexorably linked, one informing the other and setting the stage for improvement and refinement. From the SEM perspective, it is essential that recruitment and retention be synchronized.

In order to synchronize recruitment and retention, institutions must focus on both institutional and student enrollment decisions and the factors influencing these decisions. These factors fall into three broad categories: academic, administrative and service, and student life factors (see Table 8.5).

Meaningful research must inform institutional decision makers as to which of these factors influence student decisions, which need attention or enhancement, and which have a positive influence on student retention behavior. Key to altering retention statistics is the ability to identify at-risk students early enough to permit intervention strategies to work. A modern student information system is a vital strategic weapon here. By monitoring student transcripts on a term-by-term basis and flagging the records of students who exhibit at-risk symptoms, intervention can occur in time to alter the outcome. A retention classification system is extraordinarily helpful in this process.

The Retention Classification System

   I. Persisters: Currently enrolled students.

    A. Satisfactory Academic Progress:
   Defined as sufficient units attempted, units attempted in proper sequence, performance at a satisfactory Grade Point Average (GPA).

    B. Unsatisfactory Degree Progress:
   Defined as insufficient number of units attempted, or units attempted out of sequence.

    C. Unsatisfactory GPA:
   Defined as a GPA falling below a threshold or declining at an unacceptable rate.

   II. Graduates: Students have completed a degree objective.

   III. Attainers: Students have completed a nondegree objective.

   IV. Transfers.

    A. Planned: Students enrolled in a transfer program.

    B. Unplanned: Students enrolled in a degree program who request a transcript be sent to another institution prior to completion.

   V. Stop-Outs: Students who fail to register or enroll for the next logical term and make no attempt to inform the institution.

   VI. Dropouts: Students who voluntarily withdraw.

   VII. Dismissals: Students who did not enroll due to institutional action.

    A. Disenrollment: Financial nonpayment.

    B. Academic Disqualification: Academic standards are not met.

    C. Administrative Disqualification: Administrative procedures are not followed.

    D. Disciplinary Disqualification.

Academic underachievement can result from a wide variety of factors: poor academic foundation, poor study skills, poor self-esteem, or personal conflict or crisis. Each factor requires different intervention strategies. Triage has emerged as a concept and process to help ensure proper diagnosis and treatment of the symptoms of academic underachievement in students. Triage, as applied to intervention systems, is a bit different from its original battlefield definition. In this case, it sets up a central comprehensive diagnostic capability that refers students to the treatment or counseling most appropriate for them.

Intervention strategies wherein the institution takes the initiative are referred to as intrusive. Intrusive intervention usually takes the form of advising or counseling, but intrusive intervention also may involve prescriptive academic skills or tutorial programs. Preemptive intervention strategies such as summer bridge programs, freshmen orientation, and student success courses are effective in treating retention-related problems before symptoms develop. A number of retention-related intervention strategies focus, not on the student, but on faculty and staff. Development programs that focus on cross-cultural sensitivity, diversity of learning styles, cultural comfort, and effective teaching and learning environments are all effective retention initiatives.

Research shows that significant advantages exist to front-loading retention and intervention strategies, particularly at such critical times as the transition into college life and the first year of attendance. Financial aid is also a factor in retention and must be mapped against, and allocated according to, institutional SEM objectives. The key element to intervention is knowing when and with whom to intervene. Successful intervention requires a comprehensive information strategy.

REFERENCES

Bean, John C. 1996. *Emerging ideas: The professor's guide to integrating writing, critical thinking and active learning in the classroom.* San Francisco: Jossey-Bass.

Dolence, Michael G. 1993. *Strategic enrollment management: A primer for campus administrators.* Washington, DC: American Association of Collegiate Registrars and Admissions Officers.

———, ed. 1996. *Strategic enrollment management: Cases from the field.* Washington, DC: American Association of Collegiate Registrars and Admissions Officers.

Galsky, A., ed. 1991. *The role of student affairs in institution-wide enrollment management strategies.* Washington, DC: National Association of Student Personnel Administrators.

Hossler, D., and J. P. Bean et al. 1990. *The strategic management of college enrollments.* San Francisco: Jossey-Bass.

Hossler, Don. 1984. *Enrollment management: An integrated approach.* New York: College Entrance Examination Board.

———. 1986. *Creating effective enrollment management systems.* San Francisco: Jossey-Bass.

Ihlanfeldt, W. 1980. *Achieving optimal enrollments and tuition revenue.* San Francisco: Jossey-Bass.

Ingersoll, R. J. 1988. *The enrollment problem: Proven management techniques.* New York: Macmillan.

Kemerer, F., J. V. Baldridge, and K. Green. 1982. *Strategies for effective enrollment management.* Washington, DC: American Association of State Colleges and Universities.

Pascarella, Ernest T., and Patrick T. Terenzini. 1991. *How college affects students.* San Francisco: Jossey-Bass.

Tinto, V. 1987. *Leaving college: Rethinking the causes and cures of student attrition.* Chicago: University of Chicago Press.

Part IV

Admissions Tools

Part IV discusses the tools used in current enrollment management practices.

9

Research

Linda M. Clement and Teresa M. Flannery

A primary role of admissions officers as the millennium approaches is the role of the institutional researcher and marketing expert. In order to understand the competitive environment in which our institutions must survive and thrive, admissions officers have evolved into professionals with critical skills in marketing, statistics and research, and computer systems (McDonough and Robertson 1995). The demand for this research expertise, in a field that has traditionally called for experience in counseling and administration, has developed as a result of institutions' hunger for information and their need to focus efforts in an age of enrollment challenges never previously faced.

Deans and directors of admission are now called upon to assess the potential for enrollment growth from certain markets; to analyze the impact of academic policies and planning strategies likely to affect the institution's image and students' experience; to predict with extraordinary precision the composition of the next class in terms of talent, ethnicity, and financial need; and to explain reasons for discrepancies between enrollment goals (both matriculation and persistence) and actual outcomes. To assess, analyze, predict, and explain—perhaps these are more appropriate expectations for a meteorologist or a psychic. Consider these scenarios, which typify those that our admissions colleagues all over the country are expected to address:

- A governing board is threatening to cut an institution's funding significantly if it does not enroll more students from inside the state within the next year. The president, who does not want the first-year class profile to be adversely affected by such an increase in students, offers the dean of admissions a onetime, 5 percent increase in the operations budget to meet the governing board's required increase. The state has a history of losing its most talented students to flagship campuses of contiguous states. The dean needs answers. To which recruitment treatments and activities have talented, state-resident students responded positively in the past? To which of the competitors' institutional characteristics are these students attracted? At what rates can they be expected to apply and enroll?

- An institution has just received a donation of $500,000 to provide grant aid to talented students. The director of admissions knows that four-year renewable scholarship offers are what counts and that it will be important to stretch the dollars as far as possible to impact the decisions of as many students as possible. What is the smallest amount of grant aid that, when offered, will affect the enrollment decisions of highly talented students who might not otherwise enroll?

- An institution has developed ambitious goals for a significant improvement in the enrollment of students of color over the next five years. The admissions staff report anecdotally that African-American and Latino communities in the region seem to view the institution's environment as hostile and unwelcoming to their students. How can the director of admissions qualify and demonstrate for colleagues the characteristics and features of a college or university that are particularly important to these students, and how favorably or unfavorably the institution rates in their students' perceptions of each characteristic?

- The faculty of an institution have taken up the banner to move away from remedial education, which, they feel; (1) the institution has no business offering, and (2) appears to inappropriately sap resources and expand teaching loads. Simultaneously, the institution has decided to expand the size of the first-year class to increase enrollment to take advantage of a sizable projected increase in high school graduates over the next 10 years. The dean of admissions is aware that such projections indicate that the increase will come primarily from students who have not historically participated in higher education at high rates and that many of these students will be the first in their families to go to college. The president, sensing a possible conflict between these two institutional goals, seeks the advice of the dean. Who are the students who have become available as a result of the population boom? Do their needs and skills match what the institution has to offer? If admitted to realize the enrollment increase, will their preparation be different than that which has historically been expected of new students?

Such is the nature of applied research in college admissions. Far different than the theoretical research that is designed to expand the frontiers of new knowledge, the research in college admissions is practice oriented and designed for utilitarian purposes. It evolves out of real needs for reliable data that will enable the institution's decision makers to act with confidence and precision.

PURPOSES OF RESEARCH

As the examples demonstrate, there are several practical reasons for institutions and, in particular, offices of admission to initiate research efforts. The most salient purposes are to understand the impact of demographic trends, to assess the institution's position relative to its competitors, and to evaluate the effectiveness of programs and services.

Understanding the Impact of Demographic Trends

The changing demographic trends in the United States and their potential impact on institutions of higher education suggest that there will be increases in the number of potential students and significant changes in their composition (The College Board 1993). It is important that administrators understand the implications of a prospect pool that is becoming increasingly more ethnically diverse. It is also important that these same administrators assess the implications of the geographic shifts in population and socioeconomic groupings (Hodgkinson 1992). All of these changes will impact institutions of higher education differentially. Educators must understand the changing demographics in order to assess the unique positions of their institutions as they plan for the future. Research is an important tool in understanding demography.

Assessing the Perceptions of an Institution Relative to Its Competitors

A key element in institutional planning, particularly in admissions work, is understanding how an institution and its competitors are perceived. The process of identifying and comparing an institution's characteristics with its competitors is referred to as positioning (Kemerer, Baldridge, and Green 1982). The process of positioning is essential in planning for program offerings, pricing considerations, and promotional activities (see also Chapter 11).

In the process of determining an institution's position, it is important to acknowledge that prospective students are likely to differ on one or more important characteristics (Kotler 1982). Segmentation involves identifying those distinguishing characteristics and targeting different recruitment strategies to each segment (Hossler, Bean, et al. 1990). Kotler (1982) identified various ways to segment the prospective student population by geographic locations, such as states or regions; by demographic characteristics, such as age, gender, or ethnic memberships; by physiographic characteristics, such as attitudes and lifestyles; and by behavioral characteristics (e.g., parental education and the high school attended). Segmenting the population in meaningful ways allows an institution to more finely hone its understanding of students' perceptions of its programs and services. Research is an important tool for accomplishing this end.

Evaluating the Effectiveness of Programs and Services

Program evaluations have traditionally been important in student services operations. They have become crucial in the area of recruitment and admissions as institutions strive to use their funds wisely and devise ways to better serve students. In evaluating the effectiveness of different components of admissions, the two primary goals are to assess students' satisfaction with programs and services and to understand how programs and services impact their decisions to apply and to enroll.

The degree of satisfaction with programs and services is commonly obtained by user surveys and program evaluations. These tools are of limited use in isolation but can be made more powerful if linked with results from surveys of other programs. Patterns that emerge from multiple program evaluations are logical places to address areas for improvement. In addition, many admissions offices record data related to the recruitment treatments that prospective students have received over the course of the college search process. A systematic analysis of the application, admission, and enrollment rates for each program or activity, when used in combination with associated costs for each activity, may yield an excellent cost-benefit analysis. Relative measures of cost per applicant, cost per admitted student, and cost per enrolling student can be compared with admissions office goals and the institutional mission to determine whether the investment in various activities is consistent with goals and is yielding expected outcomes.

TYPES OF RESEARCH

Research can be viewed from the perspectives of two broad paradigms, quantitative and qualitative. These two approaches differ in their assumptions, their techniques, and their uses.

Quantitative Research Studies

Quantitative methods purport to collect evidence, in the form of objective observations, that supports or refutes a concept or construct. The researcher is testing whether a particular idea is true in a particular situation, and, if the idea is true, whether it can be generalized to a group larger than the subjects in a particular study (Borg and Gall 1989). For example, a researcher might test whether a group of talented students rated the engineering program of one school more favorably than that of another school. The researcher is interested in the perceptions of a sample of students about the quality of academic programs and wants to conduct a study in such a way that these findings can be generalized to a larger group. Most quantitative research studies fall into two general categories—descriptive studies and causal comparative studies. Descriptive studies are concerned with describing reality. How many students receiving a search piece will request additional information? Of students personally invited to a high school presentation, how many will attend? How many institutional competitors are using four-color brochures?

The methodology of a second type of quantitative research, causal competitive, seeks to discover causal links between two or more variables (Borg and Gall 1989). How do merit scholarships impact students' enrollment patterns? What impact does attending a reception have on students' perspectives of the institution? What type of contact (e.g., mailings or telephone calls) has more influence on students' perceptions of the institution? Researchers working with quantitative methodologies collect data via paper and telephone surveys and/or human observations. The statistical tools they use to understand the data collected frequently require the use of statistical programs. The careful use of statistical analysis and the careful interpretation of results are important elements of quantitative research.

Qualitative Research Studies

Qualitative research methods originated in the social sciences fields. These methodologies entail observation and interviews that enable researchers to understand phenomena (Burgess 1985). Researchers who subscribe to these methodologies believe that each case or situation is different, and that truth—an important assumption of qualitative research—can only be discovered by intense, interactive inquiry (Borg and Gall 1989).

Rather than using deductive reasoning to test a concept, as is done in quantitative research, the qualitative approach assumes inductive reasoning and seeks to discover unanticipated outcomes. Methods utilized in qualitative approaches involve human beings as data gatherers. Typical methods include observation, informational interviews, and focus groups. Sample questions that can best be answered with this methodology include such queries as, "How do students utilize the tools available to them in a high school guidance office?" "How do students behave when presented with a particular type of viewbook?" and "What themes emerge when students talk about the college search process?" A major analytical tool in this type of research is theme analysis, which can help researchers define important variables, provide depth and richness to existing information, and provide new complexity to our understanding of ideas and constructs.

Method Triangulation

Some researchers choose one paradigm—quantitative or qualitative—believing that one approach clearly has merit over the other. Others, who may work in the marketing and admissions arenas, believe both approaches have merit and, when utilized effectively, can complement each other. Stage and Russell (1992) advocate the triangulation of research methods from both paradigms. Such an approach allows the findings of a quantitative study to be compared and contrasted with the results of a qualitative study, and vice versa.

Suppose, for example, a survey of prospective students yields the finding that students rate the front cover of a viewbook as one of the most important factors in a decision about whether to read further. Such a finding might lead a designer of admissions publications to invest greater resources and more creative design elements on the front cover than on any other part of a new viewbook. No survey, however, could illuminate the findings of a focus group in which students were observed to pick up the viewbook, go to the back cover, and flip from back to front through the piece as if they were scanning a magazine. In this case, a qualitative method called to light something not anticipated by the quantitative method, namely, that the back cover and back pages may be important in getting a student to read further into a publication.

Similarly, imagine that a survey of admitted nonenrolling students asks respondents to rate the importance of distance from home as a factor in the enrollment decision and then to rate the institution and their first choices in terms of distance from home. The survey item might have intended distance-from-home to represent a construct relating to desired proximity to home, friends, and family. Thus, one interpretation of a finding that the institution is too far from home might be that it is perceived to be too far from familiar others to maintain family support and familiar connections. However, theme analysis of interview responses to the same question might flush out an entirely different interpretation—that the institution is too far from home to commute to campus and live at home (in order to moderate the total cost of education), while the location of the competitor allows for a reasonable commute. The qualitative finding improves the understanding of the quantitative finding. In fact, in this case, another step of method triangulation yields additional understanding: A factor analysis of all items on the original survey shows that the distance-from-home item consistently clusters with other items on the survey related to cost rather than with location items.

A synthesis of results from both paradigms can yield interpretations that are confirming, conflicting, or confounding (Stage and Russell 1992). Whether method triangulation answers more questions than either method alone or raises new questions, the interpretation of data is always richer when both methods can be applied to the same research topic.

RESEARCH DESIGN AND THE NATURE OF RESEARCH QUESTIONS

Research design is the process of developing a study that will yield answers to the specific question or issue at hand. The population of interest and the nature of the research question typically dictate the research design. In quantitative research, the design process requires the identification of at least four important components related to the research question, which will shape the choice of tools for collecting data and the analytical tools to interpret the results, including the following:

• the accessibility of a group to be studied that represents a population of interest,

• the nature and number of outcomes of interest,

- the nature of the factors thought to have some influence on or relationship to the outcome of interest, and

- the nature of the question of interest (relationship, prediction or influence, difference, etc.).

The admissions researcher shaping the research design should be skilled in the intricacies of each of these components and the consequences of design choices related to each. Alternatively, statistical expertise should be utilized to ensure that wise choices are made. Ultimately, a study will succeed only if the design is solid, the results directly address the question, and the design permits generalization to the population of interest.

After an accessible sample representing the population has been located and the outcome and factors or variables affecting that outcome have been identified and scrutinized comes the last important consideration of the research design, the nature of the question. The examples below show that different types of questions call for different analytical (statistical) tools in the design. For instance, is the issue to be studied a question about a relationship (between, e.g., SAT and first-year GPA) or a question of difference (e.g., whether first-year satisfaction differs by high school grade point average and geographic background)? Is there a question of influence or prediction (e.g., whether class rank, ACT score, and participation in an on-campus recruitment program predict or influence application behavior)? This final consideration pulls the other factors together in decisions regarding research design. Upon considering the nature and number of outcomes, the nature of factors thought to influence the outcome, and the nature of the research question, the design begins to take shape:

- A question of magnitude is answered using frequencies and percentages (e.g., How many students who attended a fall open house eventually applied for admission?)

- A question of relationship between two variables is addressed using a simple correlation (e.g., Are SAT score and first-year GPA related?)

- A question of difference with one continuous outcome, such as first-year satisfaction rated on a Likert scale, can be addressed with analysis of variance (ANOVA) (e.g., Does first-year satisfaction differ according to high school GPA or geographic origin?). If a second continuous outcome is added to this same question of difference, the design is addressed through a multiple analysis of variance (MANOVA) (e.g., Do first-year satisfaction and first-year GPA differ according to high school GPA and geographic origin?)

- Prediction questions (e.g., whether certain factors influence or predict an outcome) are addressed using regression statistics. Multiple regression analysis is used if there is one continuous outcome of interest (e.g., Do GPA, ACT score, geographic origin, size of high school class, and ethnic background predict first-year satisfaction ratings?). Other regression statistics, such as logistic regression analysis, are used if the outcome is dichotomous (e.g., Do GPA, ACT score, geographic origin, size of high school class, and ethnic background predict enrollment behavior [enrolled/not enrolled]?)

The possibilities are endless, but the basic process for building a research design is always the same. The variables must be identified, the nature of the data representing each outcome and other influential variables must be examined, and the nature of the research question must be clarified in order to make choices about statistics and address the question at hand.

STAFF STRUCTURE FOR ADMISSIONS RESEARCH

Resources to accomplish research can be organized in several ways, depending upon availability and the researcher's expertise. The approaches for staffing may range from one person in the admissions or institutional studies office to a team of campus representatives, or commercially contracted research expertise. Often, admissions offices do not have the resources to employ even one research staff member full-time, but more and more offices are finding the outcomes of an ongoing research agenda important to their ability to inform, practice, and influence institutional decisions. Thus, a range of possibilities exists.

Research Staff in the Admissions Office

One of the most effective ways to develop a research agenda and keep it moving is to designate or hire a staff member with research expertise. Such a staff member should have graduate-level preparation in research methods, practical experience in applied research, and familiarity with qualitative and quantitative research tools and software. The ideal staff member will possess an advanced degree demonstrating research proficiency. If resources do not allow for a full-time research position, a position might be shared between the admissions office and another campus department, such as institutional studies, resident life, public relations, or the counseling center. Even devoting a portion of an existing staff member's time to research may be a possibility until results can be generated and demand for research outcomes justifies the existence of such a position. Support (i.e., the hardware and software to run statistical programs, the staff time and operational costs of mailing surveys, conducting focus groups, etc.) for this type of position is also critical and costly at the point of start-up. However, over time, this approach may be more cost-effective than hiring outside expertise to conduct a study each time a critical question must be addressed. Moreover, since many institutions have scholars on their campuses who conduct research every day, there may be ways to borrow or share resources and expertise that do not require dollars to accomplish the research goals. Seeking out internal experts on campus is an excellent way to supplement research expertise in the admissions office.

Developing an Admissions Research Team

Whether immediately or eventually, the benefits of developing a research agenda to support the admissions office may become so apparent that a research team emerges as the best solution. A full-time admissions officer devoted to developing a marketing plan and to supervising the research agenda may be assisted by an undergraduate student or graduate assistant specializing in statistics and may even work with other professional staff who have some responsibility for coordinating market, demographic, or evaluative research. Such a team may also be assisted at times by clerical staff or students when surveys are to be produced or are ready to be coded and inserted into a data file. This is a more expensive option, but clearly also a more productive one, since the team can direct and sustain a research agenda. This type of staff team is responsible for the full range of research tasks, from data collection and analysis to interpretation and presentation of the results.

Commercial Options

If resources do not allow for an ongoing research agenda and a commitment of staff year round or if the complexity of the research task exceeds the expertise of internal resources, commercial enterprises can address an institution's most critical questions. Institutions that conduct little other research commonly contract for a survey of their admitted students to gain a better understanding of their institution's program effectiveness, competitive market position, and institutional image. Others routinely review the effectiveness of admissions criteria in predicting first-year outcomes. Products offered by The College Board and American College Testing are some of the more notable examples of such research services.

In addition, companies that primarily design and produce recruitment materials offer market research services. Although initially intended to support the development of brochures, these companies can be contracted by institutions exclusively for research services. The competitiveness of the higher education market has also supported the growth and development of public relations and marketing firms specializing in custom research services for colleges and universities. These are good options when expertise is critical and resources are available to address the full range of research tasks, from collection to presentation. Combinations of these staff structures are also possible. No matter how a structure is established, however, decisions should be made with the understanding that quality research outcomes will justify future investments in more permanent internal structures.

INTERNAL DISTRIBUTION OF RESEARCH RESULTS

"The sharing of results for both the criticism by competent peers and the edification of others is a fundamental norm for the conduct of inquiring in academic institutions" (Litten, Sullivan, and Brodigan 1983). This sentiment relates to the responsibility to share the results of research with colleagues. The effective distribution of research results can enhance the credibility of the admissions office. Sharing research results enables admissions officers to be seen as competent sources of consumer knowledge. When shared in proper forums, this information provides institutions with opportunities to foster understanding of how an institution is perceived. From a self-serving perspective, sharing research results can help admissions officers garner support for recruitment programs and secure resources to enhance or expand programs.

A wide variety of people could benefit from better understanding the perspectives of prospective consumers. Presidents and cabinet officials can utilize this information in their formulation of institutional policies, particularly in the area of institutional pricing. Academic deans can utilize this information as they shape academic program offerings and curriculum. Data can also help Student Affairs and Academic Services staff as they develop and fine tune services. Institutional Advancement staff may also find this information helpful in shaping their perspectives on how the general public views an institution.

As admissions officers consider how research results will be distributed, a number of considerations are important. Timing (i.e., the time in the policy and decision-making cycle when administrators, faculty, and staff are most disposed to consider this kind of information and best able to do so thoroughly and thoughtfully) could be important. It is also important to provide enough detail to make the issues substantive, but not cumbersome and overwhelming. The form is also important. Written documents, presentations, or discussions can all be effective with different populations. No matter what forum is selected, it is very important that admissions officers understand that exchange and interaction may shape the timing, level of detail, and forum that is utilized.

Sharing results is an important part of the research process. As noted at the outset of this chapter, academic institutions have a fundamental commitment to the inquiry process, in which the Admissions Office plays an important role.

REFERENCES

Borg, W., and M. Gall. 1989. *Educational research*. New York: Longman.

Burgess, R. G., ed. 1985. *Strategies of educational research: Qualitative methods*. Philadelphia: Falmer.

College Board. 1993. *Higher education's landscape: Demographic issues in the 1990s*. New York: The College Board.

Hodgkinson, H. 1992. *A demographic look at tomorrow*. Washington, DC: Center for Demographic Policy, Institute for Educational Leadership.

Hossler, D., J. P. Bean, et al. 1990. *The strategic management of college enrollments.* San Francisco: Jossey-Bass.

Kemerer, F., J. V. Baldridge, and K. Green. 1982. *Strategies for effective enrollment management.* Washington, DC: American Association of State Colleges and Universities.

Kotler, P. 1982. *Marketing for nonprofit organizations.* Englewood Cliffs, NJ: Prentice-Hall.

Kotler, P., and K. Fox. 1985. *Strategic marketing for educational institutions.* Englewood Cliffs, NJ: Prentice-Hall.

Levine, A., et al. 1989. *Shaping higher education's future.* San Francisco: Jossey-Bass.

Litten, L. H., D. Sullivan, and D. L. Brodigan. 1983. *Applying market research in college admissions.* New York: College Entrance Examination Board.

McDonough, P., and L. Robertson. 1995. Gatekeepers or marketers: Reclaiming the educational role of chief admission officers. *Journal of College Admission* 147(3): 22–31.

Stage, F. K., and R. V. Russell. 1992. Using method triangulation in college student research. *Journal of College Student Development* (November): 485–489.

10

The Development of a
Marketing Plan

James C. Blackburn

A marketing plan is an institution's plan of action for reaching its enrollment target(s). Marketing plans can be very specific and voluminous or very brief and concise. Specificity is preferable to length. Ideally, such a document includes market objectives, basic overall strategies, specific tactics/activities, evaluation criteria, and, for most admissions officers, a budget. Over the last 20 years, the use of marketing plans in college admissions has increased rather substantially. In the early 1970s, writers noted that the use of planning objectives for college recruiting was rare. In fact, the earliest known reference to marketing in college admissions seems to have appeared in 1969 (Lynch 1969).

The results of a study completed in 1979 indicate that, among a sample of 443 U.S. colleges and universities, only 204 (47 percent) reported using a marketing plan (Blackburn 1980), as opposed to more than 63 percent of a similar sample of admissions officers taken in 1988. Over 80 percent of the 1988 users indicated that marketing plans had been effective for them. Interestingly, institutions with high tuition were the most frequent users of marketing plans (Goldgehn 1989). No more recent studies seem to have been reported, but it is reasonable to assume that the use, quality, and effectiveness of college admissions marketing plans have increased over time. This section provides a very basic, how-to approach for developing a college admissions marketing plan. Prior to beginning, however, a few terms must be defined.

DEFINITION OF TERMS

As with most activities, a vocabulary goes along with developing a marketing plan. An attempt has been made to customize definitions to the college admissions setting.

Market—an identifiable and describable group of current or potential students (e.g., students enrolled at feeder community colleges).

Target or Target Market—a describable group of current and/or potential students toward which a college/university has chosen to direct some or all of its marketing efforts (e.g., the upper 10 percent of high school seniors in Indianapolis).

Position or Market Position—the place that a college or university holds in the consumers' mind relative to competitor institutions (e.g., most informed consumers of higher education believe Stanford is more expensive than San Jose State University). Other market positions in higher education are more or less objective and provable; for example, what are the relative qualities of midwestern colleges of business (is Michigan a better or worse place to study business than Indiana?).

Market Plan—a document that describes an institution's current enrollment and targeted goals as well as how that college/university intends to change or maintain its market position to achieve its measurable enrollment goals.

MARKET PLANNING: A CYCLICAL PROCESS

Developing and implementing a marketing plan is more nearly a process than a project. It is easy to determine when a project is finished. Since students must be recruited, admitted, and enrolled each year, the planning and implementing process/cycle is really never finished. Hence, college/university admissions marketing is an unending process. The following paragraphs describe and give examples of each of the broad stages of the admissions-marketing plan.

Market Audit and Market Goal Development

In college admissions, a market audit involves determining where an institution is in terms of various market descriptors. For example, how many freshmen are being drawn to the campus from each of several geographical areas? What are these students' academic qualifications? Similar questions might be asked in a market audit about transfer students.

The second part of the first stage of the marketing plan cycle involves developing market goals and determining the distance between the market goals and current reality (market audit) at that institution. In a very simplistic example, College A in Illinois has been enrolling freshmen from the northern counties who have ranked in the upper one-third of their secondary school classes and have a freshman class SAT total average of 1,050. Based upon the market audit and an institutional goal-setting process, College A has decided to enroll more students from Wisconsin and Michigan, and to raise the average class rank to the upper quintile of a high school graduating class, and to make some other similar changes. The first statement reflects where College A is (market audit). The second statement indicates the goals the college has targeted.

Similarly, a market goal-setting process might result in the need for a plan to increase or decrease the number of transfer students entering a teacher education

Figure 10.1
Market Audit and Goal-Setting Process

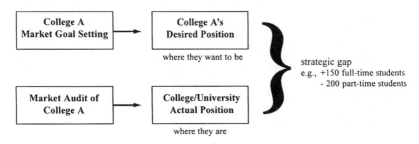

program or the geology department at College A. In either case, a market audit has determined where an institution is; the market goal-setting process has identified where the university wants to be. The difference between where an institution is and where it wants to be can be called a strategic gap. College A, for example, with a full-time enrollment of 890 and a part-time enrollment of 400 (market audit), wants 950 full- and 200 part-time students (market goal setting). Therefore, College A's strategic gap is an increase of 150 full-time students and a decrease of 200 part-time students. Graphically, the market audit and market goal-setting processes might look like the diagram in Figure 10.1.

Market Opportunity Analysis

Once the difference between the actual and desired states has been determined, it becomes possible to assess the possibilities for achieving the institution's desired positions, namely, more students, different students, or both. Admissions market possibilities are discovered by market opportunity analysis. Basically, this process involves an inventory of the institution's strengths and weaknesses vis-à-vis its actual and/or potential competitors and the marketplace. The operative questions in this process are: What do various groups of potential buyers of higher education want? Which colleges and universities are responding to those wants? How is our institution responding to these wants, and how could it better do so in the future?

Suppose for example, that interest in majoring in foreign languages at College A has declined. However, interest in international business has increased. Therefore, the opportunity to market foreign language instruction to students majoring in international business has increased. The reasons to do so may already exist at College A, since there has been a decrease in foreign language majors. By marketing international business, consumers' desires are met and the underutilized resources of the foreign language departments are constructively brought into play. Clearly, everyone wins with the success of such a plan!

Marketing opportunities can occur with any of the four ''Ps'' of marketing.

Price—What do consumers pay for their education? It is usually important to consider the net cost that individuals pay for their education; for example, total cost minus financial aid package, or in the case of U.S. service academies, net cost (almost nothing) plus military service commitment.

Place—How is the educational program provided or delivered (e.g., via in-person lecture, TV, satellite campus, at night, during the day, over the weekend, etc.)? The term *place* really refers to how the educational products are distributed. Students do not always live on campus and walk to class as they once did. For almost two generations, many other distribution schema have existed in higher education. Marketing can be changed substantially by adding other delivery systems: namely changes in distribution or place (e.g., satellite campuses, cable television delivery of instruction).

Promotion—How is information about the institution communicated to prospective students and their families (e.g., recruiting)? Promotion is the set of activities most people associate with marketing. Quite literally, promotion is any activity used by the university to tell prospective consumers about the institution. These activities can vary from press releases to paid advertisements to brochures to events to multimedia materials to telephone calls and more. What messages are being conveyed about the institution? How should those messages be changed?

Product—What curricular programs and/or cocurricular experiences are offered? Many choose to look at the degree earned via the completion of curricula as the product of higher education. Arguably, the products of college enrollment are much broader than curricular concerns. Students and taxpayers, as consumers of education, typically get much more for their educational dollars than academic/instructional programs. Any part of the university can be changed to better market the institution (e.g., the curricula, the library, athletic programs, study abroad programs, or social life).

Ideally, market goals can be achieved by manipulating one or more of the four "Ps." For example, enrollment might be increased by lowering the tuition price. However, high-achieving students might actually be attracted by higher fees if the quality of the educational experience is perceived as being better (a product/promotion consideration). Market sensitivity to any of the four "Ps" varies by region, discipline, and dozens of intangible factors.

In looking at market opportunities, University Y may discover that potential engineering majors are being lost to a university whose costs are four times higher. In such a case, publicizing University Y's academic quality and lower cost may be a good idea. University Y may also discover that a high interest in the state in teacher education or premed education is going unmet. Such information may provide a marketing opportunity for an institution wishing to develop its marketing/enrollment effort.

Setting Market Objectives

From marketing opportunity analysis (looking at an institution's strengths and weaknesses and those of competitor institutions), general notions of possible specific marketing objectives can be described. In the business world, this ex-

Figure 10.2
Setting Market Objectives

ercise is known as searching for market niches that is, unmet needs. Not all unmet needs in higher education can or should be met; institutions should select appropriately. Filling them may help meet the institution's overall market/enrollment goals (i.e., fill the strategic gap). Specific unmet needs can then be used to develop agreed-upon market objectives, as in the following example. Suppose College W has decided to raise its full-time enrollment from 800 to 950 by expanding teacher education enrollments by 50 full-time students and engineering enrollments by 75 and by drawing in 25 new (additional) premed students. The market planners at College W might further say that these three enrollment increases will happen by the fall semester of 19__. In doing so, College W will have conducted a market audit and set market goals, determined its strategic cap, analyzed some of its marketing opportunities, and stated some market objectives in measurable terms (see Figure 10.2).

Developing and Stating Market Strategies and Tactics

After writing and agreeing upon specific market objectives, an institution can develop strategies and tactics for implementing and assessing a marketing plan designed to accomplish the agreed-upon market objectives. University Z, for example, may have agreed upon increasing junior-level transfer enrollment in the school of engineering by 25 percent in two years. This is an agreed-upon and measurable objective. In assessing market planning, it will be very easy to ascertain if the university's market objective for engineering has been met by counting the number of junior-level enrolled transfers each year—something that is probably done anyway. Strategies to support the accomplishment of this objective might include improved relations and articulation with feeder community colleges, and development of internship programs with local government and industry, and so forth.

Strategies are more specific than market objectives but less specific than tactics, and they may not be as measurable as either objectives or tactics. In another scenario, X Polytechnic Institute may have agreed upon a market objective calling for raising the mean freshman ACT composite score by 4 points in two years without an accompanying drop in the size or ethnic diversity of the entering freshman class. Again, this is an example of a measurable and specific market objective. Strategies to support the institute's test score market objective might include: (a) including enriched gift aid in the financial aid packages of admitted freshmen who have scored high on the ACT, (b) launching direct mail marketing to prospective engineering students who have scored high on the ACT and have done well in secondary school, and/or (c) targeting school visits and on-campus recruitment events at feeder or additional high schools that tend to graduate highly qualified engineering majors and/or high-caliber students who have above-average test scores. Each of these possible strategies supports the institute's market objective. When the strategies are accepted by the committee or person writing the plan, specific tactics or activities can be developed and described.

Market tactics/activities should be stated in significant, measurable detail usually including assignment of responsibility and resources. For example, University Z might identify a market goal of increasing freshman enrollment from suburban Denver by 10 percent within two years. Supporting that Denver market goal, strategies for increasing Denver area high school visitation, participation in college fairs, such as the one sponsored by the National Scholarship Service and Fund for Negro Students (NSS-FNS), and recruiting by alumni might be adopted. Implementing the Denver goal/strategy tactics or activities might include the following:

School Visits	Responsible Person	Budget
Cherry Creek, Smoky Hill, Aurora, and Jefferson County high schools will be visited twice per year	Alyce Spooner, Assistant Director, Admissions	$8,000 in travel

College Fairs	Responsible Person	Budget
Z University will be represented at NACAC and NSS-FNS fairs in Denver	LeRoy Brown, Admissions Counselor	$4,000 in travel fees and printed matter

Recruiting by Alumni	Responsible Person	Budget
The Z University alumni club will host a reception for accepted applicants in late April	Jorge Ontiveros, Assistant Director, Admissions	$2,000 in travel, $600 in refreshments, $1,000 misc.

Direct Marketing Tactic	Responsible Person	Budget
Via the spring search from the College Board's student search program, 205 potentially admissible African-American high school juniors will be reached	Susan Kawakami, Associate Director, Admissions	$3,600 in mailing, $4,000 in materials, $2,000 in follow-up costs—$9,600 subtotal

Expressing tactics/activities in a tabular/matrix format facilitates concise descriptions and quick determination of the tactic/activity, responsibility, funding, and so forth.

Implementing of the Marketing Plan

Obviously, the most time-consuming and expensive step of the market planning cycle is the implementation phase (usually about 18 months), when tactics/activities implement the major portions of the plan. Hopefully, each person involved in implementing the plan will have had some role in the development of the plan and, therefore, more investment in the wisdom of the plan and its success. There is debate about who should be in charge of implementing the admissions marketing plan. It seems best that reporting lines be kept simple (e.g., the person in charge of admissions should supervise the plan's implementation and report regularly to a committee or her or his supervisor).

Assessment of the Marketing Plan and Its Implementation

The final portion of each revolution of the market planning cycle is assessment, but it is important that assessment not be a completely summative (i.e., occurring only at the end) activity. Much formative or along-the-way assessment can and should be built into the plan and its implementation. Specific assessment can take place when goals and tactics are stated in measurable terms. This part of the market-planning process produces a "glazing over of the eyes" for many admissions officers and even some faculty. Stating and assessing measurable goals and activities is probably not the most exciting facet of admissions and records work. However, without goals that can be measured and activities with specified details, it is essentially impossible to tell if success has been achieved. Moreover, it is manifestly impossible to determine where or when a plan or its execution failed.

University Z's goal of increasing freshman enrollment from the more affluent suburbs of Denver could be summatively evaluated by a yearly count of the enrolled freshmen whose home addresses fall within specified Denver zip codes. Formative (along the way) assessments could be made by counting admissions contacts, inquiries, applications submitted, admitted applicants, and deposits received, as sorted and counted by high school, zip code, and/or county code. Specific activities supporting the Denver goals can be counted and evaluated by periodic activity reports of visits made or events hosted. Such periodic reports are part of a formative evaluation. For example, the April marketing activity report for the university might include follow-up visits made to Smoky Hill and Wheat Ridge High Schools (87 pending applicants contacted) and alumni hosting a reception in Aurora, Colorado (65 applicants and 87 parents present); total expenses, $2,725.

Reporting mechanisms should be brief, simple, and specific to the plan's goals and activities. Otherwise, the paperwork can become more time-consuming than the implementation of the plan. The goal of a marketing plan is to achieve the college/university's market objective, not to generate paper reports. At the end of each admissions marketing cycle (usually in the fall), a summative assessment should determine if each tactic/activity has been accomplished and to what results. Which goals have been achieved? Again, the stated measurability of the goals and the specificity of the activities make the assessment process both possible and fairly simple.

Beyond the score keeping function, a subjective assessment portion is needed. It is one thing to accomplish goals; it is quite another to determine if other goals might have more appropriately capitalized on the institution's marketing opportunities. As is the case with most marketing efforts (and, indeed, admissions work, in general), the assessment phase leads directly back into the internal planning process for the next cycle. The results of the initial marketing plan and its implementation become the parts of the market audit and market goal-setting process for the next cycles.

In using the results of the market plan to assess measurable goals as input for the next market audit and goal-setting process, the first revolution of the cycle of college admissions marketing is completed. The cycle can then begin for the next enrollment period or academic year. Since most admissions marketing cycles are about 18 months long, there are likely to be overlapping marketing plans. As the Class of 1998 is being admitted, initial contacts with prospects for the Class of 1999 will be made with 11th graders in the secondary schools. The actualities and complexities of admissions marketing for transfer or graduate students are even more likely to overlap and confuse both planners and implementers of admissions marketing.

Nonetheless, and despite the work and possible confusion, the development and use of an admissions marketing plan are worthwhile activities. This is not to suggest that important enrollment-related events do not happen outside the plan. Indeed, predicting the future with accuracy is likely always to be impossible. Unexpected opportunities and challenges occur in academia and elsewhere. Nonetheless, dealing successfully with the unexpected as well as the expected seems easier with a plan.

SOME CAVEATS AND SUGGESTIONS

In a very pragmatic vein, some of the following ideas may be useful to first-time users of a marketing plan.

1. If the institution has never used a marketing plan, it may be best not to proceed too quickly. It is better that the marketing effort gain wide support than lie dormant on someone's shelf. Creating documents that may polarize the campus into unproductive controversy may not be useful either.

2. Word processors and electronic mail are tremendous boons to the planning process. These devices make it possible to test ideas with colleagues and to circulate drafts

for comment in a small fraction of the time and effort that such processes used to take.

3. If the whole campus cannot or will not support marketing or market-planning initiatives, it may be wise to work with a subset of the college/university (e.g., the nursing department or the school of agriculture). If the smaller marketing efforts are successful, other units are more likely to join in during subsequent admissions cycles.

4. Patience is essential in the planning process. By its nature, planning is a collaborative process involving more than a few people. Compromises will have to be made and remade. The jargon of marketing (e.g., targets, products), is potentially unpopular with academicians. Some find the whole notion of marketing college enrollment distasteful. It may be prudent to use more familiar or generally accepted terms, such as *prospective students* and *academic programs* rather than speak of *target markets* and *educational products*.

5. Most colleges and universities move/change directions in a manner more nearly like steamships than sports cars. Institutions of higher education do not move fast or maneuver quickly. Therefore, it may be wise to select modest goals, measures, and ample timeframes. Much can be gained via marketing, but it is wise not to promise more than can be delivered, given the resources, time allotted, and the ancient nature of the academic enterprise.

6. Admissions market planning is best when all segments of the campus are involved. It is essential that the leadership of academic affairs, fiscal affairs, and student services be onboard early and involved throughout the processes and cycles. Any major segment of the college/university community can derail the marketing plan and processes. Consequently, getting everyone in on the game, if possible, is wise.

A diagram of the overall Admission/Marketing-Planning Process is included (Figure 10.3). Also included is an example of an admissions-marketing plan.

APPENDIX 10.1: Overshoe State University (East Dakota) Admissions Office, Basic Undergraduate Marketing Plan for 1995–1996

I. Objective: Prospective students will be provided with information and encouraged to apply. The qualified prospects will be admitted and enroll at Overshoe State University (OSU).

Standard: New students (freshmen and transfers) will enroll for Fall 1996 in at least the quality (GPA/SAT) equal to that of Fall 1995. Total number of transfer and freshmen will be 10 percent greater than that of Fall 1995.

II. Target Populations

A. Freshmen

1. Primary: Freshmen will be sought primarily from 80+ secondary schools in Alpha, Baker, and Charlie counties, with heavy emphasis upon metropolitan Atlantis as well as the Lima, Mike, Oscar, and Papa metropolitan

Figure 10.3
The Admissions/Marketing-Planning Process

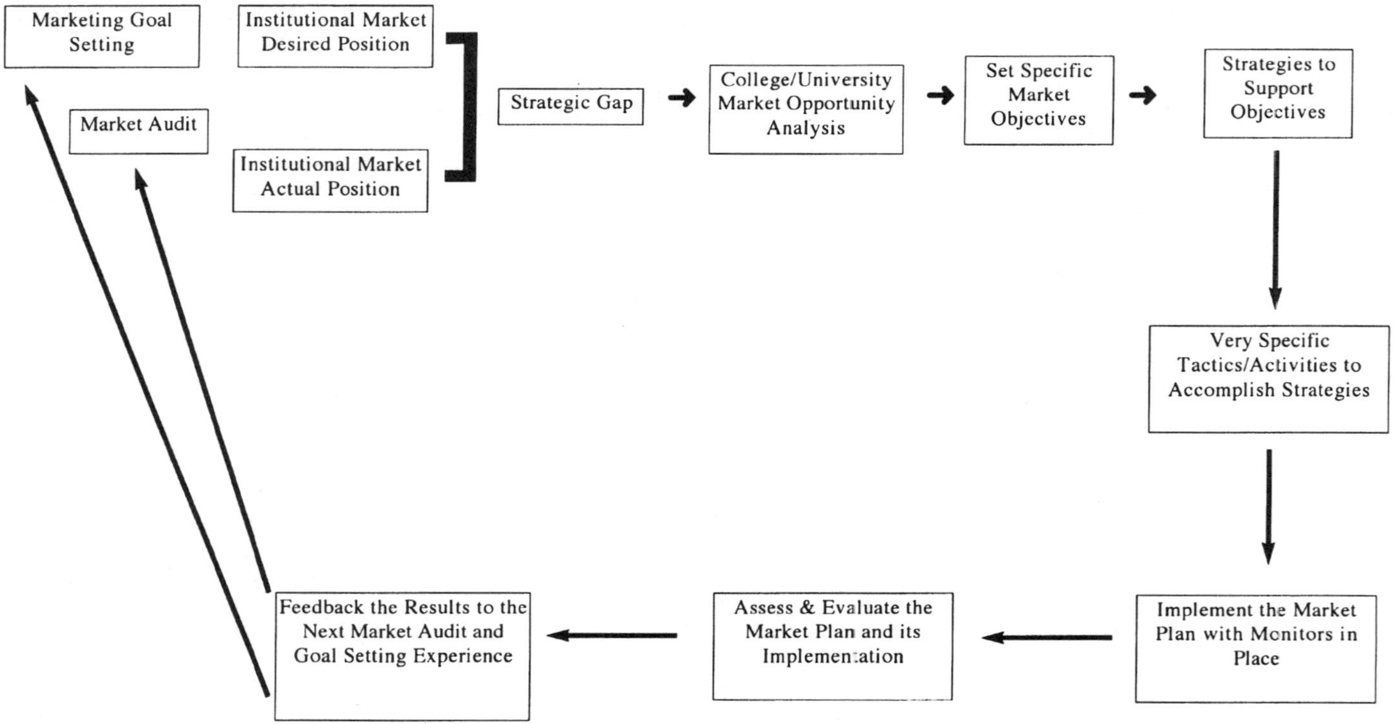

Adapted from Zikmond and D'Amico (1989) and Geotsch (1979).

areas. During recent years, a large percentage of the undergraduate population at OSU has come to the university from the metropolitan Atlantis area.

2. Secondary: Freshmen will also be sought from the western mountain regions, as well as the eastern plains and the southern Styx Valley. Less attention and different strategies used to recruit in these regions of our state will be designed to maintain Overshoe's current market share among the high school seniors of those regions.

3. Tertiary: Freshmen will be sought from carefully targeted out-of-state markets. The criteria for target selection will be those which describe large population centers where affluent communities exist from which students might have some motivation for enrolling in an out-of-state college or university as full-pay students. Examples include "Chicagoland," Omaha, Albuquerque, selected cities in California and New Jersey, and Oahu in Hawaii. Freshmen will also be sought from selected areas of Kansas.

   Note: In the case of the tertiary markets (i.e., nonresident students) there is significant financial gain (full-pay, nonresident tuition) to the university upon the enrollment of such students. It is therefore possible to spend more money on recruitment of those students and yet incur similar financial benefit to the university. It is also well that out-of-state students be enrolled at the university to guard against possibilities for provincialism on the part of the university's undergraduate community.

B. Transfer Populations

1. Primary Transfer Market

   a. Transfers will be sought from the community colleges in the Atlantis area and on the eastern plains. The two-year colleges to be targeted first include: Northeastern Junior College, Quayle Community College, Atlantis-Auraria Community College, Front Door Community College, Sioux Junction Community College, and the Community College of Polaris.

   b. The second target group will include Gamma Junior College, Grenada Junior College, and Alexander Community College. "Courtesy" visits will be made to Overshoe Northwestern Community College, and the Mountain Empire College campuses; these are specific OSU programs (e.g., recreation and community health) for which OSU has potential "corners on the market."

2. Transfer students will also be sought from two-year institutions in adjoining states (Kansas and Minnesota).

3. Transfer students will be East Dakota residents who began but did not finish their education at other regionally accredited colleges and universities. Transfer students will also be sought from the group of students who applied to Overshoe as freshmen, did not enroll, and are currently attending two-year colleges.

C. Reentry Students: Older students who may be either freshmen or transfer students will be sought from the recruiting area (25 miles). This market, by some reports, currently accounts for nearly 10 percent of the university's headcount enrollment.

D. International Students: Academically and financially qualified non-American nationals will be encouraged to enroll at OSU. The Admissions Office is coordinating with the International Student Advisor various ways to approach marketing problems with regard to recruiting foreign nationals. We are utilizing such sources as the United States Information Agency, educational foundations, U.S. embassies, Overshoe international student alumni, and so on.

E. Ethnic Minority Students: Special efforts will be mounted to address the recruitment of minority students (see specific marketing plan for the recruitment and retention of black and Hispanic students).

III. Strategies for Target Markets

A. Freshmen Activities

1. a. College Days across East Dakota. The Admissions Office staff will participate in college days and night programs across the state and in other specific markets. A copy of the schedules for recruiting is available from Jorge Trujillo or Jerry Feinstein, assistant directors of admission.

   b. September–December 1995
   College Day/Night programs
   Nike County high school programs—55
   Out-of-state recruitment programs (9 weeks)—108 high schools
   Out-of-state college fairs (4 weeks)—100+ high schools
   Upward Bound programs—high schools—81
   Follow-up visits to major high schools (Dec. 9)—21
   State college fairs—3
   Reentry student programs
   (East Dakota firms and agencies)—25
   NSS-FNS College Fairs—2
   Atlantis high school visits—35
   Counselor Clinics—6
   Parent/student home visits (underrepresented students)—27
   Minority student fairs, e.g., MESA—2
   Other programs (high school counselors invited OSU representative)—24
   Total programs—410

2. Direct Mail Marketing (n = 30,000)

   a. Both Student Search Service (SSS) of the College Board and the Educational Opportunity Service (EOS) of the American College Testing program will be used as sources from which names of prospective students may be bought. The university will continue to participate in some direct mail marketing to talented juniors and seniors.

   b. The Admissions Office will also send a special mailing concerning the nonresident scholarships. By February 1996, over 30,000 students should receive such mailings.

    c. Outstanding out-of-state secondary school juniors will be reached via the purchase of names from the Student Search Service (SSS) of the College Board.

3. Individual Follow-up on Inquiries: Letters, telephone calls. A variety of individual follow-ups will be made to students inquiring about the university. A letter is addressed to every prospective student who contacts the university either by telephone or letter. The same is true of family members, friends, and counselors who contact the university on behalf of prospective students.

4. Follow-up visits to major feeder high schools ($3 \times 80 = 240$): Winter–Spring 1996.

5. Campus Visitation Days (e.g., Fall Visitation Day, Minority Visitation Day, Math-Science Day, Foreign Language Day, etc.).

6. Campus Tours (more than 100 per month).

    a. The visitors' center section of the university Admissions Office provides tours of the campus to students, their families, either individually or in groups, four times a day, Monday through Friday. More than 100 persons take these tours each month. Follow-up is accomplished with each person who visits the campus in this manner, and, whenever possible and/or requested, visits are made to academic departments, financial aid, ar ˙ so on.

    b. Evening and weekend visitors to the campus are encouraged to contact the information desk in the University Center for admissions materials as well as a self-directed tour.

7. a. Community-based financial aid workshops, hosted jointly by personnel of the Admissions Office and the Office of Student Financial Resources, will be attempted. These events have taken place in the Atlantis area and are an effort to reach out to persons in that metropolitan area who may not be reached via the school and community college visitation program(s).

    b. The Office of Student Financial Resources provides and will continue to provide financial aid workshops to local secondary schools.

8. a. A list of out-of-state high schools with counselor names has been prepared to inform the counselors of the nonresident awards.

    b. The telephone follow-up to the counselor letters will be accomplished by the Admissions Office.

    c. Letter writing campaigns have consisted primarily of letters generated over the signatures of department heads through the use of the word processor and sent to students accepted for admission.

B. Transfer Activities

1. Winter and Spring 1996 visits will be made to each of the first group of two-year colleges.

2. The second group of feeder institutions will receive visits slightly later in the year (e.g., Spring Quarter 1996).

3. Remotely located two-year colleges will be reached via mailings to key persons (counselors, junior college faculty members, etc.). Especially important among these mailings will be the recently revised and expanded *Overshoe Transfer Guide.*

4. In the case(s) of the community colleges located in Atlantis, groups of OSU faculty and/or administrators will be included in informal articulation conferences hosted by the Admissions Office.

C. Reentry Student–Marketing Activities

1. Reentry students will be reached via the media and cooperation with The Division of Continuing Education and/or the Office of Evening and Summer Programs. The retooling of programs and/or program delivery strategies would be extremely useful to the marketing of the university of reentry students. Historically, standard curricula, which OSU offered from 8:00 A.M. to 2:00 P.M., may not be appropriate to this target market.

2. A media strategy is imperative for success in attracting reentry students. Purchasing ad space and time is dependent upon funding.

3. The phonathon efforts staffed by Reentry Center personnel and currently enrolled older students will be continued.

4. An assistant director of admissions will spend the equivalent of one working month developing and monitoring contacts with the personnel departments of every local business which employs more than 50 people. If time remains, some networking with social agencies should be accomplished.

5. Working with the College of Education, the Graduate School, and others, strategies for serving the needs of persons seeking to reenter the university for teacher recertification or perhaps initial certification.

D. International Student Activities

1. Via English language schools (e.g., Overshoe English Institute) and foreign consulates, information on OSU will be disseminated.

2. Large scale efforts to recruit international students seem unwarranted in view of the paucity of services available to such students at OSU.

3. Many of Overshoe State's international students are enrolled at the graduate levels. Recruiting activities may well originate in the Graduate School.

4. In addition to the recruitment of new students, it is important that currently enrolled international students be helped to feel good about Overshoe State University. Such feelings will engender word-of-mouth advertising abroad.

E. Minority Student Activities

1. OSU participates in all of the Associated College/Career (ACCESS) programs. These programs are designed to increase the college going rate(s) of the state's disadvantaged youth and to furnish those students with information about collegiate/career opportunities. More than 90 such events are planned for 1995–1996.

2. Working with representatives of OSU and other institutions, funding will be acquired for a college fair affiliated with the National Scholarship Service and Fund for Negro Students (NSS-FNS).

3. Ethnic minority group members will continue to be featured to the highest degree possible in OSU publications (e.g., "Overshoe—A Diverse Community" brochure and the OSU admissions bulletin "It Doesn't Get Better Than This").

4. Mailings will be sent to identifiable minority populations in our state (e.g., by way of the College Board and ACT).

5. The recruiting of minority students will be accomplished via a matrix of activities supervised by the associate director of admissions.

6. Undeclared majors will be recruited and served via cooperative efforts involving the admissions staff, the Director of Academic Advising, and the Director of Career Development and Testing.

   a. Letters, telephone calls, and flyers will be used to reach prospective undeclared students.

   b. Orientation will include mention of and emphasis on OSU's services to undeclared students.

IV. Publications

   A. As supports to the marketing effort several publications either are available or will become available.

   1. Departmental brochures (nearly two dozen have already been published). The departmental brochures have been primarily financed through academic departmental monies. If a student visits with an admissions officer at a college day, a general brochure is furnished that student. If that student indicates an interest in a specific Overshoe State program, the departmental brochure is mailed to him/her as soon as possible along with the follow-up letter.

   2. OSU Financial Aid brochure "Drachmas for Your Degree" is ready and will be freely and widely distributed.

   3. Catalogue/Bulletin "It Doesn't Get Any Better Than This" (revised for the upcoming year).
   Each of these publications will feature, on its cover, a photograph of Carnegie Library and the proximity of the Big Mogul Mountains in the background. The basic theme of these publications is that Overshoe State University is large enough to be diverse, yet small enough to be personal. OSU's location and the attractiveness of nearby Wobegon will also be stressed. Academic quality must be emphasized, whenever possible.

V. Admissions Activities to Involve OSU Faculty in Recruiting

   A. Alumni receptions: two in Atlantis, one in Beta, one in Gamma, and one in Upsilon. These events involve taking Overshoe State faculty, staff, alumni, and students to meet with accepted students and their families. Nearly 700 persons participated last year in OSU alumni–new student receptions.

B. Letters or names/addresses furnished to departments for letter writing to accepted students. Each department which offers at least one major should have a letter for each major. Such letters will be sent personally to each student accepted to or expressing an interest in each program.

C. Faculty will continue to be encouraged by the Admissions Office and others to nurture relationships with secondary school and community college counterparts.

D. Visits with Overshoe State professors by prospective students will be and are scheduled by the Admissions Office.

E. The Admissions Office will work with academic departments in the planning and implementation of special days for prospective student visitations, e.g., Math-Science Day.

VI. "Company Line." In portraying the university to prospective undergraduate students, the following descriptors (i.e., "company line") should be used:

A. Overshoe State is large enough to offer a diversity of curricula, student lifestyles, and experiences.

B. Overshoe State is small enough to offer students a degree of personal attention unmatched by other nearby state universities.

C. OSU is located in a pleasant community situated near both the metropolitan and Big Mogul Mountain areas of East Dakota.

D. Specific Overshoe State programs which have state, regional, or national appeal should be stressed (e.g., jazz, ceramics, special education). Examples, including data, should be supplied to substantiate each of these features. In addition, the following features should be used for specific populations.

E. Out-of-state (e.g., Nebraska, California, and Illinois)—OSU's proximity to the mountains should be stressed graphically.

F. Metropolitan populations in East Dakota—OSU offers the total student experience. This may be contrasted with the commuter experience.

G. Reentry (age 25+) students—The presence of older students at OSU and the services provided for those persons should be mentioned and stressed. Testimonials are often especially useful in such cases.

H. The following "company line" statement has been adopted by the department heads in University Relations. "As a public university, OSU offers diversified academic programs and highly personal service to the people of East Dakota and our region. The people of East Dakota work constantly to update programs which are moderately priced and which meet the changing needs of students."

Surveys of enrolled and accepted but unenrolled students have indicated that these are the features that are both attractive and demonstrable.

VII. Evaluation Procedures

The standards of evaluation will include:

A. the completion of each of the above activities,

B. the quantity and origins of applications of admission,

C. postenrollment determination of the qualifications of the new students, and

D. subjective and objective responses from the target markets and the university.

VIII. Conclusion

A. Inherent in the contents of this marketing plan is the assumption that the marketing of Overshoe State University is everyone's business. In a manner not unlike the business world, the marketing of a university has the dimensions of planning, product development, pricing tactics, distribution techniques, and promotional activities. This plan deals most directly and almost entirely with the promotional aspects of the marketing of OSU. The work of the Enrollment Management Council has begun to address some of the other aspects of marketing.

B. It is extremely obvious that all of the promotional activities imaginable would fail to produce consumer satisfaction if the other parts of marketing (e.g., product development) are ignored. Specifically, the university's academic offerings, long range planning, and the delivery of the classes, workshops, and so on, must always be done with significant attention paid to consumer satisfaction.

REFERENCES

Allen, B. H., and W. H. Peters. 1983. The status of strategic marketing in higher education. College president's viewpoint. *Proceedings of the American Marketing Association Educators Conference* (August).

Aslanian, Carol. 1985. Market analysis is the key to finding adult students. *Admissions Strategist* 3.

Baldridge, J. O., F. R. Kemerer, and K. C. Green. 1982. *The enrollment crisis: Factors, actors and impacts.* AAHE-ERIC/Higher Educational Research Report No. 3. Washington, DC: American Association for Higher Education (AAHE).

Barton, D. W., Jr. 1978. *Marketing higher education.* San Francisco: Jossey-Bass.

Basin, W. H. 1975. A marketing technique for student recruiting. *Research in Higher Education* 331 (January): 51–65.

Bean, J. P., and R. Bradley. 1986. Untangling of satisfaction-performance relationship for college students. *Journal of Higher Education* 57: 393–442.

Behrs, D. G. 1995. The chameleon effect: Enrollment management beyond the year 2000. *Journal of College Admission* 149 (Fall): 5–7.

Berry, L. L., and B. H. Allen. n.d. Marketing's crucial role in institutions of higher education. *Atlantic Economic Review* (July–August).

Bickers, Doyle. 1986. For marketing success, plan, plan, plan. *Admissions Strategist* 7.

Blackburn, J. C. 1979. Marketing techniques used by admissions officers. Unpublished doctoral thesis, Indiana University.

————. 1980. Marketing in admissions: A perspective on its use. *College Board Review* 116 (Summer).

Borden, U. M. H. 1995. Segmenting student markets with a student satisfaction and priorities survey. *Research in Higher Education* 36 (February): 73–88.

Brooker, G., and M. Noble. 1985. The marketing of higher education. *College and University* 60 (Summer): 191–99.

Bruker, R. M., and L. E. Taliana. 1983. The institutional self study: First steps in a viable marketing program. *College and University* 60 (Winter): 32–42.

Campbell, Roger. 1979. Marketing: Matching the student to the college. *College and University* 54 (Summer): 591–604.

Caren, W. A., and F. R. Kemerer. 1979. The international dimensions of institutional marketing. *College and University* 54 (Spring): 173–88.

Carter, V. L., and C. S. Garigin, eds. 1979. *A marketing approach to student recruitment: The best of CASE* Currents. Washington, DC: Council for Advancement and Support of Education.

Chait, Richard. 1979. Mission madness strikes our colleges. *Chronicle of Higher Education* (July 16): 36.

The College Board. 1976. *A role for marketing in college admissions.* New York: The College Board.

———. 1980. *Marketing in college admissions: A broadening of perspectives.* New York: The College Board.

David, C. A. 1980. The myopic marketeers of academe. *Chronicle of Higher Education* (April 28).

Erdman, D. G. 1983. An examination of factors influencing student choice in the college selection process. *Journal of College Admissions* 28 (Summer): 3–7.

Geotsch, H. W. 1979. *How to prepare and use marketing plans for profit.* St. Charles, IL: Marketing for Profit.

Glover, R. H. 1986. Designing a decision-support system for enrollment management. *Research in Higher Education* 24 (Winter): 15–34.

Goldgehn, L. A. 1985. Audit your marketing program for success. *Currents* 11 (September): 36–39.

———. 1988. The interpretation of marketing in colleges and universities in the United States. Unpublished paper, University of San Francisco.

———. 1989. Admissions standards and the use of key marketing techniques by United States colleges and universities. *College and University* 65 (Spring): 44–55.

Grabowski, S. M. 1981. *Marketing in higher education.* AAHE/ERIC Higher Education Research Report No. 5. Washington, DC: American Association for Higher Education (AAHE).

Hossler, D., and K. S. Gallagher. 1987. Studying student college choice: A three-phase model and implications for policy makers. *College and University* 62 (Fall): 207–21.

Huddleston, Thomas, Jr. 1980. In consideration of marketing and reorganization. *NACAC Journal* 25 (July): 18–24.

Hugstad, Paul. 1975. The marketing concept in higher education: A caveat. *Liberal Education* 65 (December): 506–12.

Jefkins, F. 1973. *Dictionary of marketing and communications.* 5th ed. Aylesbury, U.K.: International Textbook.

Johnson, J., and D. Sallee. 1994. Marketing your college as an intangible product. *Journal of College Admission* 144 (Summer): 5–7.

Kotler, P. 1975. *Marketing for nonprofit organizations.* Englewood Cliffs, NJ: Prentice-Hall.

———. 1991. *Strategic marketing for nonprofit organizations.* 4th ed. Englewood Cliffs, NJ: Prentice-Hall.

Kotler, P., and G. Armstrong. 1991. *Principles of marketing*. Englewood Cliffs, NJ: Prentice-Hall.

Kotler, Philip, and K. F. A. Fox. 1985. *Strategic marketing for educational institutions*. Englewood Cliffs, NJ: Prentice-Hall.

Kotler, P., and P. Murphy. 1981. Strategic planning for higher education. *Journal of Higher Education*. 52: 470–89.

Krachenberg, A. R. 1972. Bringing the concept of marketing to higher education. *Journal of Higher Education* 43 (May): 369–80.

Lay, Robert, and John Maguire. 1980. Identifying the connection in higher education. *College and University* 56 (Fall): 53–65.

Litten, L. H., and A. E. Hall. 1989. In the eyes of our beholder. *Journal of Higher Education* 60 (May/June): 302–24.

Lucas, J. A., ed. 1979. *Developing a marketing plan*. New Directions for Institutional Research No. 21. San Francisco: Jossey-Bass.

Lynch, R. G. 1969. Marketing the small college. *College Management* 4 (September): 56–58.

Marshall, J. F., and J. M. Dalman. 1984. The development and implementation of a market research plan for educational institutions. *College and University* 58 (Fall): 316–33.

———. 1985. Researching institutional image: The development and implementation of a market research plan for educational institutions. *College and University* 59 (Fall): 371–79.

McDonough, P., and L. Robertson. 1995. Gatekeepers or marketers: Reclaiming the educational role of chief admissions officers. *Journal of College Admission* 147 (Spring): 22–31.

Muston, R. A. 1985. Role ambiguity in institutional marketing and enrollment management. *Research in Higher Education* 22 (Fall): 371–79.

Nielsen, R. P. 1983. University strategic market planning socioeconomic trends. *Proceedings of the American Marketing Association Educators Conference* (August).

Paate, W. S. 1993. Consumer satisfaction, determinants and post-purchase actions in higher education. *College and University* 68 (Spring/Summer): 100–107.

Sevier, R. A. 1989. Creating a marketing plan. *College and University* 64 (Fall): 393–402.

———. 1994. Image is everything: Strategies for measuring, changing, and maintaining your institution's image. *College and University* 69 (Winter): 60–75.

———. 1996. Those important things: What every college president needs to know about marketing and student recruiting. *College and University* 71 (Spring): 9–16.

Smith, L. R., and S. T. Cauasgil. 1984. Marketing planning for colleges and universities. *Long Range Planning* 17: 104–17.

Stevens, R. E., D. I. Loudon, and W. E. Warner. 1991. *Marketing planning guide*. New York: Haworth Press.

Topor, Robert. 1983. *Marketing higher education: A practical guide*. Washington, DC: Council for the Advancement and Support of Education.

Welki, A. M., and F. J. Navrtil. 1987. The role of applicants' perceptions in the choice of college. *College and University* 62 (Winter).

Zikmund, W., and M. D'Amico. 1989. *Marketing*. New York: John Wiley and Sons.

11

Recruitment: Student Outreach
Strategies

Joyce E. Smith

Recruiting students for undergraduate admission is perhaps the most visible aspect of the college admission process. Most people do not truly understand what it takes to identify, recruit, and retain a class. With increased competition for traditional and nontraditional students, reduced recruitment budgets, staffing cutbacks, and the admissions process under greater scrutiny, it is important to design effective outreach and on-campus activities to maintain or increase enrollment and also maintain academic quality. This chapter will explore the components that lead to effective on-campus and outreach programs, namely, planning, understanding consumer behavior, trends in marketing and student recruitment activities, stages of contact and targeted recruitment activities, and evaluation.

THE IMPORTANT ROLE OF PLANNING

While other authors address marketing plans, budgeting, and the changing student market in greater depth, this chapter looks at the activities and programs that make on-campus and student outreach programs successful. It begins with an understanding of marketing, effective planning, and budgeting.

Too often, recruitment programs are ill-conceived and ineffective because research, planning, marketing, and budgeting were inadequate. In Chapter 10, Jim Blackburn writes, "A marketing plan describes an institution's plan of action for reaching its enrollment targets." Ideally, such a document includes market objectives, basic general strategies, specific tactics or activities, and evaluation criteria. An admissions marketing plan is most successful when all segments of the campus, particularly academic affairs, fiscal affairs, and student services, are onboard early and involved throughout the process. Any major segment of the college or university can derail the marketing plan and processes. Therefore, if possible, it is wise to get everyone in on the game from the beginning.

All segments of higher education today are experiencing a reduction in funding. Programs, publications, and outreach activities in admissions are extremely important to the health of the institution in that admissions must attract a new class of freshmen and transfer students. However, the admissions office, as is the case throughout the institution, today has to do more with less. Developing cost-effective programming that will yield a greater return on an investment will be the challenge ahead.

A study of recruitment efforts conducted by the National Association of College and University Business Officers (NACUBO 1989) found that 52 percent of the colleges surveyed had not changed the focus of their recruiting efforts in the last five years. The most important goals of the recruitment effort, in order of importance, were maintaining the quality of accepted students, increasing the quality of accepted students, and increasing the number of enrolled students. The goals somewhat important in the recruitment effort included expanding geographical range, enhancing diversity, and increasing minority enrollment. Regarding recruitment costs, the study found that, of the colleges responding, 74 percent had a long-range plan for the recruiting function; the trend in most colleges had been to increase recruitment funding at a rate faster than or similar to that of other college activity funding; and most colleges included the traditional and obvious expenses when reporting recruitment costs (travel, entertainment, office supplies, phone, postage, publications, salaries, and advertising). However, most colleges did not include such expenses as computer-related costs, marketing consultant costs, employee benefits, and nonstaff travel and entertainment. Of the colleges surveyed, 16 percent did not include staff salaries in their recruitment expenses and 19 percent did not include advertising expenses.

The primary goal of recruitment programs and activities is to influence the behavior of prospective students, their parents, and significant others in the college admissions process. Programs and activities can be conducted at different stages in the admissions process to (a) generate initial student inquiries and interest, (b) identify serious potential candidates, (c) convert prospects to applicants, (d) convert applicants to deposits, and (e) convert deposits to matriculants. These stages are usually referred to as an admissions funnel (i.e., starting with a large pool and reducing through each stage to the final matriculants).

As planning programs and activities begin, admissions professionals should consider their role—whether as a director, associate, assistant, or admissions counselor—and their level of responsibility in planning discussions, decision making, designating assignments, or budget development. They should consider the institutional, presidential, or admissions office's goals and objectives for student body composition; identify outreach initiatives, visibility, and so on in planning; and review research results to ensure appropriate student markets have been selected.

It is crucial that the program planner know the priorities within the institution's primary, secondary, and tertiary markets so as to stay within the recruitment budget by reviewing profiles from feeder schools, admissions testing data, enrollment-planning services, or institutional data to monitor the persistence of currently enrolled students; by reviewing evaluations from past events to measure their effectiveness in generating action from prospective students; by considering the cost-effectiveness of past or planned recruitment events; and by meeting with interested parties, such as student group leaders, faculty, and other administrators to ensure their cooperation on recruitment outreach efforts. It is important to keep everyone informed. These planning tips can positively influence the effectiveness of campus-based and outreach programs and activities.

UNDERSTANDING CONSUMER BEHAVIOR

For students and parents, the cost of a college education is a major investment of time and money. In the same way colleges recognize the admissions funnel (prospects, applicants, acceptances, deposits, matriculants), consumers go through stages in their college decision-making process. High school counselors advise prospective college students to begin with a long list of colleges that they may be interested in considering for admission. They normally encourage students to apply to at least four colleges and universities considered to be either safe (academically and financially), competitive, selective, or a long-shot, based on the student's academic credentials and the competitiveness of the institutions.

Prospective students and parents may have many different needs that will influence their college decision making. Admissions professionals will want to be aware of those needs as they consider effective program and recruitment outreach activities. Kotler and Andreasen (1991) present Maslow's Hierarchy of Needs as one way of looking at the criteria consumers might apply in making a particular decision.

Maslow contends that people's higher needs are *self-actualization* (self-development and realizations) and *esteem needs* (self-esteem, recognition, and status). Moving toward the middle and lower hierarchy of needs are *social needs* (sense of belonging, love), *safety needs* (security and protection), and finally, *physiological needs* (food, water).

Maslow held that people act to satisfy their lower-level needs, such as safety and physiological needs, before satisfying their higher needs, such as social, self-esteem, and self-development. What are the basic needs in relation to college choice? Kotler and Andreasen suggest that students may be concerned that they will not be able to meet their basic needs for food and adequate housing. Others wonder how safe they will be away from home. Still others are concerned with whether they can find people they like and who like them. Finally, at the highest level of the hierarchy, others are concerned about self-esteem or self-actualization needs. Colleges, contend Kotler and Andreasen, cannot give attention to all these needs. Rather, they found, colleges may cater primarily to the need for belonging (for example, small colleges with small numbers in the classes, a caring faculty, and a good social life), to students' need for esteem (such as "name" recognition colleges and universities), and to students' needs for self-actualization (through the performing arts, quality writing programs, and strong technology programs).

Kotler and Andreasen also recognized the influence of others who often bear the title of significant others or referents. These individuals can provide information on the criteria individuals use to form their personal attitude toward an act. They can have direct influence on behavioral intentions. How does all of this affect student recruitment outreach and activities? Consideration of these factors and the individuals who influence behavior may shape the types of outreach activities that are developed, may suggest those who should be invited to participate, and may determine the messages expressed. The admissions professional should know why students and parents are invited to the campus, for example, for an open house and make certain their needs are addressed when they are there.

Typically, college admissions officers focus on the benefits of attending their school which, if shaped to address the audiences' needs and concerns, will be effective. Admissions professionals, however, must also understand that students may use factors such as cost of tuition, public versus private, colleges versus universities, large versus small student populations, religious versus secular orientation, single sex or predominantly of one race, and student-teacher ratios to differentiate institutions. Admissions officers should know their institution's strengths and emphasize them as they prepare programming for target audiences. Parents, counselors, and others are encouraging students to apply for admission to more colleges. Students and parents are cost comparison shopping as they review admission and scholarship offers and financial aid packages. They are submitting multiple deposits for housing or orientation; and many are committing to more than one school. In addition, parents and students increasingly want to know about careers or jobs to help in the selection of majors, what professional or medical schools accept the college's graduates, what types of companies recruit on the campus, where graduates are hired, and the starting salaries of recent graduates.

These are only a few practical queries that admissions professionals must be prepared to address when planning recruitment campaigns or hosting prospective applicants at special events.

TRENDS IN RECRUITMENT AND MARKETING

A survey, jointly sponsored by several educational organizations in 1979, 1985, and 1992, provides a 16-year profile of trends in admissions practices. *Demographics, Standards, and Equity: Challenges in College Admissions* (1986) and the latest report, *Challenges in College Admissions* (1995), chronicle policies and practices in two-year and four-year institutions, including trends in

Table 11.1
Institutions Reporting "Very Frequent" Use of Various Recruiting Practices

Recruitment Practices	1979	1985	1992
High School Visits by Admissions Staff	76%	81%	81%
Visits to Campus by Students and Families	38%	75%	82%
Visits to Campus by High School Personnel	24%	21%	21%
*Recruiting Visits Outside Local Geographic Area	---	---	38%
*Recruiting Visits Outside the United States	---	---	4%
College Nights with Invited Institutions	64%	67%	63%
College Fairs that Charge for Participation	---	31%	37%
Visits to Noninstitutional Central Locations	15%	13%	12%
Displays, Booths in Public Locations, Malls	---	15%	9%
Direct Mailings to Prospective Students	64%	72%	72%
Telephone Calls to Prospective Students	36%	43%	53%
*Toll-Free Lines for Incoming Calls	---	---	48%
*Online Information Services	---	---	12%
Advertising on/in:			
Billboards, Posters	5%	9%	7%
Commercial Radio/TV	11%	20%	20%
Public Radio/TV	3%	8%	14%
Local Newspapers	26%	36%	32%
High School Newspapers	5%	6%	7%
Magazines	3%	10%	12%
Promotional Audio Visual Products	12%	20%	26%
*Computer Searches	---	---	19%

*New questions asked in 1992 survey.
Source: Challenges in College Admissions (1995).

applications, admissions and acceptances, qualifications of students, recruitment and marketing efforts, special services provided, use of admissions tests, and much more. Of particular relevance to this discussion is the section on recruitment, marketing, and financial aid, which highlights the frequent use of traditional and new programs and activities in the area of student recruitment (see Table 11.1). Admissions professionals considering the use of various methods of recruitment reported in the survey results should consider the profile of those responding to the questionnaire in the designated years (see Table 11.2).

From 1979 to 1992, the survey results suggest, virtually every category

Table 11.2
Number of Institutions Responding to Surveys

Year	Two-Year Institutions		Four-Year Institutions		
	Public	Private	Public	Private	Total
1979	401	81	333	648	1,463
1985	745	218	413	827	2,203
1992	705	169	366	784	2,024

Source: Challenges in College Admissions (1995).

showed an increase in recruitment activity. The results also imply that the primary techniques used—high school visits, visits to campus by students, college nights, direct mailings, and telephone calls to prospective students—continue to be important recruitment strategies. The respondents are doing more of what they have traditionally done and increased their use of such techniques that were once used sparingly. From the 1992 survey, respondents were asked to write in additional recruiting practices not listed in the response options.

• Respondents at two-year public institutions reported using techniques such as advertising in community college newspapers, church publications, mobile recruiting programs, bus tours, speakers' bureaus, home visits, booths at powwows, programs on campus for students in kindergarten through ninth grade, sponsorship of community teams, young scholars programs, middle school visits, and the formation of special interest groups.

• Two-year private institutions reported using portfolio days, phone book advertising, receptions in homes of alumni, cafeteria visits, slide shows, athletic programs, trade conventions, weekend experiences, and educational consultants.

• Four-year public institutions reported using guidebooks and rating magazines, alumni receptions, academic achievement awards, and college newspapers.

• Four-year private institutions listed church and synagogue publications, college guides, home visits, camps, announcements and posters in high schools, fax information, public concerts, conventions, receptions in homes of alumni, referrals by staff and alumni, special weekends, ads in telephone book yellow pages, and variations of recruitment programs and activities already listed.

STAGES OF STUDENT CONTACT AND TARGETED ACTIVITIES

Conducting research will help enrollment managers realize immediate savings by eliminating costly, ineffective strategies and concentrating resources on those that pay off. Research areas that are critical include segmentation to define groups of potential students; studies of currently enrolled students or recent alumni to capture concerns that can be used to appeal to prospective students;

studies of nonenrolled students to understand why they did not enroll; enrollment decision research to detect influential factors; image research to understand perceptions about an institution's reputation and awareness of their desired student populations; and positioning research to identify who competitors are and how an institution can differentiate itself from others.

Most four-year institutions typically conduct special recruiting activities for student subgroups. *Challenges in College Admissions* (1995), the survey, jointly sponsored by the American Association of Collegiate Registrars and Admissions Officers (AACRAO), the College Entrance Examination Board, Educational Testing Service, and The National Association for College Admission Counseling (NACAC), reports that over half of the responding institutions directed special recruiting efforts toward academically talented students (67 percent), racial/ethnic minorities (67 percent), athletes (60 percent), adults (60 percent), students with special talents such as art and music (51 percent), and international students (42 percent). Other targeted groups included relatives of alumni, relatives of faculty/staff, the disadvantaged, students with disabilities, out-of-state/district, part-time, veterans, military personnel, students who can pay full cost, and resident aliens.

In *Achieving Diversity: Strategies for the Recruitment and Retention of Traditionally Underrepresented Students* (NACAC 1993), admissions professionals shared strategies to enhance their recruitment of multicultural students. The activities and special initiatives listed below can be developed with other offices on campus or with student leaders.

- Mentoring programs for multicultural students (new freshmen with seniors)
- Summer studies or enrichment programs
- Direct mail information on services, programming, or organizations for multicultural students
- Special bus trips to campus for overnight visits in the dorm/special weekend events
- Church visitations for discussions with parent and student groups
- Partnerships between the university or college and area high schools with a high concentration of multicultural students
- Invitations to currently enrolled students to accompany admissions representatives during visits back to their hometown schools to discuss students' college experience
- Use of multicultural alumni for interviews, special local events, or alumni weekends
- Emphasis on the institution's historic commitment to the admission of students of color in recruitment materials
- Work with the members and staff of the National Association for Equal Opportunity in Higher Education Upward Bound programs on campuses to retain student participants
- Development of advisory groups from multicultural communities to enhance the college and community relationship as college students participate in local community activities

• Scholarships for multicultural students

• Powwows and career days, information sessions for Native Americans

GENERATING INITIAL STUDENT INQUIRIES AND INTEREST

The following examples of programming may be incorporated at different stages of the admissions funnel.

Direct Mail

These activities might best be categorized as casting-your-net opportunities for the greatest exposure to as many prospective students as possible. After identifying the audience or subgroups and the activities, the admissions professional may consider the best student lists to receive the college's letters, invitations, announcements, publications, videos, and application software or paper applications. Most marketing experts say that the best mailing list is always an individual institution's own list of inquiries. This list may be garnered from students who have expressed interest in the institution through unsolicited phone or mail contacts or through interest cards collected from prior events and admissions-testing agencies. Generally, all accredited colleges and universities are eligible to participate in the Educational Opportunity Service of ACT or the Student Search Service of the College Board. Both testing agencies have more than a million students completing their questionnaires when they register for their respective admissions tests each year. The information from these questionnaires serves as the database for variables for segmentation. Lists may be segmented by many variables including gender, race, states, zip codes, and prospective college majors.

Travel

Increased travel expenses over the years have not deterred the importance of visits to high schools. This activity remains an extremely vital component of the recruiting process. Admissions office representatives can meet the counselors, update information in the school resource center about their institution, collect the latest profile information about the secondary school, and meet personally or in a group with prospective students. They leave with a greater understanding of the potential of the applicants from that school. That understanding is communicated via trip reports shared with others in the admissions office. Survey reports suggest that colleges establish territories based on their primary or secondary feeder schools or the new market areas they wish to cultivate. More colleges and universities are organizing tours for invited high school guidance counselors to visit their campuses, tour their facilities, and participate in information sessions. This falls in the area of informing "influential" partners in the admissions process.

International recruitment to identify American citizens living abroad and encourage student interest from diverse cultures around the world is at an all-time high. Admissions professionals are encouraged to participate in training experiences before they set out to recruit international students. The same tactics used within the United States may be perceived differently in other cultures (i.e., direct mail and marketing strategies conducted by educational institutions may be perceived negatively). The admissions professional should obtain publications that describe the educational systems in the countries from which they plan to recruit students and be prepared to explain not only the colleges' curricular or admissions requirements but also matters of safety, politics, language assistance, or other types of available support services. AACRAO's Office of International Education Services and AACRAO along with the National Association of Foreign Student Advisors: Association of International Educators (with the participation of the College Board) publish several series of reports on foreign educational systems.

International students are not eligible to receive federally funded student financial aid, and they must prove through documentation that the family has funds available to fully support its student's educational experience in the United States. Because many may seek academic scholarships, the recruiter needs to understand the institution's policies regarding international students and financial eligibility for scholarships, jobs, and so forth. For Americans living overseas, admissions recruiters need to understand issues of state residency as they pertain to in-state or out-of-state tuition assessment, admissions testing, and much more. Private and public institutions alike report degrees of success in international recruitment, with schools increasingly sending representatives independently or on sponsored recruitment tours throughout the world.

College Fairs

College fairs are yet another activity designed to give institutions greater visibility with many students and parents. The fair site typically showcases many educational institutions with table-top displays in a large facility that invites prospective students to browse and collect information. Some fair sites offer sessions on financial aid, college selection, or topics of greatest concern to the local community. NACAC offers more than 32 sites for National College Fairs and 15 Performing and Visual Arts College Fairs across the country each fall and spring. Other professional organizations offer specialized fairs for multicultural students or graduate admission for adult students. In addition, state and regional organizations, as well as local schools, sponsor fairs on a smaller scale.

Visits to Campus

Many college admissions professionals suggest that if they can get students and their parents on the campus grounds, the campus will sell itself. Colleges invest a great deal in maintenance of the grounds, buildings, and facilities. Welcome centers, kiosks, information booths, and good signage are also important. Admissions offices are encouraged to have organized campus tours available to give visitors a firsthand view of the campus. A video should also be available in case of inclement weather. The best tours have trained student volunteers who are aware of what to emphasize as they share their knowledge and experiences as currently enrolled students. Special summer camps for middle or high school students are yet another means to present a campus experience for prospective students. While not always directly connected with the admissions office, many colleges welcome summer camps for the student exposure they bring to sports, math, science, or computer training, as well as early enrichment programs on the campus. These camps offer students the opportunity to live on campus, become familiar with the facilities and enjoy a good experience that will encourage them to apply for admission when they become high school seniors.

TECHNOLOGY AS A RECRUITMENT TOOL

In the 1992 survey (AACRAO, CEEB, ETS, and NACAC, 1995) of those responding, only 12% reported having "on-line" services, and 19% reported offering computer searches. The use of technology in the college admission recruitment process has since taken off in leaps and bounds, and institutions not keeping pace will lose out. The Internet provides you with essentially global advertising of your institution's programs and services and makes good use of this revolutionary tool to recruit, admit, and retain students. It is predicted that if secondary schools gain greater access to the Internet and the increase in the purchase and use of computers in households continues, many of our traditional ways of recruiting in the college admission process may go by the wayside. There are issues concerning the need to have information available both electronically and in print while everyone catches up, but that time may be sooner rather than later.

Internet Guide for College-Bound Students. Hartman (1996) states that in early 1996 nearly three-quarters of the colleges in the United States, both two-year and four-year, were on the Internet. By the end of this century all colleges and universities are expected to be on-line. Hartman states, "colleges recognize the power and ability of the Internet to provide vital information and services to enrolled students and faculty, but also to recruit prospective students." Students are already using the Internet to search for colleges, conduct research for school projects, and much more. College admission professionals must adjust recruitment strategies and practices to maximize use of this evolving medium.

Increasingly colleges now offer multiple web sites for different audiences, such as currently enrolled students who want to know about on-line registration for classes, and alumni and members of the general public, who want information about campus activities, museums, or special library collections. Prospective students can click onto many college sites and visit dorm rooms, listen to the campus student orchestra, download catalogues, or locate admission and financial aid applications to complete and submit electronically. Hartman encourages students to use web sites to select information about colleges, find out about financial aid and scholarships, exchange information with other interested students through chat groups, contact faculty or administrators, apply for admission, or explore information about majors and careers. If your campus has a web site, keep it current to encourage multiple visits that engage and inform prospective students and parents. Provide information year-round about the admission calendar so they can be reminded of important deadlines, policies, and practices.

Using technology as a recruitment tool is a permanent fixture in the landscape of college admission and professionals must consider ways to maintain the "counseling" aspect of the jobs while utilizing these new media.

IDENTIFYING SERIOUS POTENTIAL CANDIDATES

After initial unsolicited contacts with prospective students, those who respond—by returning a card, e-mailing, electronically visiting your web site, calling the office for more information, or visiting the campus—are indicating some continuing interest in the institution. After a contact designed to support a student's interest, admissions offices may utilize recruitment strategies, such as sending a monthly student newspaper, an invitation to campus events with a calendar, or follow-up letters or phone calls. Students who come for a campus informational visit or those who request an interview are seeking an opportunity to understand the uniqueness of the campus and to share their own special qualities. In exchange, the admissions professional has an opportunity to get to know the student and showcase the campus.

CONVERTING APPLICANTS TO MATRICULANTS

After the applications have been read and admissions decisions reached, the admissions professional's job in the recruitment process is still not complete. Increasingly, colleges have developed strategies to influence prospective students and parents during the difficult decisionmaking period. Institutions may plan on-campus or outreach events to address the negatives. Were the students friendly? Did another institution offer a better financial aid package? Will the faculty members be accessible? Is the campus too large and impersonal? These types of concerns might be answered in a telephone campaign that uses currently enrolled students to field such questions of admitted students. A campus visitation program (overnight or weekend) to permit students and parents to discuss housing, financial aid, and future careers in an open-house format might be offered. Faculty representation at this type of event is very important. Alumni may host events in cities across the country, inviting locally admitted students to meet others in the area who have been admitted. These types of programming and activities that best portray an institution and are helpful to the students and their families can influence the final decision of admitted students.

SUMMARY

Today's competitive market environment makes it important for colleges and universities to plan, monitor, and evaluate the effectiveness of their recruitment functions. Kotler and Andreasen refer to this as understanding the marketing mix. These authors suggest that colleges be clear about what response they are seeking from the target audiences throughout the development of the marketing mix. "Typically, the response is movement forward through the stages of awareness, knowledge, liking, preference, conviction, and action" (Kotler and Andreasen 1991). Recruitment advertising, visiting cities around the world, direct mail, publications, use of new technologies, such as web sites, CD-ROM programs, and electronic applications all require fine tuning as the students to recruit are changing. Recruitment programs and activities may be evaluated by the participants, by the admissions office or campus administrators revisiting their goals and objectives or from a cost-effectiveness approach. Is it important to measure the effectiveness of events by the number of applications received or matriculants enrolled? What does it cost to recruit a new freshman? Traditional evaluation tools such as response cards, surveys, staff evaluations and institutional research are important annual investments for the admissions professional to consider before another cycle of recruitment programs, both on and off campus, begins.

REFERENCES

American Association of Collegiate Registrars and Admissions Officers (AACRAO), The College Entrance Examination Board (CEEB), The Educational Testing Service (ETS), and The National Association for College Admission Counseling (NACAC). 1986. *Standards and equity: Challenges in college admissions: Report of a survey of undergraduate admission policies, practices and procedures.* Washington, DC: AACRAO, CEEB, ACT, ETS, and NACAC.

————. 1995. *Challenges in college admissions: A report of a survey of undergraduate admissions policies, practices and procedures.* Washington, DC: AACRAO, The College Board, ETS, and NACAC.

Hartman, K. 1996. *Internet guide for college-bound students.* New York: The College Board.

Kotler, P., and A. Andreasen. 1991. *Strategic marketing for nonprofit organizations.* 4th ed. Englewood Cliffs, NJ: Prentice-Hall.

National Association for College Admission Counseling. 1993. *Achieving diversity: Strategies for the recruitment and retention of traditionally underrepresented students*. Washington, DC: NACAC.

National Association of College and University Business Officers (NACUBO). 1989. *Assessing the cost of student recruitment at smaller independent colleges and universities*. Washington, DC: NACUBO.

12

Applying Technological Tools

David H. Stones

One will seldom encounter a more personable, outgoing, caring lot than the admissions officers at colleges and universities. Why would such a warm and friendly group want to be associated with cold, unfriendly, unintuitive machines that turn their prized possessions, prospective students, into impersonal numbers? Why, indeed? Survival despite a diminishing budget? Service to the student? Speed? Effectiveness in recruiting? Accountability? Strategic advantage to the institution? A better fit with the faculty and the mission of the college/ university? Providing the best data to facilitate retention? For the sheer fun of it?

But how does an institution decide what to do and how to get there? There is no single answer for any one institution, and there are many differences between institutions that might lead to different decisions. The answers lie somewhere between quill pens and lasers, the U.S. mail and satellite telecommunications—and between counselors and robots. It is crucial to focus on "What's the question?" before asking "What's the right answer?" An institution's admissions system will not automatically solve specific problems nor match a specific wish list, unless the admissions officers get involved, make their thoughts known, and work side-by-side with those delivering the systems.

A FEW GOOD PRINCIPLES

A few truths should be self-evident and should be considered when evaluating technological options.

1. Electronic Highway + Standard Formats = Access, Speed, and Efficiency. If people always spoke in the same universal language understood by our computers, and if

they could connect directly and eliminate delays in collecting data and in disseminating results, they could reduce their efforts and time requirements to a fraction of current levels.

2. A time-honored analysis technique breaks systems into input, process, and output. Input and output are directly related to data collection, communication, and notification. Most new technologies provide alternative methods for improving input and output. Most traditional automation benefits come in the process section. Knowledge of which components are affected by which innovations is important.

3. The greatest technological advances are not those in which manual actions are automated, but rather those in which technology allows existing procedures and practices to be streamlined or discarded entirely.

Reengineering and automation of the workflow are more complicated and involve rethinking and change, but they provide the biggest payoffs. People spend much of their time perfecting their current operations, making sure they do the same old things right. This includes straight automation and increased accuracy. Drucker suggests that "the executive is, first of all, expected to get the right things done" (Drucker 1966).

TRADITIONAL SYSTEMS FOR AUTOMATED ADMISSIONS PIONEERS

The use of computers to assist in automating the admissions process began in the mid- to late 1960s, and the early stages continued though the 1970s. The tools and techniques of this era have not received much press of late, but the functionality achieved by these traditional systems is often still necessary. For schools just beginning to automate—or more likely, thinking to scrap existing systems and reautomate—these basics should still receive attention.

The old admissions system was driven by process and output. The production of computer-generated letters of admission eliminated considerable typing and typos and introduced an upper-case form that left little doubt of its origin. Bulky batch reports on wide paper with green bars allowed staff to see what was in the database for all students, since there was little direct on-line access. One very significant development was that admissions staff entered not only data pertinent to the admit decision, but also the core data needed by the registrar for registration processing and, later, for the on-line official record. This front-end load was a heavy price for admissions offices to pay. However, it showed an institutional investment toward a better overall system, even though time and expense for admissions personnel may have increased. In lockstep cases with firm criteria, the admit decision process was automated, providing a bit of a payoff to weary admissions officers. Automation of other time-consuming processes such as grade point average (GPA) calculation was held up because of the data entry needed to precede them.

The tools available to offices of admission underwent major improvement.

ACT Service and the Educational Testing Service (ETS, processor of the Scholastic Aptitude Test, for the College Board) provided much more information than just test scores when they began delivering scores to institutions on magnetic tape. This additional information on applicants included personal identifiers (name, Social Security number, date of birth), demographic data (race, citizenship, address), and answers to many questions regarding academic and extracurricular activities and abilities. Many of these data elements, including information on schools attended, were coded and allowed computers to process the received records. The testing agencies also provided to colleges, roughly at cost, these same institutional code sets, which were very useful at a time when storage costs for full school names were prohibitive. All of this allowed some schools to reengineer their procedures to have the test score receipt (along with all the coded data) as the first step in the application process. The schools could then send a confirmation letter back to the prospective student, collect a few bits of additional data, and make the admit decision.

Another major advance in admissions-processing systems was the creation, at a few schools, of transfer evaluation systems that allowed the storage of data tables showing relationships between courses taken elsewhere and the equivalent courses when they were received in transfer. Automatic matching and equation was made much simpler by improved database management systems (DBMSs). These DBMSs allowed faster inquiry and analysis, as well as easier file modification. Colleges and universities also began to install more "dumb terminals" (full-screen IBM 3270 terminals), providing computer access to more staff.

A NEW PLATEAU

The 1980s brought radically different expectations for computerized admissions systems. The focus shifted from automating office processes to manipulating data in order to provide useful management information. As administrators became concerned with data-driven strategic planning, decisions such as outcomes and accountability suddenly needed to be measurable. Degree audit systems, which were on the increase, also required much more data and much more precise data on courses, both home and transfer, which admissions officers were called on to supply. This represented another need for institutional investment, with the student, academic advisor, and degree checker receiving the benefit of the office of admissions' toil.

The basic processing of documents came under increased scrutiny as lost documents and slow admit decisions resulted in letters of complaint to presidents and boards of regents. This led to demands for more accountability and to more direct intervention from on high. A little access also leads to a lot of demand. The solutions were still data driven, and the data had to be entered one character at a time. Fully comprehensive "kitchen sink" reports were still expensive to produce. Fortunately, the opportunity to implement new technology came at a time when state and school budgets were being slashed.

Several major advances in technology provided extra functionality to the admissions office. Among these were personal computers, touchtone telephone/voice response (TT/VR) technology (originally billed as telephone registration), and electronic data interchange (EDI).

Personal Computers

Personal computers (PCs) arrived in full force in the 1980s. They quickly furnished a set of tools for quick development of a complicated system, and they provided the data needed only by the operator of the PC. Generally, data stored in PC systems were not accessible to other offices or individuals. Among the many side effects were the following:

- Managers and administrators became accustomed to quick development and user-friendly systems on PCs and Macintoshes and expected the same features from mainframes—and they were usually disappointed.
- Those dissatisfied with development time and priority on the mainframe developed many stand-alone, PC-based systems, which often contained data that would later need to be merged with mainframe data, even though the data were collected with different audits and assumptions.
- Local area networks (LANs) proliferated, allowing PCs to be connected together if in close proximity.
- Network managers and technicians were needed to oversee operations of the LANs.
- New technologies, protocols, and languages arose to allow the PCs, LANs, and mainframes to communicate with one another.
- Desktop publishing, spreadsheets, and presentation graphics made admissions offices completely independent of many of the outside offices and companies they had dealt with for years.
- The simplicity of PC-based data communications paved the way for exponential growth in electronic mail (E-mail, with Bitnet and Internet) and EDI.

A complicated picture began to develop, but one could select the most appropriate tool for each particular task and then tie a series of tasks together. All staff members were now involved with the computer, and this set the stage for client-server systems.

Touchtone Technology

Touchtone was interesting in two respects. First, it involved an intermediate computer—generally a minicomputer or a group of microcomputers (call it Harold)—connected to the mainframe. Callers (students) dialed into Harold, and merely answered questions asked by a program already running with connections to a session of the mainframe. That is, students were controlled by a program and were thus unable to write programs or execute any commands not provided through the TT/VR script. This was a major security enhancement. Second, students could enter data into the system in machine-readable form (the numeric digits from the touchtone phone pad). This eliminated staff data entry and gave students a chance to review and possibly change the results of the entry before leaving the system.

The *telephone registration* system rapidly led to the development of other uses, from bulletin boards to grade reports. At least two possibilities were very important for admissions, namely, the provision of prerecorded voice answers to many commonly asked questions and of systems to provide direct information on credentials received or missing. Both of these applications left staff free for processing and tasks other than telephone duty. TT/VR brought many new components into the admissions systems, including authentication of the caller identity generally via a personal identification number (PIN), or password, the switch to a more client-server-like relationship between the voice response boxes and the mainframe, and universal access (via phone) versus the limitations of prerecorded speech.

Many new and innovative tools have arrived on the scene during the 1990s. Once perfected, these approaches, which deal primarily with communication, will once again revolutionize the way traditional transactions are processed.

Electronic Data Interchange

Electronic data exchange (EDI) provides a tremendous tool for today and the future. EDI provides standard formats for sending information regarding standard business transactions in processable form from one computer to another. Coded data can be sent directly to the receiving institution's computer systems, opening the door to both straight automation and reengineering of systems. For offices of admission, EDI was first utilized in the development of what is now known as the SPEEDE/ExPRESS electronic transcript.

The SPEEDE/ExPRESS development story is interesting and important. *SPEEDE* stands for Standardization of Postsecondary Education Electronic Data Exchange, the college component, which was sponsored by the American Association of Collegiate Registrars and Admissions Officers (AACRAO). *ExPRESS* stands for Exchanging Permanent Records for Students and Schools, the prekindergarten–grade 12 part, which was funded by the National Center for Education Statistics, a branch of the U.S. Department of Education. Following successful efforts in the early 1980s by schools in Texas and Florida to develop new (non-X12) formats for the exchange of transcripts, a joint project was started in 1988 to develop a national standard. Automotive and financial industries began using EDI in the late 1960s, with the American National Standard Institute's (ANSI's) Accreditation Standards Committee (ASC) X12 overseeing the development and maintenance of data standards for EDI.

SPEEDE/ExPRESS led the charge for educational EDI and also beat health insurance, defense, and government to the top, placing education in a very good position to set enterprise-wide data standards that could also be used by government and business. Work on standards for the verification of enrollment, applying for admission at educational institutions, sending financial aid transcripts, and exchanging course inventory information has demonstrated this very well.

The benefits to admissions of receiving SPEEDE/ExPRESS transcripts are numerous:

- envelope handling, data stamping, sorting, distribution, data entry, and coding are completely eliminated;
- the workload is decreased during peak processing periods;
- security and quality assurance improve;
- service to students is faster, allowing earlier notification of decisions;
- electronic feeds to credentials-tracking systems can provide instant data for answering student inquiries, and the same format covers high school as well as college transcripts;
- the calculation of hours and GPAs, and evaluation of transfer coursework can be made automatic;
- admissions has complete data, enabling a more thorough analysis of such items as high school unit requirements; and
- when paper is needed, schools can print the desired information in the most appropriate format for their purposes.

In the ideal situation—a reality at several SPEEDE/ExPRESS sites—after semester grades are posted, hundreds of transcripts are received in an electronic batch from a large feeder school. That same night, before human hands have touched them, the transcripts are matched with the admissions database, the credential is marked as received, staff are notified if this document completes the file for admissions purposes, and, depending on the application and enrollment status of the student, up to three different GPA and hour calculations are done and the transfer courses are automatically equated to the numbering system at the receiving school. The results are stored on-line, with exceptions flagged for staff review. Meanwhile, the equivalent work is available the next day for use in degree audit, advising, and prerequisite checking. The most remarkable aspect is that these benefits come from a solution that is quite cheap in terms of the actual dollars required and number of staff who have to be involved in implementation.

In the near future, EDI will become more refined and more pervasive. From college and university campuses, where it was implemented fairly early, EDI will be extended to more secondary schools and school districts, thus allowing a much more detailed and individualized approach to both admission decisions and academic placement. EDI will continue to be used for transmission of large batches of transactional data, but interactive EDI will become much more common, with data delivered and questions answered in near "real time." The data standards behind EDI will also allow computerized systems to handle many of the tasks now delegated to frontline staff. The day is near when a student will be able to use EDI to apply for admission, housing, and financial aid and to request that transcripts be sent. In return, the student will be able to receive confirmation of decisions and aid awards plus information about how the evaluated transfer courses fit the requested degree program.

EDI will also be used for reporting purposes and for obtaining data from central sources. Institutions are already beginning to see this within education, with the development of a clearinghouse for student loan information, increased interest by the National Center for Education Statistics (NCES) in standards for surveys and reports, and in a request for expansion of the transcript format to accommodate vocational and training needs for government and business purposes. This technology remains strategic for many reasons, including the way it combines data standards with improved data delivery on the information superhighway, supports automation through reengineering, and supports better workflow management.

Data standards inherent in EDI have a very attractive side effect. Standardizing the way in which data are imported into, or exported from, software systems is important. This standardization should make data interface problems less frequent and easier to solve. It should also allow vendors to produce software for a lower price. An important example is the application for admission in which tens of commercial agencies began marketing primarily diskette-based services that would allow students to apply "magnetically" to colleges and universities. In 1994 when the SPEEDE Committee proposed ANSI ASC X12 "national EDI data format standards" very similar to those for transcripts, the proposal was generally accepted by the software vendors. The result may well be that admissions offices' automated systems will need to support only a single format rather than one for each vendor.

The Electronic Superhighway

The *electronic superhighway* is supposed to provide easy, fast, and powerful connections between computers and individuals. It has received huge amounts of press, but what will it do for admissions? The electronic superhighway, or Internet, can be compared to the interstate highway system in the United States. The interstate was designed to allow large numbers of vehicles to move quickly and easily from one region to another. Within the regions, connections met specified requirements to allow the interstate highways to attach to other U.S. highways, state highways, city streets, and eventually, to individual driveways.

The information superhighway works the same way and to a great extent already exists, but not as a single entity. Just as the interstate is not a single entity, neither is the Internet. Instead, it is an organized protocol for the connection of regional Internets, which consist of defined Internet nodes and transmission media, among other things. Each of these nodes is a self-contained unit that generally runs its own internal mail and networking system. For instance, a university might have a single node that in turn connects to several mainframes and hundreds of local area networks (LANs). The protocol on this machine allows the individual person or office to connect easily to the larger Internet community. The local "streets and driveways" are much more expensive, but an essential component.

The importance of the electronic superhighway can be tied to basic communications. An instant connection of individuals and institutions to other individuals and institutions can streamline existing communication and expand the amount and quality of information shared. The challenge is to find a common language to facilitate that communication. EDI and the data standards inherent within it complete a large part of this second piece, which will lead to potential speed, accuracy, and efficiency in processing information. Toward this end, a dedicated Internet EDI server was placed in public service by the University of Texas at Austin in November 1995 to provide free, encrypted delivery facilitation for schools using a variety of Internet protocols.

The Internet has several forms and several functions, which will be discussed throughout this chapter. The two primary types are Simple Mail Transmission Protocol (SMTP) and File Transfer Protocol (FTP). FTP requires the machine to support a communications protocol known as TCP/IP (Transmission Control Protocol/Internet Protocol). It can be used to obtain documentation, participant tables, or other nontransaction information to support processes such as a SPEEDE/ExPRESS transcript exchange. The Serial Link Internet Protocol (SLIP) allows a lone user with a PC and modem to attach to the Internet and use some of its services. Options such as TELNET let the Internet provide the connectivity so that a remote user on a single PC or on another network can log into a system and act like a terminal in full screen mode (3270 screen protocol).

Gopher is an Internet-based tool in which various sites (schools) provide menu-driven and keyword-driven systems to open access to specific data from the administrative mainframe. Likely candidates for Gopher development include faculty-staff-student directories (including E-mail addresses), course schedules, and transfer equivalence formulations by feeder schools. Most of these will make an institution more compliant with Americans with Disabilities Act (ADA) requirements. Gopher allows an Internet user to interactively connect with text and database information at other locations; many schools make course schedule information available in this manner.

Mosaic is more like the Macintosh Hypercard feature and goes even further, allowing a text passage (or a menu) to reference a file that resides on another machine in another city or even country. The referenced file may include more text, a document image of a picture or painting, or even an audio-video segment. The use of Mosaic could even obviate use of the sacred viewbook.

If E-mail IDs and accounts were established for prospective students sufficiently early (prior to enrollment), schools could achieve incredible savings in printing and postage and could speed communication with the applicant. After enrollment, student electronic accounts could support an electronic homeroom used to dispense information.

World Wide Web

The World Wide Web (WWW) has made enormous recent advances, extending the functionality introduced by Mosaic. It has brought uniform text and graphical presentation modes and Internet access to the masses. It has been used for making information easily available to the public, for allowing individual interactive connections, and for providing a launching pad for a variety of Internet-based services. It is used for commercial transactions. Encryption capability is developing nicely, which is good news for those concerned with the Family Educational Rights and Privacy Act (FERPA). It mixes well with Gopher, FTP, and E-mail, and it supports forms for collecting data. Tools such as Java allow the development of Web front ends to data on our (separate) administrative computers. It will change in a positive direction before this book is published, so watch it closely. In the foreseeable future, it—or its vastly improved successor—could provide an inexpensive replacement for our catalogues and viewbooks, college search services, test sign-ups, and applications for admission. It could also replace some of our classrooms.

Campus-Wide Information Systems

Campus-wide information systems (CWISs), also called distributed access systems, have emerged from a time in which a few individuals on a few machines in a few offices had log-on IDs and direct access. CWISs enabled individual students, and sometimes John Q. Public, to interact with the administrative database. With the proper security—which includes identification, authentication (password or PIN), authorization, and secure transmission medium—CWIS could allow students to view academic and other personal information (grade reports or degree audits, for instance) and perform the data entry function in those instances where the student provides information or makes decisions. The latter has the additional benefit of encouraging the student to audit and correct the transaction before it is finalized.

Pioneers in this area have used dedicated, hardwired public access terminals, ATMs (automatic teller machines), and kiosks (which are also useful for multimedia displays of general information, such as maps) (Gwinn and Lonabocker 1996). Advances in the Internet and/or the information superhighway should soon give students virtually limitless access to some system within (or connected to) the administrative computer system. Full-screen display will overcome the vocabulary and timing limitations of touchtone/voice response systems. All of these remote connections help further the development of *client-server* architecture, which provides structure and protocol for software routines designed to provide answers to specific questions stored on a different machine. It is also very important in providing integrated data systems when individual databases are maintained on disparate machines and systems.

Direct connection goes even further. It can reduce the need for interactive EDI by simply allowing the student to answer questions directly and storing the answers in coded form in the database. The Georgia Institute of Technology was an early pioneer in this area. An applicant could provide, electronically, most of the information collected on the application for admission. While additional items such as application fees and the student signature might still be needed, recruiters could, early in the process, identify a very interested prospective student and thus reduce the data entry task. Housing and scholarship applications could be collected in the same manner.

This system makes it easy for an institution to ask its own questions, rather than the standard questions that might be used by a third-party application service. The direct connection also provides a superior tool for posting (on a "bulletin board") general information about a school as well as the answers to frequently asked questions. If E-mail IDs and accounts could be established for prospective students prior to enrollment, schools might be able to achieve incredible savings in printing and postage and also speed communication with the applicant. After enrollment, direct connection would support an electronic homeroom through which information could be inexpensively and accurately given to each student.

Document Imaging

Document imaging, while in existence for some time, has only recently become affordable to the typical office of admissions. Installation of imaging systems onto LANs has allowed offices to eliminate file cabinets and paper and create databases of indexed fields for keyed document searches. It has also provided improved security over straight paper systems against fire and other natural disasters (see Perkins 1996).

Imaging can go much farther, though. While expense and programming requirements would be much greater, by extending imaging to a fully integrated part of campus-wide student information systems, institutions could gain remote as well as simultaneous access and parallel, rather than serial, processing. The prospect of treating a document image of a transcript, application (with signature), letter of recommendation, design diagram, artistic creation, or picture like any other kind of data in the student file is very attractive. Imagine being able to see, on a split screen, the notation that a document has been received and the actual document. The picture on the student ID could also be viewed, as well as, for example, an image of the picture taken when the student took the TOEFL exam. Such an integrated system could place a burden on the requirements for speed and security on the campus computing infrastructure. However, library and research applications for the school with an image-enabled system for viewing research materials and books could support a structure that opens the door to enterprise-wide imaging for admissions and records. The institution would thus have a strategic technology that provides great access speed and an opportunity to reengineer systems to support a good workflow model.

Smart Cards

Smart card technology could be a major player on several fronts. Most have heard of the innovative new ID card systems implemented at many schools— Florida State University being the first—which incorporate several new uses, including telephone access, magnetic stripes for dorm entrance, a vendor stripe, and banking (a charge or debit card). In order to make this a truly universal card serving staff, students, faculty, library users, and spectators at fine arts presentations and athletic events, some schools have moved away from the traditional Social Security number and have initiated new numbering schemes, some of which are based on International Standards Organization (ISO) taxonomies—a 15-digit number, with the first 6 digits identifying the institution. The card becomes a smart card if a computer chip, approximately $\frac{3}{4}$" in diameter, is embedded in the plastic. In 1994 this chip was roughly the equivalent of an IBM PC/AT, with intelligence, a few thousand bytes of memory, and, possibly, hard-disk storage capacity. The basic card gives benefits to the student. Schools might sign contracts with long distance telephone companies and banks that are financially attractive to the school. Cards provide students with standard access to ATMs and allow the use of ATMs for campus-wide information systems.

What does the smart card feature add? Part of the memory can be made "read only" for most purposes, meaning it could not be altered or erased. A reserved location in memory could store a value for the most recent semester in which the student paid the recreational sports fee (traditionally, the student would need to bring the card to the proper office after payment to have it updated). This solves the replacement problem for multicolor stickers that have been affixed to ID cards in the past. A second feature of the smart card could be its possible use for authentication purposes. With the intelligent chip, an extremely secure *digital signature*, next to impossible to duplicate, could be stored. The pitfalls of traditional personal identification numbers that allow the student to store bits of information known only to him or her could thus be avoided. This would increase the security value of the card and lead to more reliable verification of the bearer's identity.

Finally, the student entering an open-enrollment school could have stored on his or her chip some secure information, bearing the digital signature of another college, that shows the degree earned at that college and a nuts-and-bolts summary of the financial aid record at the other school. It would then be possible to process the registration and financial aid of the student without either an academic transcript or a financial aid transcript from the other school. While the inclusion of full transcripts may have some drawbacks (like the reluctance of a student to have the results of a bad last semester posted to the card), the ability to carry bits of information could be very useful.

Multimedia data storage as part of the computerized record of the student or prospective student has all kinds of possibilities. In addition to standard coded data and short-answer text, writing samples, letters of recommendation, essays, and pictures of architectural and engineering constructions could be viewed. Musical performances and orations, which may complete the picture of a student and allow a more informed decision process, would also be possible.

Touchtone Technology

Telemarketing fits nicely into the technology delivered by the touchtone/voice response "telephone registration" systems. Some individuals are taking advantage of the technology and converting from a data collection point of view to an outreach or problem resolution mode. Some institutions have long used the telephone to follow up on missing credentials and solicit applications. Staffing for these projects costs real dollars. Schools might consider having these touchtone boxes, driven by a batch process, use some of their paid-for-yet-idle phone lines to call and remind the student of the approaching deadline and missing application fee.

Thus, many tools support an institution's ability to provide better service and decrease the number of staff performing mundane and repetitive tasks. Admissions processing staffs may become smaller, but the individuals remaining will need to be well-educated, trained, and comfortable with the use of technological tools.

NEW TECHNOLOGY AND THE EFFECT ON SECURITY

With all this new technology, the world has changed to one with computerized records, demand for access and information, and both distributed and automated transaction processing. Institutions cannot forego these options? The good news is that the new technology allows institutions to perform more effectively, faster, and at less cost. The bad news is that much of this technology is new, and *not even the problems, much less their solutions, have been fully documented.*

The admissions officers' jobs regarding security are still to identify resources to protect, list possible hazards, develop cost-effective solutions, and continue the process. Possible damages from a security breach include:

- *Destruction.* A database file or a record could be deleted or trashed, compromising the ability to do the job (run automated systems) or to produce the required records.
- *Modification.* Records could be changed illegally and intentionally, to the advantage of some individual. They could also be altered accidentally, leading to invalid conclu-

sions or actions and to a loss of logical integrity or public confidence in the data. The cost of restoring lost data and public confidence could be quite high.

- *Revelation.* Release of administrative data could threaten the strategic position of the school. Personnel information is also sensitive. If reasonable steps are not taken to protect student records, the institution may break the law, namely, the Family Educational Rights and Privacy Act (FERPA), which prohibits unauthorized release of any part of the student file except for a few types of data which may be labeled "directory information."

Some general maxims regarding security apply to low-tech applications as well as leading edge operations:

- Security is in the eye of the beholder—we have different comfort levels.
- The cost of security must be balanced against the estimate of damage from a breach of security, weighted by the likelihood of such a breach.
- You can achieve absolute security—but to do so may prevent the satisfactory execution of a job.
- Data are more often destroyed or otherwise rendered useless, or even harmful, by people making mistakes than through dishonesty or malice.
- It is of the utmost importance when considering the potential for damage by dishonest or malicious people to keep in mind that the vast majority of all white-collar crime is committed by employees, not outsiders.
- People whose loyalty and honesty are unquestioned but whose judgment and competence leave much to be desired are our greatest enemies.
- If systems protected against accidents and against ourselves, we would have little cause for alarm regarding malicious actions.

Many of the new technological advances deal with distributing the input and output processes involved with collecting data and communicating results. In dealing with data and system access, consider these four ingredients:

1. *Identification*—How do I tell you who I am? What is my ID (student or log-on)? What is my name?
2. *Authentication*—How do I prove that I am who I say I am? This depends on a password or personal identification number, or knowledge of secret or personal information.
3. *Authorization*—Given that I am who I say I am, what am I allowed to do?
4. *Detection*—If I cannot always prevent the occurrence of "bad things," either accidental or intentional, how do I find out about them after the fact? If I suspect misdeeds, how can I determine what happened?

For some specific situations, how would an institution:

- restrict the actions persons can take once they get into the system: Can they write and execute programs or are they restricted to certain options or certain menu choices?

- determine user identity: Will we use the Social Security number (SSN) in every case? Should we consider a new ID number?

- authenticate the identity: Will an institution have one password—the most common method of authentication—for all uses or one per application? How is the password to be entered? Are there any controls against repeated (programmatic) attempts to provide the password using a systematically incremented sequence?

- safeguard the authentication information: Are passwords ever passed over insecure networks? Might a "Trojan horse" scheme be used to capture passwords? When collected on a screen, is the password displayed during its entry? Should encryption be used? Will encryption keys need security of their own?

- terminate sessions or depersonalize screens: What happens when a user leaves without sign-off? Can the new user conduct business in his or her name without additional authentication? Can passers-by see the SSN and name (identifiers) and confidential data on the screen? Can an abandoned screen reveal meaningful information to the next viewer?

- protect the new ID card as it acquires increasing functionality and value: Should the SSN be visible? Should you consider requiring authentication whenever possible? Should you look toward the digital signatures possible with smart card technology?

- trust the Internet, with all the news about Internet break-ins: Where are you most vulnerable? Have you considered the authenticity question and then thought twice about universal, multipurpose passwords and not trusting those that are accessible via the Internet?

- trust a SPEEDE/ExPRESS transcript: If the proper protocol is used, they are light years ahead of paper systems. Routine acknowledgment to the certified acknowledgment address for each transcript, followed by recipient reconciliation against a record of transcripts sent, guarantees authenticity as well as proof that the transcript has not been modified.

ADMISSIONS TECHNOLOGY AND STRATEGIC ENROLLMENT MANAGEMENT

Just about every admissions office activity is important, or else funding for them would never be approved. Many fit every definition of strategic management, including identifying prospective students, recruiting them, and tracking the contacts. Correctly and efficiently processing the various credentials in the applicant file is certainly something that every institution will find vital. The high-profile aspects of strategic admissions activity are generally driven by data. They fit into the general category of management information. These allow you to be flexible, and to respond to, marketplace variation.

Unfortunately, management information is best produced using tools far different from those that best support record (application) processing and office automation and that must generally provide the data to feed the analyses. Taking it a step further, the admissions office generally adds considerable data that are not necessary for the admission function but are needed to support the ongoing educational experience of the enrolled student. All of these costs must be met, and the office of admissions must be recognized as a vital component with important needs.

With so many data-driven activities, investment in a "data person" would be wise. This person should either "belong" to, or have priorities controlled by, admissions and should be an analyst on the enrollment management team. He or she should:

- know the processes, trends, when what changed, and why,

- know the data sources and meanings,

- know that the student records system was designed for the automation of processes rather than the management of information,

- maintain (flat) files of pertinent data in usable form (such as a biweekly tape replica of the master database file for students),

- capture (retain) comparable data and produce summary reports at benchmark points in the same format each semester (such as a headcounts on-line file updated weekly and at the end of the semester, or an archival tape of all applicants),

- use tools for analysis (including software programs such as SAS, dBASE, Lotus 1-2-3),

- possess knowledge of data systems across office boundaries (registrar, admissions, financial aid, housing, and so on), and

- finally—and this is very important—this person should have sufficient staff backup, with activities and procedures that are sufficiently well-documented, to protect data and information-generation capability against the possible loss of this position.

OTHER VIEWPOINTS

The automation and technology fields may be viewed from many different perspectives. Functional components, hardware, software, and connectivity are all important and can be briefly studied as separate pieces.

The traditional *functional model* for records-processing systems broke every system into the three steps of input, process, and output. Most systems involve all three steps, which may often be studied independently, as they affect different populations. Input includes the collection, as well as the entry, of data. It may be extended to include requests for, as well as delivery of, applications for admission, test scores, transcripts, essays, letters of recommendation, and even pictures. Process may include coding, calculation (of GPA, say), translation (of transfer courses), decisions, generation of additional communication (asking for missing documents), and answering applicant requests for status checks. Output consists of decision notification (correspondence), feedback to institutions, requests for follow-up data needs (final transcripts), feedback to students (course evaluation, applicability to degree programs), and printed reports used by staff for various purposes.

Early traditional developments dealt more with the process section. More recent developments with Internet, touchtone/voice response, imaging, ID cards, and campus-wide information systems have concentrated on the input and output areas. EDI is nearly unique in the way it revolutionizes all three areas.

Hardware, once the primary hurdle to automation, is still important and increasingly complex. The old assumption that an IBM mainframe was the only possible solution is no longer valid. The raw processing power and affordability of various brands of personal computers provide attractive alternatives for data storage and manipulation. The advance of local area networks (LANs) has allowed many such machines to be linked within an office or a building.

For many user applications, the problem stops at this point. For others, though, the need for access from remote locations or separate systems makes these new advances far more difficult to use. If integrated corporate data are needed on a frequent basis or hundreds of simultaneous users are anticipated, the mainframe remains very attractive. Data management needs are present in cither case. If a diverse, decentralized, or distributed processing environment is used, physical connectivity and the ability to support various forms of logical connectivity become paramount concerns. Good functionality for the support of client-server and other access methods, along with the physical hardware, will provide the necessary infrastructure for corporate or institutional data delivery.

Software may well have replaced hardware as the most expensive single item. The key issues in making decisions for the purchase of software systems are the degree of interactivity and whether to purchase vendor-supplied systems or develop them in-house. The smaller in scope the system, the fewer users it has to satisfy, causing the development cost to go down accordingly. An umbrella system that must simultaneously meet the needs of accounting, alumni relations, personnel, financial aid, and admissions and registration will be much more difficult to generalize and will run into more problems with institutional differences. The integration and access needs must be addressed in any case. The reality is that vendor software can generally be installed and run much more quickly than an institution could develop it, and the former is likely to have more secondary functions and more polish than a home-grown system. From that point on, however, maintenance needs and the desire for an institution to use innovative approaches to recruitment, enrollment management, and classroom teaching, start to tip the scale in favor of the in-house system. It can never be assumed that a purchased system will meet all needs or eliminate the need for substantial programming support. If possible, systems and annual maintenance upgrades should be purchased for those pieces that are most complicated and likely to change due to external reasons. Then, a way to plug these modules into interfaces with "in-house" systems should be found. One rule of thumb indicates that if a project requires one unit of development time the first year, it will require one-half unit for maintenance the second, one-third of a unit the third year, and then start increasing again as underlying needs and rules diverge from those upon which the software was defined.

Location of the systems support resources is another important issue. Maintaining and upgrading the institutional data infrastructure and handling institutional priorities are always critical, but user offices are often lost in the shuffle, and an admissions office may wait for years for the central data-processing support team to reach its priority items. If at all possible, the admissions office should try to gain control of the priorities of one or more systems persons. This may well require the payment of salary and benefits, but it can be well worth the cost. As systems become more automated, some clerical positions might be switched into programming positions. Work with the central data-processing team might help ensure that plans become reality.

Connectivity remains an extremely critical issue. In the past, it has been approached from within the school. Is admissions connected to registration and financial aid? Is student accounting connected to registration and the library? The answers depended on the type of mainframe architecture in place. This internal focus is still important, with terminal emulation, the ability to upload and download, and the ability to access remote data via client-server calls providing the answers.

Connections outside the college are increasingly important. Not only whether a school is on the Internet, but how it connects (from mainframe or PC) and which protocol is supported (SMTP or FTP) become critical questions. Can staff participate easily in E-mail, EDI, Gopher, and Mosaic? They certainly need to, and systems must be able to support these activities without overlooking security requirements.

CAVEATS TO NOTE

In the face of this imperative for change, a few caveats stand out, and they deserve special attention.

1. The structure of hardware and software systems may take any of dozens of different forms. Regardless of the form, the proper systems need to be accessible, and able to talk to each other (student records to student accounting to library to financial aid to institutional reporting, etc.). Ample programming resources and support for the infrastructure that must carry the data and the inquiries must be provided.

2. Management information capabilities as well as traditional processes and their automation must be covered. They have different needs, and they may well be served best by different structures that are physically disjointed, although logically connected at specified points in time. Both needs must be met.

3. The need for privacy and security in a more open environment must be remembered. New technology takes information out of the locked office and allows access from every corner of the planet. Data must be protected to keep automated systems oper-

ational, permanent records inviolate, and academic records private. New awareness and methods will be required to provide this protection.

4. On security and management information, the cost of an action must be weighed against the risk it is intended to eliminate. Obtaining absolute security and advance answers to every conceivable question are unlikely. Instead, reasonable steps to guard against likely problems and to answer the most likely questions must be taken. Data structures and systems must be developed to allow the detection of breaches, repair of problems, and research of additional questions. These solutions will require physical (hardware and files), logical (software tools), and human (trained staff) solutions.

THE ONCOMING TRAINS

Needs are generally evaluated on the basis of what has happened in the past and the information that is already available. In planning automated admissions support systems, the assumption has been that universities will continue to be organized in the same manner as they have been in the past and they will continue to deliver the exact same product. However, we might be wrong.

Consider the way software system implementation has been approached in the past. Each school studied its needs and made a decision to purchase a software package, develop one in-house, or do some combination of the two. Consider also the way state budgets are often cut deeply year after year and the decreasing amounts that are left for higher education. "People costs" being what they are, legislators balk at providing system development funds for similar functions at multiple schools. With institutional differences and faculty prerogatives, no two institutions are exactly alike and no faculty committee appreciates letting policy be driven by software. However, the forces of legislative budgets and institutional uniqueness continue to clash. Knowing which traits are sacred and which might truly be manageable using common software systems or common modules; looking at centralized processing, connected but distributed processing, and shared software investments; and studying the overhead involved in development, ongoing maintenance, and preservation of the ability to react quickly to strategic needs will be critical.

Before quickly applying existing technology to the administration of colleges and universities as they exist now, thought needs to be given to how these same technological tools will change the very institutions themselves. The largest share of college personnel budgets goes to the faculty. The ability to deliver real-time multimedia presentations to remote locations should lead to increased use of the best faculty, with total numbers greatly decreased. Internet mail and conferencing facilities should keep these classes from being simply large lecture sessions, as interaction with faculty and other students will be stressed. What effect will that have on admissions processes? Will institutions admit more students, but to just a few "logical universities" that teach the student electronically and remotely? With imaging technology and the payment of a few modest royalties, institutions can shift from purchasing 100 copies of one book for placement in 100 locations to the purchase of 100 books, to be placed in one location for unlimited simultaneous access. Will this change universities? Will it change admissions?

CONCLUSION

Without question, change is terribly disruptive, but the necessity of change is of equal certainty. To move ahead and to take advantage of those tools that support strategic initiative, an investment must be made in both change and technology. The right people in place with the proper training and support in their task of managing change must be assured. These key staff and their tools will allow institutions to keep what they need to keep from old records, systems, and functionality, while discarding or revamping those parts that must be altered to take advantage of new technology.

REFERENCES

American Association of Collegiate Registrars and Admissions Officers. 1994. *A Guide to Implementation of the SPEEDE/ExPRESS Transcript.* Implementation guide. Version 2 draft, April. Washington, DC: AACRAO.

Drucker, Peter F. 1966. *The effective executive.* New York: Harper and Row.

Gwinn, Donald G., and Louise Lonabocker. 1996. *Breakthrough systems: Student access and registration.* Washington, DC: AACRAO.

Palmer, Barbara H., and P. Betty Wei. 1993. SPEEDE made easy. *College and University* 29 (Fall): 4–13.

Perkins, Helen L. 1996. *Electronic imaging in admissions, records, and financial aid offices.* Washington, DC: AACRAO.

Stones, David H. 1994. On the strategic nature of SPEEDE/ExPRESS, scalability, and applicability of EDI in the workplace. *SACRAO Journal* 8.

13

Policies and Procedures

M. Overton Phelps, D. Parker Young, and Timothy D. Letzring

POLICIES

Admissions professionals regularly address and monitor admission and evaluation policies. Each institution must develop a philosophy of admissions and annually establish admissions goals and standards. A faculty admissions committee (FAC), representing as many units of the institution as possible, ensures that all areas contribute to admissions standards and decisions. The FAC should query the top administration—the president and vice president (either academic or student services) to whom the dean or director of admissions reports—on the ideal number and quality of new students desired. At the lower division level, these numbers may represent an institution-wide uniform standard. At the upper division and at the graduate and professional levels, the various majors or units may establish the desired number and quality of students. The decision makers should schedule quarterly meetings. Annually, the president should attend and give the charge (i.e., the goal for the upcoming years).

Directives from chief administrators that tell the FAC to increase the number and quality of students as much as possible put admissions officers in an untenable position and usually result in rapid turnover in the admissions leadership. A reasonable administration determines the desired number and quality of students at each level and instructs the FAC to work with the admissions office to set standards that will produce the desired number and quality of students. Facilities, personnel, and the budget of the institution are considered when these decisions are made. The desired number of each major or unit is a joint decision made by the faculty of the unit and the chief academic administrator. Having this kind of periodic exchange and input from representative faculty ensures support, interest, collaboration—and even pride—in admissions goals and achievements.

PROCEDURES

The director of admissions and the admissions staff develop a calendar to implement the procedures throughout the enrollment period. Recruitment efforts begin some 24 months before the date of enrollment of the student. For beginning freshmen, this date will coincide with the middle of the junior year of high school. When admissions processing personnel begin receiving completed applications for admission on a specified date, the standards established by the FAC are applied.

Some institutions are basically open-door and admit all students who apply. Some institutions are semiselective and have certain minimum admissions standards a student must meet to be admitted. In these institutions, the applicants arrange themselves in three categories—clearly admissible, borderline, or clearly not admissible. Only a few institutions are highly selective, and most of their applicants are clearly qualified to do acceptable academic work, so a variety of factors predetermined by the administration, the FAC, and the admissions staff are considered in determining admissibility. Factors will generally include the usual criteria of high school grade point average and standardized test results, with additional consideration given to the high school program of studies emphasizing Advanced Placement courses; interview results; high school recommendations; student essays; ethnic distribution; geographic distribution; alumni connection; athletic, artistic, or musical ability; and any other factors deemed important to the particular institution.

Processing of applications is relatively simple in open-door institutions. All applicants who apply and meet basic minimum standards such as high school graduation are sent admissions letters—usually soon after the application is received. Semiselective institutions have a somewhat more complicated system of processing. Generally, applications must be received by a prescribed date. These applications may be reviewed as they are received and clearly acceptable candidates may be sent admissions letters on a rolling basis as soon as the application file is complete. Applicants whose credentials clearly do not meet predetermined standards may be denied admission as soon as the application is complete so that these applicants can make alternate plans for additional education. Borderline applicants may be held for a predetermined date, and the best of these applicants will be admitted as long as space is available. Often these applicants are given a date by which to send additional grades and test scores to increase their chance for admission.

Applicants to highly selective institutions may apply for early decision acceptance and, if fully qualified, may receive an acceptance letter by a predetermined date—usually in the late fall of the student's senior year. These applicants must agree to apply to no other institution. The bulk of applicants for these highly selective institutions will need to complete their applications by a certain date—usually in mid-winter of their junior year. The admissions staff or committee reviewing these files will carefully consider all factors. Notification letters for this group will be sent by April 1 each year. The admitted students will be asked to notify the institution by May 1, if they are planning to enroll. Some of the students not admitted on the April 1 date may be placed on a waiting list, to be considered later if space becomes available.

Transfer applications are usually processed in somewhat the same manner as freshman applications. Standards for transfer admissions are established by the FAC, and applications are processed by the undergraduate admissions staff. Some admissions offices have the responsibility for the evaluation of transfer credit, which, in a school with a large transfer population, becomes a major part of the processing procedure. Graduate applications are usually processed by a graduate admissions staff, and graduate admissions decisions are made by the various coordinators of the graduate programs. Admissions applications to professional schools may be processed by the undergraduate or graduate admissions staffs or by the professional school staff. However, decisions concerning admissions are made by personnel in the professional school.

Admissions committees should develop procedures to process applicants with unusual types of situations. These applicants may include nontraditional students; international students; students with physical handicaps; applicants who are, or who have been, incarcerated; applicants with a history of mental illness; visiting students; students applying for joint enrollment or early admission; students who are not in good standing at another institution; and students who are applying for readmission. The processing of applications has been facilitated by the use of data processing and computers. Additional progress will be noted with the increase in the electronic transmission of data between high schools and colleges and between colleges.

LEGAL ISSUES

Over the past few decades, the entanglement between legal issues and higher education has increased dramatically. The courts, the legislatures, and the regulating agencies have steadily encroached on the activities of higher education institutions, including the area of admissions. State and federal legislatures constantly draft laws affecting admissions policies, and agencies adapt rules and regulations to enforce these laws. While colleges and universities continue to enjoy some autonomy from judicial interference, the courts have set precedents important to admissions. The Family Educational Rights and Privacy Act (FERPA) of 1974 and its subsequent amendments; the *Hopwood v. Bakke* addressing affirmative action decisions which, while they affect only three states, have major policy implications for institutions; recent Americans with Disabilities Act (ADA) regulations; and the student right-to-know and the higher education reauthorization issues considered in 1997 are among the laws directly impacting institutions. With the onset of the information superhighway, the educational opportunities now available as distance education puts learning at every student's doorstep. With education providers springing up in every corner of the globe, higher service expectations by the public at large created by technological advances, and easier access to records of all kinds, educators must grapple with an array of changing and challenging issues. Every admissions officer, therefore, must understand what is permissible and legal to better avoid the risk of litigation.

Public-Private Distinction

The question of permissible admissions practices depends first upon the classification of the institution involved. Admissions policies in public colleges or universities are grounded in two legal theories. The first is a constitutional concept based upon the application of the Bill of Rights to the states through the 14th Amendment. Under this theory, public institutions have a constitutional duty to provide consistent and rational admissions criteria. The second theory is contractual; it requires the institution to abide by its part of the contract and places certain requirements on the prospective student. In the area of admissions, the college catalogue or bulletin is an invitation to apply. The application and fee from the student are an offer, and the college's taking of the fee is an acceptance that forms a contract between the applicant and institution.

For the private institution, the relationship between the college and the applicant is purely contractual and is created in the same manner. Therefore, private colleges and universities are only required to abide by the terms of the contract. The one exception to this rule arises if the college or university is engaged in state action. State action occurs when a private institution is so entangled with a government entity that the institution is acting on behalf of the government. This is rare and usually occurs when the government is somehow involved in the governance of the private institution.

Because of the application of the contractual theory to both public and private institutions, neither type of institution can discriminate against a person in the admissions process. The civil rights laws provide that everyone has a right to freely enter into a contract.

Admissions Criteria

Generally, colleges and universities can decide the criteria upon which admissions decisions are based, provided the criteria are legally permissible. These criteria can include objective criteria such as grades and test scores, and more subjective criteria such as an interview process, extracurricular activities, and demonstrated leadership potential (see Chapter 6).

Once an institution has determined its criteria, the college or university must make these criteria known to potential applicants. Legal constraints also require that the institution apply its published criteria to every applicant equally. One apparent exception to the general rule requiring equal application of the admissions criteria revolves around the application of affirmative action programs. In an effort to increase admittance of underrepresented groups, institutions have initiated programs that take the race or sex of the applicant into consideration. Setting fixed quotas for a particular group is unconstitutional. However, the law does allow a college to use criteria that measure an individual's potential for academic success against his or her achievements and past social, cultural, or economic disadvantages. The critical factor in administering an affirmative action program is that an institution cannot use race, national origin, or sex as the deciding factor in the admissions decision. Also, the admissions process cannot involve dual systems that apply different standards to different classifications of applicants. The law allows such classifications to be one of many factors, but an institution cannot use them as a decisive criterion. Every applicant must be judged by the same criteria (see Chapter 15). Colleges and universities must continually reassess their admissions criteria against new and changing regulations.

It is also permissible to provide an alternative program for applicants who do not meet the regular academic standards. These special admissions programs allow applicants with educationally disadvantaged backgrounds an opportunity to demonstrate their academic potential. These special programs usually involve probationary periods, remedial requirements, and proof of academic progress before the student moves on to the mainstream academic programs. Again, the law requires that the institution apply the policies concerning the admission to such programs equally, following the published criteria.

Due Process and Denial of Admission

A due process claim can only arise from an incident in which a public or private institution is involved in state action. As long as the college or university follows its published admissions criteria, there is no violation of due process when an applicant is denied admission. Thus, the rejected applicant does not have the right to a hearing regarding the rejection and denial of admission issues. Of course, if the published admissions standards were not followed uniformly, a due process claim could be made. This would primarily occur when a public college or university is accused of practicing illegal discrimination.

Discrimination

Colleges and universities discriminate every day in the admissions process. The issue is whether such discrimination is legal. Institutions of higher learning classify and discriminate against applicants based on grades, test scores, interview scores, letters of recommendation, athletic ability, and many other permissible grounds. Private institutions can even go further and classify applicants on the basis of their parents' alumni status, religious classifications for church-related institutions, and sex for single-sex institutions. Even state institutions can require higher standards for applicants from out of state. The problems arise when groupings and discrimination are made on the basis of suspect or quasi-suspect classifications defined by the United States Supreme Court.

These suspect and quasi-suspect classifications generally include such criteria as race, color, national origin, ethnicity, and sex. No institution, public or private, can deny admission to an applicant based on one of these criteria if the institution receives federal money, directly or indirectly. For example, if an institution has students receiving any federal financial assistance, all of the institution's programs (degree or nondegree, credit or noncredit) are covered by the federal antidiscrimination laws. A primary exception to this requirement is the private single-sex institution. Men and women's private colleges may discriminate against applicants based on sex without violating laws. Recent court decisions, however, have ended the ability of institutions receiving federal funds to limit admission (e.g., to male students in the case of the Citadel Military College of South Carolina and the Virginia Military Institute; and in three states affected by the *Hopwood v. University of Texas* decision of the 5th U.S. Circuit Court of Appeals to use race as a selection procedure). Other instances exist where a college or university has successfully justified denial of admission to an applicant. A prime example involves a medical school that denied admission to an applicant because of old age.

Another example involves discrimination against a person with a disability. While federal laws make it unlawful for institutions of higher learning to discriminate against individuals with disabilities, these directives only apply to "otherwise qualified" disabled persons. This allows a college or university to make sure the applicant will meet the academic and physical standards necessary to achieve success in spite of that person's disability. For example, a nursing school may reject a deaf applicant because wearing a mask in the operating room renders reading lips impossible, thus posing an unreasonable danger to patients and others.

Revocation of Acceptance and Readmission

Once a public institution accepts an applicant for admission, the student has acquired a property interest that cannot be taken away unless the institution provides due process, which is a constitutional requirement. In this context the college or university must provide the student, whose admission is to be revoked, with notice of the revocation outlining the reason or reasons why, and give the student an opportunity to rebut the given reason. In addition, the institution's reason for revocation cannot be arbitrary, capricious, or without a rational basis.

For the private school that wishes to revoke an acceptance, the issue falls under pure contract theory. If the acceptance is revoked, the student can claim the college breached the contract that the initial acceptance formed. However, many instances exist under which a private college can revoke an acceptance under contract principles. If a student misrepresented his qualifications on the application and these misrepresentations were not discovered until after acceptance; if the student did not meet a condition of the acceptance or did not abide by the terms of the contract formed (e.g., final grade requirements or meeting fee deadlines), the school could claim the contract was induced under fraud. Such reasons justifying the revocation of an acceptance also apply to the public institution that deals in both constitutional and contractual principles.

Liability

The area of admissions can also create problems of liability. One involves bringing high school students to campus, individually or in large numbers, for high school weekends. For large planned activities such as dances, parties, picnics, and the like, admissions officials must make sure adequate supervision is provided to minimize any risk. Instances that might lead to litigation range from slip-and-fall injuries to injuries resulting from the consumption of alcohol. The university must constantly monitor the activities of its minor guests for both the institution's as well as the students' protection.

The use of alumni as recruiters can also create liability problems for colleges and universities. Because they are not paid recruiters and, therefore, are not properly trained nor completely familiar with the school's admissions policies, the promises they make can cause an applicant to rely on false information. In some instances, an applicant could sue under an agency theory which, if successful, would require the university to abide by the terms the alumni offered. Even if the university successfully defended such a suit, litigation itself is a cost that should be avoided, if possible, by taking proper precautions when allowing alumni to recruit.

SUMMARY

Since the area of admissions is not insulated from legal issues, it behooves those involved in admissions to keep abreast of current legal parameters within which decisions should be made and actions taken. When in doubt, the admissions officer should seek competent legal advice. Following risk management principles and practicing preventive law will help admissions officers avoid potential legal pitfalls.

Part V

Admissions Programs

Part V details institutional programs that accomplish enrollment management goals.

14

Targeting Diversity

Diana Guerrero

Diversity, access, equity, multiculturalism, pluralism—these complex issues confront communities daily and are continually addressed on campuses across the nation. Changes in demographics, personal and social values, family structures, the workforce, technology, and the world economy are prompting institutions to reevaluate themselves and the populations they have traditionally served. Institutions must reflect these demographic, economic, technological, and social changes if they are to be relevant and competitive in the twenty-first century.

The Report of the Commission on Minority Participation in Education and American Life (American Council on Education 1988) predicts that by the year 2000, one-third of all Americans will be members of minority groups. One out of eight persons in the United States now speaks a language other than English in the home (Roberts 1994), and yet ethnic minorities are underrepresented at every educational level. On many campuses the "traditional" student is now an older, minority female who commutes part-time.

UNDERSTANDING INSTITUTIONAL CHANGE

Institutions that have begun to deal effectively with these realities recognize that a proactive institutional commitment to diversity and equity and an understanding and appreciation of the cultural differences new populations bring with them are required to change the complexion of a campus. Recruiting techniques and admissions policies must be modified, and role models, mentors, and minority alumni must be actively involved. Creative financial aid packaging must be available, precollegiate programs and academic and student support services must be implemented, curricular offerings must be modified, and effective assessment and retention programs must be in place.

Securing institutional support and committing resources to diversify a campus are formidable tasks if the institution is resistant to change. There are traditions, governing boards, faculty, administrators, alumni, students, and communities to consider. What will their reactions be, and what effect will the inclusion of unfamiliar elements have on institutions as they are known? But the admissions officer must challenge institutional policy makers. Where does the institution see itself in the next century? Whom should it be serving? How will its graduates fare in a changing, competitive global marketplace? What is the institution's responsibility to the public good? Access does not mean lower standards or open admissions; it does not guarantee degrees. Access does mean giving motivated, committed individuals the opportunity to succeed and requires the support these students need to achieve their full academic potential.

In the mid-1960s, B. Alden Thresher, director of admissions emeritus at Massachusetts Institute of Technology, presented a threefold thesis in his *College Admissions and the Public Interest*:

First, one cannot tell by looking at a toad how far he will jump; second, the process of admission to college is more sociologically than intellectually determined; and third, to understand the process one must look beyond the purview of the individual college and consider the interaction of all institutions with the society that generates and sustains them. (Thresher 1966)

These thoughts are still relevant as institutions face the challenges of a new century. How can an institution develop the talents of all students? What can these students bring to the institution to enhance its mission and to contribute to the educational and social experiences of its student body? Developing a clear picture of how a more diverse institution can serve both its own and the public's interest helps pave the way for change.

Institutions that have successfully begun to diversify and to offer access to underrepresented populations have first assessed their mission, strengths, weaknesses, and attitudes toward groups that are different from those who normally populate their campuses. Diversifying a campus affects the institution at almost every level, with campus climate being a primary contributor to an institution's success or failure in retaining students. Schools whose recruitment plans focus only on numbers will face serious problems if support services, cultural awareness, and instructional issues that can contribute to a student's sense of inclusion are not addressed. Students who have been actively recruited may ultimately leave because of a sense of alienation, even if they are doing well academically.

A genuine institutional commitment to eliminate the barriers to minority and nontraditional student participation in higher education must exist. This commitment must extend from the institution's highest to its lowest levels. The president, faculty, administrators, and staff must, continually and publicly, tele-

Table 14.1
Persons 18 to 24 Years Old by High School Graduate Status, College Enrollment, Race, and Hispanic Origin, 1993, 1983, and 1973 (Numbers in thousands)

	All Persons			
		High School Graduates		
Race and Year	All Persons	Percent	Percent Enrolled in College	Percent Dropouts
All Races				
1993...............	24,100	82.0	41.4	12.7
1983...............	28,580	80.4	32.5	15.4
1973...............	25,237	80.7	29.7	15.7
White				
1993...............	19,430	83.4	41.8	12.2
1983...............	23.899	82.2	32.9	14.3
1973...............	21,766	82.8	30.2	14.2
Black				
1993...............	3,516	74.8	32.8	16.4
1983...............	3,865	70.9	27.0	21.5
1973...............	3,114	66.8	24.0	26.5
Hispanic Origin[1]				
1993...............	2,772	60.7	35.8	32.7
1983...............	2,025	54.8	31.4	37.5
1973...............	1,285	55.2	29.1	38.9

[1] May be of any race.
Source: U.S. Bureau of the Census (1994), xvi.

graph a message of inclusion. An institution must want these students, believe in educational equity, and understand that diversity brings with it new cultures and ideas, different needs, and opportunities for mutual growth. The challenge is how best to integrate these new elements into everyday campus life.

In addition to institutional commitment, there must be a dedication of resources to more flexible learning systems and to support services for these new student populations. Resources must also be allocated to help faculty and staff to develop sensitivity to the cultural, academic, and socioeconomic issues affecting underrepresented groups.

If a school decides to target students of color, admissions and recruitment staff should be familiar with population demographics and high school completion and college enrollment rates. The minority high school graduation and the college enrollment rates shown in Table 14.1 illustrate the disparity in minority advancement that still exists, in spite of the gains that began in the late 1960s as a result of the civil rights movement and legislation increasing the availability of financial aid and veterans' benefits.

While Hispanics are numerically the fastest-growing minority group in the

United States, their high school completion and college enrollment rates are among the lowest. African-Americans have made the greatest gains, but they have not closed the gap between their rates and those of the white population. Census information on American Indian and Asian-American educational participation rates are not collected on an annual basis, but American Indian graduation and college enrollment rates are extremely low. Levels of educational attainment of Asian-Americans exceeds that of all Americans (O'Hare 1990), but these students still have needs that must be addressed. As minority advancement in higher education continues to lag behind that of the white majority, colleges must increase their efforts to narrow the gap that marks disadvantaged racial and ethnic populations.

Population geographic and enrollment trends should also be studied. Harold Hodgkinson notes that by the year 2010, one-third of the nation's youth will live in Texas, California, Florida, and New York, and more than half of them will be minority (Hodgkinson 1992). By 2010 it is projected that the nonwhite youth populations in the following 12 geographic areas will range from 92 to 40 percent: Washington, DC; Hawaii; Texas; California; Florida; New York; Louisiana; Mississippi; New Jersey; Maryland; Illinois; and South Carolina (Hodgkinson 1992). The 1991 status report on minorities in higher education indicates that California and Texas high schools graduate more than half of all Hispanic youth, south and south central states have the largest number of African-American graduates, and more than half of all Asian-American graduates live in the West (Carter and Wilson 1992). Additionally, 82 percent of students of color attended public institutions of higher education in 1993, compared with 62.7 percent of white students (Carter and Wilson 1995). Familiarity with such trends helps target minority recruiting areas as yearly travel schedules are prepared.

UNDERSTANDING THE CULTURAL DIFFERENCES OF STUDENTS

Institutions must develop an awareness and appreciation of the different cultural characteristics of minority populations. The Crayola crayon company quit calling one color "flesh" because no one could agree on what color flesh is (Roberts 1994). By the same token, there is no such thing as a typical minority. Each ethnic or racial group is comprised of subgroups, whose internal differences may go unnoticed to outsiders. While some segments of our minority populations are well educated and financially successful, many segments are not. Hodgkinson suggests that "with the establishment of sizeable populations of middle class blacks, Hispanics, and Asians, many racial problems are actually issues of race *and* class. The single factor that holds the most children back is poverty, regardless of race" (Hodgkinson 1992).

When working with minority populations, it is important to use the accepted name for each group: African-American, black; American Indian, Native American; Asian-American, Asian/Pacific Islander; Hispanic, Chicano, Latino, Mexican-American; people of color. Consensus is difficult, and may be impossible, even within groups. Schools that recruit in different geographic regions should seek guidance from colleagues familiar with those areas. Membership in national, regional, and state professional organizations; participation in relevant workshops and conferences; and familiarity with professional literature provide a wealth of information. And enrollment services professionals throughout the country are always willing to share their expertise with others who need information or are trying to develop new programs.

Choosing to go to college is a very difficult decision for many students of color. Many have recently arrived as immigrants or refugees and, as first generation college students, share similar problems with other first generation students. Many are under great pressure not to lose their cultural identities. Hispanics may often be urged not to leave home. African-Americans may feel guilty if they do not attend a predominantly black institution. American Indians may be faced with an educational environment very different from anything they have ever experienced. Asian-Americans (possibly the most diverse of America's major minority groups, with more than two dozen different subgroups that do not share a common language, religion, or cultural background) may feel a tremendous pressure to succeed. These latter students are often unfairly viewed as the model minority, are often considered overrepresented, and are not actively recruited by many institutions (Suzuki 1989). The different value systems these students have shape the attitudes, perceptions, and expectations they bring with them to a campus—and these values may conflict with the institutional values they encounter and act as barriers to their success.

Individuals who are bilingual and bicultural are multitalented, but these skills are often viewed negatively by the majority population. Stereotypical images of these students need to be dispelled, differences need to be appreciated, and different value systems need to be recognized and understood. When these first-generation, ethnic minority college students do not act or respond as expected, college personnel should look beyond their personal experiences to see if any of the following factors may be influencing behavior or performance. Issues or barriers can be handled more effectively once they are understood.

Importance of the Family

For many students of color, the family—immediate and extended—is the one constant in their lives. It is the one place where they have a definite role, know what is expected of them, have an ever-present support system, and always "belong." Compared to the family, institutions are usually cold, imposing, impersonal, and intimidating and can cause individuals to lose the confidence they might demonstrate in more familiar situations. Humanizing the institution is vital when dealing with individuals who value belonging and relevance. Processes need to be simple, with as few barriers as possible. Applicants may be distrustful of bureaucracies and may not know enough to ask the right questions. Therefore, it is important that applicants' first contacts be with warm, helpful individuals, because they might not pursue admission if their sense of alienation is overwhelming. The bonding agent may be a faculty member, admissions clerk, custodian, advisor, food services worker, or another student, but the key is a caring, responsive person who can confirm that the student has made the right college choice.

Many students have a deep sense of personal pride and a fear of failure, because failure may be seen not just as a personal shortcoming, but as a failure to meet the expectations of family and any supporters met along the way. In addition, many students are often reluctant to burden the family with their problems and have the added responsibility of knowing that their success or failure may influence their siblings.

If students are made to choose between family and school, they may put family first because self-worth is tied to the decisions they make. A female student may miss class to take care of a sick brother or sister because there may be no money for day care, it is unthinkable for the father (if present) to miss work, and if the mother misses work she may have no vacation or sick leave and the wages lost may be the week's grocery money. This means not that school is unimportant, but rather that overriding family pressures take precedence within her value system.

Parental Support

Most parents want their children's lives to be better than theirs. Some work at several jobs to keep their children in school. Many minority parents who have had no college experience are supportive of higher education, even when they do not quite understand what it means. A regret parents often express is that they want to help but do not know how. Others may be supportive until college conflicts with economic realities, whereupon they may pressure their children to drop out to help support the family. Other parents may not support the idea of women in higher education, particularly when attending college means leaving home.

Importance of Financial Aid

Economic factors are often seen as insurmountable barriers to higher education. Many parents and students are working to provide basic essentials for the family rather than to support a preferred lifestyle. These factors may cause promising students to postpone or abandon plans to attend college, or it may cause them to settle for a school that is not their first choice. Institutions must creatively package financial aid, using grants, scholarships, and work-study first.

Minority scholarship programs are also essential. Loans should be used as a last resort because of the hardship that future indebtedness creates.

In 1994 the Texas Guaranteed Student Loan Corporation conducted focus groups with parents and students, whom they found wanted early access to simple, understandable financial aid information so they could plan more effectively and enable students to see higher education as a reasonable, attainable goal. They identified the transition between middle and high school as an appropriate time to begin learning what the application process involves, what the financial obligation will be, and what savings or outside resources must be tapped to meet those costs. They also indicated that bilingual information would be especially helpful to parents who do not understand English (Alexander 1996). Until financial aid is seen as a possibility, application to college may not become a reality for many minority students.

Work-study and on-campus employment are extremely effective retention tools and should be used whenever possible. Opportunities to work closely with staff, faculty, and peers help students develop social and professional skills, allow them to see how systems work from within, put them in helping positions, and build confidence in their own abilities. These work opportunities also demystify the institution, make it relevant to their lives, and prepare them for the professional workplace.

Response to Authority

Many students of color are taught to respect authority, whether it be a parent, an elder, or a titled individual. Students may be apprehensive about approaching institutions, or they may be afraid to challenge a policy or procedure out of respect for the authority represented. However, there is a fine line between respect for authority and students getting what is rightfully theirs. Students may not know what is expected of them or how to use the system to their advantage because they have no history of academia in the home. They may not understand the values of the system they are buying into or their rights or options within that system.

Minority students may be reluctant to approach faculty, even if they need help. Some may think they should be able to take care of their own problems and should not bother professors. (After all, professors have more important things to do; why would they know one student from another in the class?) Students may have an unrealistic assessment of their own progress, may wait too long to ask for help, and may be embarrassed if they are in academic difficulty, even though their grades are salvageable. These students may leave or wander in and out of the system because they do not understand their options or do not know how to approach those individuals who can help them. Faculty members who work closely with their students, who are skilled at identifying students in academic difficulty, and who are willing to reach out and engage those students to get them back into the classroom are an institution's greatest asset in retaining students who might otherwise be lost.

Competition

Many students of color come from environments where cooperation, rather than competition, is stressed and sharing whatever one has is a way of life. Women in particular are often taught to care for others first and themselves last. While these values may make students appear passive, unmotivated, lacking in self-esteem, or unable to handle the rigors of college life, these same students may be very competitive among their peers and within the systems they understand. Stereotyping students' academic abilities based on superficial observations must be avoided, and studies indicate that "there is almost zero evidence that failure to learn is tied to low self-esteem or that massaging the psyche can improve learning. In fact, one common finding in the literature is that high self-esteem is often linked to low performance" (Leo 1996).

Some students may say that being number one is not particularly important; nor are money or public recognition. But having people whom students care about know they did their best is important, just as not disappointing the family is important. Victories and accomplishments may be measured in more personal or universal terms—doing something one believes in, having a purpose, or making a difference in human terms. When faced with an important decision, the question asked might be, "At what cost?" If an option goes against a deeper personal value, the student may choose not to act, which may be difficult for others to understand.

Some individuals may not feel a need to draw attention to or promote themselves, and self-promotion may not be highly regarded. Even after they have completed their degrees, students may have difficulty preparing resumes that extol their talents or understanding that some self-promotion is beneficial and expected. Well-qualified students may not apply for fellowships, grants, or internships because they do not relate to the lofty language in advertisements. Yet these students are often much more accomplished than they realize. Career services and leadership development programs can help polish their skills.

Goal Setting

Most students know that education is the fastest way to change their lives and rise above the struggles and sacrifices their parents may have had to endure. Yet these college seniors may not think about graduate or professional schools. Considering the quantum leap they will make from their parents' socioeconomic status to their potential earning power, they may well ask, "What will a master's degree get me that a bachelor's degree can't?" These students are very marketable in today's economy and they must be aggressively recruited into post-baccalaureate programs with attractive fellowships, scholarships, internships, and teaching/research assistantships, or they will be lost to the workforce.

UNDERSTANDING RECRUITMENT METHODS

Traditional recruiting, admissions, and retention methods are not successful with most minority populations. For this reason, supplemental recruitment programs should be used to reinforce contacts made thorough regular channels and to create new ones.

- Avenues through which minority students and parents can be reached—such as high school and church groups, minority political interest groups, community development agencies, tribal councils, minority professional organizations, minority chambers of commerce, community centers, sports organizations, or minority alumni chapters— should be tapped. As these groups are approached, recruiters should be aware of protocol and group politics, and they should use available resources to identify leaders within the organizations to provide introductions.

- Networking and forming partnerships with selected groups can make a difference. A president, for example, could host periodic receptions, breakfasts, or luncheons for selected community leaders; outline how diversity fits into the institutional mission; and invite these leaders to serve in an advisory capacity to the college or university. An activity such as this addresses the institution's commitment to minority education and helps establish the lines of communication needed to work effectively within the community. Even if a school recruits outside its geographic area, the insights these local leaders provide can be invaluable. These groups must ultimately see progress in the institution's efforts to make its campus more accessible to students of color or the administration's rhetoric will ring hollow.

- The English language may be intimidating for minority parents. They may be afraid to ask questions because they do not understand and do not want to embarrass their child. Jargon-free information programs developed to explain admissions, the college experience, the time commitment their children will have to make, and the importance of a college degree will ease their minds. Presenting admission and financial aid forums in a nonthreatening environment, conducting programs in the language with which parents are most comfortable, and helping fill out financial aid forms can be instrumental in initiating the admissions and financial aid processes.

- When speaking with parents, recruiters should recognize that the content of a conversation may be less important than the rapport, feeling of trust, and comfort level that need to be established before business is discussed. It may be easier to let parents set the tone, beginning with small talk about family, the weather, personal backgrounds, or sporting events. Honesty, sincerity, and respect are highly valued. Hospitality is also important, and if an offer must be declined, it should be refused graciously.

- Role models are extremely effective in getting students to identify with an institution. Using minority students in presentations and having people of color as members of the faculty and staff demonstrate an institution's commitment to diversity and help create a relevant environment for the student.

- Programs that involve parents and students, such as a mother-daughter program, can encourage grade school students to pursue higher education and can also result in parents enrolling and earning degrees.

- High school and middle school teachers can be used as resources to identify students with academic potential but who might not actively be recruited because of lower grade point averages or test scores.

- Minority alumni can augment a recruitment program by handling programs in cities where institutions may not be able to send full-time staff. They need to be well trained, but their enthusiasm for their alma mater and their professional successes will be invaluable.

- Phone calls or personal contact from other students, faculty, and staff are more effective than mailings when working with minorities. Having a bilingual staff is essential in frontline offices if large minority populations are served. Information brochures, handouts, videotapes, diskettes, and radio and television announcements targeting specific ethnic groups are also helpful.

- Special care should be taken with targeted mailings. Middle and upper class minorities may be offended or feel patronized if they are selected to receive non-English publications based solely on their last names. For these mailings to be more effective, the recruitment database should include information about the family's socioeconomic level, the occupation of the parents, or the language spoken at home.

- The campus visit is an excellent way to familiarize young people and parents with a college or university and create a bond with the institution. If it is within a school's mission and capabilities, outreach programs that extend down into the grade schools and programs that continually champion the "stay in school" message help students recognize higher education as an attainable goal. It also takes the institution into the community and demonstrates its commitment. Bringing families on campus for academic programs, cultural events, movies, athletic activities, or trips to the museum allows them to see themselves as part of the institution and higher education as part of their future.

- As students get older, summer preparatory programs in engineering, science, or the arts that involve staying in the residence halls give them a preview of college life. Participants could be paired with college students and allowed to shadow them for a day. They could sit in classes and take notes or talk to professors in small groups about what they teach and what kind of research they do. Grants could be sought to fund bridge programs designed for these students, and an institutional office that oversees contracts and grants may be able to lend assistance. Successful outreach programs are investments in the future and require continual coordination between the institution, school districts, and community agencies.

ADMISSIONS CRITERIA THAT ENHANCE QUALITY AND DIVERSITY

Many students of color are very accomplished and will thrive academically and socially in any situation. But traditional yardsticks for measuring college success are not good predictors for most minority students. Many do not perform well on standardized admissions tests, some have language problems or are underprepared, some needing remediation may never have been exposed to the course content because of their school's lack of resources, and some may have had teachers whose expectations of them were always low—all of which reflect a disadvantaged socioeconomic status. Hodgkinson suggests,

Show me a minority child raised in a suburb and whose parents are college graduates, and I will show you a child whose educational performance is roughly the same as that of a white child raised in a suburb by parents who are college graduates. (Hodgkinson 1992)

In spite of these barriers, many minority students can perform where it counts—in the classroom. Admissions officers should look beyond traditional admissions criteria when making decisions concerning these students. Recommendations from individuals who have worked closely with the students are helpful, as are personal statements, interviews, and a review of extracurricular activities. A student's level of maturity is also important. Many students have had to assume responsibilities beyond their years because of their family situations, and those coping skills can serve them well in a higher education environment. If a variety of measures is used, the lowest may be disregarded as students are considered in light of their total experiences. Students want an equal opportunity to succeed, unimpaired by obstacles that others do not have to face.

Schools may also consider targeting students whose academic achievements are more modest and who would normally not be actively recruited by more selective schools. This forgotten middle is a group that with proper nurturing could develop into a successful college population. Schools with a significant minority population may find an extremely valuable tool in the development of local admissions test norms for that population. By knowing the test scores for an admitted minority group and how that group performed at the end of a specified period, reference to the norms can be made during the admissions decision process. Admissions officers may find that students who would normally be rejected because of low test scores can perform at an acceptable academic level when given the opportunity. Institutional research offices or social sciences departments may be able to prepare such data, or one of the admission testing agencies may provide assistance.

Recruitment and retention work hand in hand, and a successful recruitment plan must support the institution's retention efforts. Interest in an institution must be cultivated and maintained during the recruitment process. Once college selection has been made, continued efforts are required to retain those students recruited. Once enrolled, institutional fit is a primary consideration in a student's decision to stay at a school. A good match between a student and an institution helps develop and maintain a comfort level that assures the student his academic, financial, and social needs will be addressed and met by the college or university selected.

RETENTION METHODS THAT WORK

Orientation is critical to helping students make the transition from high school to college, to making them feel welcomed, and to addressing their initial academic and social needs. A strong parents' orientation program reinforces the institution's commitment to their children's education. Minority parents possess a wealth of knowledge and skills for which they often do not receive credit. Mothers can particularly influence students' decision making, and parents should be regarded as allies and resources in an institution's recruitment and retention efforts.

Highly structured programs that concentrate on the freshman year help high-risk students develop the academic and social skills they need to succeed. Ongoing orientation, testing, assessment, advising, learning assistance, student activities, intervention, and retention components of these programs should be continually monitored and evaluated to measure their effectiveness.

Student programs and organizations that address the interests and needs of minorities and that celebrate multiculturalism should be designed with student input and supported by the administration. Commencement speakers and special programs involving people of color should be part of campus life. Disciplines such as fine arts, history, political science, sociology, languages, linguistics, education, and health sciences provide rich backdrops for the inclusion into the curriculum of relevant materials that reflect the wisdom, traditions, and cultures of all Americans. In such settings, effective teachers "help students make connections between their community and national, ethnic, and global identities" (Ladson-Billings 1990). Faculty and staff orientations that include language training and cultural awareness seminars also promote an understanding of diverse populations.

Students must see minority role models within the faculty and administration. Faculty mentoring of students is an excellent retention tool. If a minority affairs division is established, its administrator must be in a position of real power that cuts across reporting structures and is supported by all departments. Other institutions may find it more advantageous to make access and diversity the responsibility of every office and to build accountability into that charge. The institution's Affirmative Action/Equal Education Opportunity officer could meet periodically with faculty and administrators about increasing minority representation within their ranks. Faculty and staff could be home-grown over a period of time. Departments could be rewarded for their efforts in recruiting and hiring minorities by being given additional faculty positions or additional teaching assistants after minorities are hired. Accountability can be built into faculty and staff recruitment by making women and minority hiring efforts part of the personnel evaluation process.

Four-year institutions may also have a special interest in recruiting transfer students. Special efforts need to be taken with minority populations, because the community college can be a terminal educational experience even when students say they plan to transfer. Two- and four-year institutions should work together to prepare articulation agreements and transfer guides for feeder institutions. These agreements give students specific information about the transfer process and how credit will be accepted toward a specific degree by the four-year schools. Transfer centers established on community college campuses can actively promote the transfer of qualified students. They can be staffed by representatives from the two- and four-year institutions and can provide preliminary transfer evaluations to its visitors. Ongoing information programs at the community colleges and campus visits at four-year schools can familiarize students with the transfer process. Orientation programs are very important, particularly those that address the applicability of credit toward the university degree. Students also benefit from support groups such as transfer student associations, and these students can also serve as resources to help the recruitment staff with future community college presentations.

Faculty can jointly participate in the development of parallel curricula that facilitate the transfer process. Proactive joint articulation committees composed of faculty and staff can oversee areas of mutual concern, plan institutional directions, and address specific issues as they arise. Periodic meetings or luncheons with key administrators, hosted by presidents and articulation committees and focusing on a variety of topics, can keep lines of communication open and make the transfer experience a reality for the community college student.

SUMMARY

As institutions look with excitement toward the next century, they need to integrate key segments of our population into their campuses so that everyone can fully participate in the prosperity of American life. Currently, ethnic minorities carry the full burden of adapting to the majority campus culture and simply co-exist within the majority population. Colleges and universities must work toward creating pluralistic campuses where the burdens and rewards are equally shared (Eaton 1989, viii). They need to continually ask whom they serve, what works and what doesn't, and how they can couple their efforts with local, state, and federal resources in partnerships and consortia to help them do what they do even better. Institutions need to become even more creative in developing ways of insuring inclusiveness in the midst of current legislative action and political climates that threaten to close the doors to minority participation in higher education and to reverse the small, but significant, advances that have been made over the past thirty years.

Many individuals who are currently outside our system of higher education have finely honed survival skills. These people made it through public school even though the odds were against them. They possess an incredible amount of raw talent and potential; they are tenacious and resilient. It takes institutional commitment and effort to motivate these students, cultivate that talent, and retain them. Tradition will not do it, multimillion dollar research facilities will not do it, the publication record of the faculty will not do it, and good grades will not do it. Commitment and a sense of purpose must permeate the institution and must be reflected through its actions and its representatives. Colleges and universities have a future if they can empower all their students, celebrate the convergence of cultures, honor new ideas, and take the best of all worlds to forge a better, more inclusive one.

REFERENCES

Alexander, Kim, Texas Guaranteed Student Loan Corporation. 1996. Interview by Diana Guerrero, El Paso, Texas, 25 June.

American Council on Education. 1988. *One-third of a nation: A report of the commission on minority participation in education and American life.* Washington, DC; American Council on Education.

Canchola-Flores, Anthony. 1987. Target Hispanic students: A growing potential college market. *The Admissions Strategist* 9: 17–22.

Carter, Deborah J., and Reginald Wilson. 1992. *1991 minorities in higher education: Tenth annual status report.* Washington, DC: American Council on Education.

———. 1995. *1994 thirteenth annual status report on minorities in higher education.* Washington, DC: American Council on Education.

Downing, Karen E., B. MacAdam, and D. P. Nichols. 1993. *Reaching a multicultural student community: A handbook for academic librarians.* Westport, CT: Greenwood Press.

Eaton, Judith S. 1989. Foreword to Madeleine F. Green, ed., *Minorities on campus: A handbook for enhancing diversity.* Washington, DC: American Council on Education.

Gollnick, William A. 1990. The reappearance of the vanishing American. *The College Board Review* 155 (Spring): 30–36.

Hikes, Zenobia Lawrence. 1993. Decoding college admission for first-generation families. *The Admission Strategist* 19 (Fall): 9–13.

Hodgkinson, Harold. 1992. *A demographic view of tomorrow.* Washington, DC: Center for Demographic Policy, Institute for Educational Leadership.

Hudson, J. Blaine. 1994. Democracy, diversity, and multiculturalism in American higher education: Issues, barriers, and strategies for change. *Western Journal of Black Studies* (Winter): 222–26.

Jackson, Marshall. 1987. Effective strategies for recruiting minority students. *Admissions Strategist* 9: 11–16.

Kobrak, Peter. 1992. Black student retention in predominantly white regional universities: The politics of faculty involvement. *Journal of Negro Education* 61 (Fall): 509–30.

Ladson-Billings, Gloria. 1990. Culturally relevant teaching: Effective instruction for black students. *College Board Review* 155 (Spring): 20–25.

Leo, John. 1996. Let's lower our self-esteem. *U.S. News and World Report* (17 June): 25.

Magner, Denise K. 1993. Colleges faulted for not considering differences in Asian American groups. *Chronicle of Higher Education* (10 February): A32, A34.

O'Brien, Eileen. 1990. Indian students' needs not the same as those of other minorities, advocates say. *Black Issues in Higher Education* (6 December): 22–23.

O'Connor, Patrick J. 1994. The needs of adult university students: A case study. *College and University* 69 (Winter): 84–86.

O'Hare, William. 1990. A new look at Asian Americans. *American Demographics* (October): 26–31.

Rendon, Laura, and Richard O. Hope. 1996. *Educating a new majority: Transforming America's educational system for diversity.* San Francisco: Jossey-Bass.

Richardson, Charles. 1993. A baker's dozen: What a president should know about recruiting and retaining students of color. *ACCESS: The newsletter for recruiting and retaining students of color* 1 (July): 4–5.

Richardson, Richard C., Jr., and Louis W. Bender. 1987. *Fostering minority access and achievement in higher education: The role of urban community colleges and universities.* San Francisco: Jossey-Bass.

Richardson, Richard C., Jr., and Elizabeth Fisk Skinner. 1991. *Achieving quality and diversity: Universities in a multicultural society.* New York: Macmillan.

Roberts, Sam. 1994. Who we are. Interview on Good Morning America, ABC-TV, July 4.

Suzuki, Bob H. 1989. Asian Americans as the "model minority": Outdoing whites? or media hype? *Change* (November/December): 12–19.

Thresher, B. Alden. 1966. *College admissions and the public interest.* New York: College Entrance Examination Board.

U.S. Bureau of the Census. 1994. *School enrollment—Social and economic characteristics of students: October 1993.* Current Population Reports, Series P20, No. 479. Washington, DC: U.S. Government Printing Office.

15

International Students

Clifford Sjogren

The diversity of American higher education is dramatically illustrated by the ethnic composition of U.S. college student populations. No other country hosts more international students and few compare with the United States in the number of its citizens who have studied abroad. Americans and non-Americans alike have benefited immeasurably from the internationalization of the U.S. campus environment.

During the past three decades, the definitions of foreign student and international student have become somewhat clouded as the movement of the world's people across national borders has greatly accelerated. No longer are the terms *foreign* and *international* used interchangeably. Foreign students are those who enroll in institutions in a second country, usually on temporary visas, with the intent to return home at the completion of their studies. International students are those who, for whatever reasons, have completed a portion of their education in a second country. Thus, all foreign students are international students, although many international students are not foreign. All students, therefore, may be classified as either international, or domestic, the latter defined as those who have completed all of their education in their home country.

These definitions are important because of the many subgroups that fall within the three general classifications. Serious legal and moral issues arise when campus administrators seek to simplify the processes by lumping all foreign students in one category. Refugees and legal immigrants (green card holders) are entitled to nearly all of the privileges of natural born citizens, including admission consideration and financial eligibility. Some states have even afforded undocumented, or illegal aliens, similar rights. Many Americans have completed all or most of their education overseas, either in U.S.-type or foreign schools. And many foreign students have completed their secondary education in the United

States as exchange students or as children of foreign diplomats assigned to U.S. posts.

College administrators must carefully assess an applicant's credentials and citizenship status before determining the candidate's need for special treatment in both the admissions and enrollment processes. English is a second language for literally millions of Americans, and thousands of native English-speaking foreign applicants seek enrollment in American universities each year. Thus, generalizations on the student's academic readiness, English proficiency, eligibility for financial aid, and personal factors should not be made on the basis of some simplistic category title.

THE CONSEQUENCES OF FOREIGN STUDENT ENROLLMENTS

When the foreign student admissions functions are handled properly, many good things happen to both the student and the university. Campus life is enriched and enrollment numbers are often strengthened by well-conducted foreign student admission and placement processes. Institutions, whose mission statements frequently include terms such as *ethnic diversity, internationalization, the global community*, and others that are fully compatible with, and enhanced by, foreign student enrollments can proudly proclaim the achievements of their foreign alumni, many of whom have risen to distinguished levels in the physical sciences, economics, health sciences, social engineering, and government service in their countries. The overwhelming percentage of foreign students who enroll in U.S. institutions are academically prepared, complete their programs successfully, and leave fully qualified to enter their professions. U.S. higher education deserves accolades for its unselfish willingness to share its resources with bright young foreign students, who have contributed significantly to making the world a better place.

Regrettably, however, there have been far too many undesirable incidents associated with the admission of foreign students. A predictive, deadly combination of ignorance and greed at a few institutions has resulted in the enrollment of ill-prepared or inadequately financed students which, in turn, has led to both institutional and national embarrassments. It is common for the U.S. student who fails college work to leave for a time and return at some later date to resume studies. Unsuccessful foreign students, however, face a far different future. When admitted, they assume—usually confirmed by college catalogues— that only well-qualified students are admitted and that comprehensive student services are available to all students. Often forgotten in these reassuring terms are the students who, at great financial sacrifice and with the hopes and dreams of families and friends, have traveled thousands of miles, only to be met with frustration and serious learning barriers. The result for the university is wasted funds, damaged image, loss of a student, and possible litigation. For the student it can mean wasted talent and energy, damaged dreams and expectations, loss of face, and possible severe psychological and other health problems.

A well-conceived and well-managed foreign student admission and enrollment policy, carried out in a professional manner, will yield highly satisfactory results to both the student and the institution.

ADMINISTERING A FOREIGN STUDENT ADMISSIONS PROGRAM

Before an institution seriously considers enrolling foreign students, a number of administrative procedures must be in place. Provisions must be made for increases in the operating budget for additional personnel and office space. Because wrong decisions can often prove costly for the university, staff training and the collection of reference materials must be assigned high budget priorities. Following are some essential administrative elements that are central to a successful foreign student admissions program.

- A foreign student admissions coordinator (FSAC) should be appointed. (It is common to have a coordinator for the undergraduate level and another for the graduate school, although the two positions can be combined into one office.) At least two other staff members should work part- or full-time with the coordinator to ensure administrative continuity should the coordinator leave the position.

- The FSAC should be encouraged and supported to affiliate with two professional organizations at both the regional or state, and the national levels. They are the American Association of Collegiate Registrars and Admissions Officers (AACRAO) and NAFSA: Association of International Educators. Both organizations (located in Washington, DC) prepare and distribute essential publications that describe foreign educational systems, sponsor national and regional workshops and professional presentations that aid the FSAC and staff, and provide a network of resource people who willingly share their time and knowledge with their professional colleagues.

- The FSAC should oversee the creation and distribution of several admissions information pieces and forms (using lightweight paper for cost-efficiency), including a brief description of the institution, a condensed preliminary application for foreign students, an outline of special admission requirements for foreign students, a statement on English language proficiency requirements, and a statement on institutional costs and financial aid probabilities. Examples of these forms and statements can be obtained from professional admissions personnel located at institutions that enroll large numbers of foreign students.

- Because of the expense incurred by both the institution and the student during the application process, the institution should design and circulate a preliminary application that provides applicants with an opportunity to describe their academic qualifications, English-language proficiency, and financial resources before they submit documents and sit for examinations. That information should then be reviewed by the FSAC to determine whether or not the student should be encouraged to apply. (Most foreign applicants require financial assistance and justifiably assume that a complete application is necessary before they can be considered for aid. The preliminary application would advise the student of aid possibilities before the costly application process.)

- The FSAC should inventory and update foreign student admission and placement references. The number of references required will be somewhat dependent upon the number of foreign applicants typically served, the nature of the programs offered, and levels of instruction at the institution.

  Several good bibliographies have been prepared and distributed by professional organizations and agencies. Because the reference lists are constantly being revised, these resources are not listed here. Most professionals agree, however, that every reference library should include, either in hard copy or on CD-ROM, the volumes of AACRAO's international education series and the numerous reports sponsored cooperatively by AACRAO and NAFSA, with participation by The College Board, through the joint Projects for International Education Research (PIER) committee.

- An institution should offer admission to non-native English speakers only if there is strong evidence, as measured by a reliable testing program, that a reasonable level of English language competency has been attained by the applicant. Further, the language proficiency should be revalidated when the student arrives on campus. However, if the institution sponsors a strong program of English for nonnative speakers at all levels of proficiency, it would be appropriate to admit students with deficiencies in English as long as the applicant is advised that several months of intensive and costly English-language training might be required before admission to a degree program is offered.

- Institutions must have carefully crafted and comprehensible costs and financial aid policies for foreign students. Estimates of annual as well as school year costs should be included with initial communications to prospective students. Administrators must recognize that immigration laws greatly reduce employment opportunities for visitors on temporary visas. Further, a substantial portion of institutionally administered financial aid is from state and federal sources available only for Americans and legal immigrants.

- After their enrollment, foreign students require specialized services that an institution must provide. Special advising services that are staffed by culturally sensitive and competent professionals will contribute to a mutually beneficial relationship between the institution and the students. Of particular importance is a staff member or convenient community resource who can provide legal services on immigration issues. The complex and continuing changes in laws pertaining to foreign visitors require serious attention by the institution.

THE ADMISSIONS DECISION

Central to a successful international student admissions program are the institutional policies and practices that relate to admission decisions. Admission should be offered only to those students who possess strong academic qualifications in appropriate areas, present evidence of at least adequate English language proficiency, seek a curriculum offered at the admitting schools, and show evidence of ability to meet all financial obligations associated with their study.

If any of these conditions are not met, the applicant should not be admitted. Admissions personnel must avoid the temptation to admit an Olympic-class swimmer from Norway or the child of Middle East royalty unless all other factors in the admissions process are fully satisfied.

The FSAC should be responsible for preparing policies and procedures for review by faculty and senior administrators. Institutional guidelines that cover such areas as desired number of entering non-American students, geographic distribution (if any) of those students, financial aid policies, and related matters should be created and approved by the faculty and senior administrators.

Institutions with small numbers of foreign student applicants may use one of several excellent professional credential evaluation services. AACRAO's Office of International Education Services (OIES) evaluates foreign educational credentials for the Association's member institutions. The National Association of Credential Evaluation Services (NACES) consists of services that have met rigorous professional standards. These services offer document translations, and educational level and course analyses of educational systems throughout the world. The student, the college, and the society in which the graduate's talent is applied benefit immeasurably when a good admissions decision is made.

RECRUITMENT OF FOREIGN AND U.S. INTERNATIONAL STUDENTS

The ingenuity of American student recruitment procedures has been successfully applied to programs designed to attract international students to U.S. campuses. Admissions offices employ a variety of strategies to identify and encourage enrollment of overseas candidates, including specially designed publications, overseas trips, and alumni recruitment projects. Recognizing the need to make honest and unambiguous U.S. college information available to prospective students, professional organizations such as the College Board, various U.S. government agencies, and private services have cooperated with the higher education community to encourage the enrollment of well-qualified foreign students in U.S. colleges.

The common and most effective means of attracting foreign students is a well-designed system of communications, including publications. Of utmost importance is the institution's knowledge and willingness to use modern technology to facilitate communications. A quick and thorough response time to inquiries will give an institution a distinct advantage in the recruitment process. The following are examples of some useful technologies:

• Facsimile (fax) machine: Mail service in many countries is poor. Many foreign students have been denied the opportunity to study at an institution of their choice because mail to and/or from the college was either seriously delayed or never received. Institutions should be willing to send and receive applications and documents, along with credit card account numbers for fees, by fax. All communications with the candidate must emphasize, however, that before final permission to enroll is awarded, official, or true, copies, of all documents must be received, carefully reviewed, and verified for authenticity by the institution.

- The Internet: Electronic mail (E-mail) addresses, preferably of the reviewing admissions officer or FSAC, should be prominently displayed in all publications and on the office letterhead. Some institutions allow, even encourage, students to apply through electronic mail. Oftentimes, alumni located in the applicant's city can be a helpful resource. This highly efficient way of communicating with prospective students should be seriously considered.

- Floppy diskettes: An increasing number of institutions now give students the option of applying on a computer diskette. This is especially practical for overseas applicants. Several students can apply on a single floppy and can include recommendations and essays. Diskettes that can be easily copied could be sent to United States Information Agency offices, international schools, and other sites where there are concentrations of prospective international students. It is suggested, however, that a foreign candidate for admission first supply to the college with a preliminary application form, which might also be included on the diskette. A diskette or an accompanying CD-ROM might include institutional promotional information with color graphics and sound.

International schools located throughout the world are important sources of both American and non-American students. International schools are privately funded, although about 90 are provided some financial assistance by the U.S. Department of State. These schools are generally located in urban centers and offer a strong U.S.-type curriculum. Typically, the student populations of such schools consist of Americans, host country nationals, and students from 25 to 35 other countries whose parents are in the diplomatic corps or international business community. Non-Americans who have attended U.S.-type overseas high schools will have normally taken a strong college preparatory curriculum, taught in English by American teachers. Most are from middle- to upper-income families and have long planned on attending a college in the United States. Because of their frequent association with American students in a U.S. educational setting, these students usually adjust quickly to U.S. campus life.

College admissions personnel may secure a directory of these international schools by writing to the Office of Overseas Schools (A/OS), Room 245, SA-29, U.S. Department of State, Washington, DC 20522 7800. Research sponsored by the A/OS reveals that graduates of international schools assisted by the office are excellent candidates for an American higher education program.

Hundreds of other overseas schools offer an American curriculum taught in English as the language of instruction. Most of these schools have a religious affiliation. A valuable reference for brief descriptions of over 500 overseas schools that employ the American curriculum is the *ISS Directory of Overseas Schools*, published annually by International School Services, 15 Rosedale Road, P.O. Box 5910, Princeton, NJ 08543.

Further, many well-qualified foreign students graduate each year from private boarding and day schools located in the United States. The umbrella organization for these schools is the National Association of Independent Schools, 75 Federal Street, Boston, MA 02110. Most foreign graduates from U.S. public schools and those on exchange student visas will be required by immigration regulations to return to their home countries for a period of time before they are eligible to return for further study. Nonetheless, many of those students will eventually seek enrollment in U.S. institutions and can be successfully recruited.

Finally, many institutions have found overseas visits productive, especially those administered by professional services that promote and organize trips for U.S. admissions personnel. An example of a popular service is Linden Educational Services, 2802 Cathedral Avenue, NW, Washington, DC 20008. During 1994, Linden reported that it led 120 college admissions officers to 30 countries on four continents, where 30,000 prospective students were seen.

SUMMARY

International students, when properly recruited and professionally serviced by competent and caring college staffs, will add a desirable dimension to a campus environment. While the financial reward to the institution can be considerable, the mere presence of well-qualified and properly placed students from throughout the world is a far more significant and visible benefit for the college or university.

16

Collegiate Telecounseling and Recruitment Videos

Joe F. Head

TELECOUNSELING

Perhaps the four most powerful mass communication tools introduced to humankind are Gutenberg's moveable type printing press, Alexander Graham Bell's telephone, RCA's television, Charles Babbage's computer. These advancements have tightly coupled the information age with the communications explosion and have thrust the world of higher education onto the information superhighway. Universities, corporations, and private foundations are contributing to the knowledge base so rapidly that the public is suffering from information overload. In view of this phenomenon, how does the admissions professional effectively communicate with its audience and maintain a personal relationship in a high tech environment?

Innovative enrollment management professionals from across the nation have discovered the productive enrollment power of telecommunications. Increasing state-of-the-art technology and new awareness of how to use the telephone more effectively in the college recruitment industry have placed a customized communications tool in the hands of enrollment professionals. The added value of phone power and associated telephony has given higher education an alternative marketing method to quickly reach prospective students.

Since 1980, a new breed of technologically savvy enrollment managers has emerged to expand telecommunication applications beyond the early role of traditional, outbound recruitment calling. In the broadest scope, collegiate phone power has evolved to facilitate a variety of enrollment services ranging from recruitment and retention telethons to touchtone registration.

Following World War II, American higher education was underprepared for the tidal wave of veterans who would take advantage of GI Bill benefit programs. In addition, postsecondary institutions did not foresee the enormous baby boom that would follow the GI generation. This sudden demographic change dramatically overloaded existing college campuses, and forced state and federal government into action in response to public demand for higher education access. Secondary school curricula, faculty, and facilities were also blindsided by the onslaught of post–World War II baby boomers. High schools were poorly connected to colleges and lacked programs to transition college-bound students efficiently to the hallowed halls of unsuspecting institutions of higher learning.

A national rush to expand existing college campuses and construct new ones to meet the enrollment demand soon swept America. But, again, the higher education system was caught off guard. Large numbers of entering students were ill prepared; remedial programs became a priority. Colleges had to gear up to support large enrollments which meant adding more faculty, staff, and capital improvements. In two decades, the baby boom had moved through the educational system, and colleges began to experience lean enrollments. Enrollment planning by the mid-1970s was nonexistent for most colleges; long-range forecasting was a fresh concept. Soon keen competition for the traditional student population became a reality. Colleges, left reeling from the enrollment declines, faced some uncomfortable decisions regarding operational downsizing or adapting to a changing academic environment where fewer traditional students were becoming customers.

Many colleges submerged academic egos and took aggressive marketing action to stem the threatening enrollment decline. Central administrations approved stand alone admissions and/or recruitment offices. Reorganization brought in consultants, advertising firms, and experts to deal with the enrollment monster. Soon colleges were moving from recruitment activities to marketing strategies. In less than a decade a media mix of direct mail, road trips, billboards, radio, newsprint, and television advertising became acceptable. For lack of better models, colleges often emulated the marketing methods of corporate and retail sectors and applied similar techniques to reach student audiences. In hindsight, this copycat marketing may have confused some colleges' telemarketing or phone-a-thon practices.

HISTORY AND DEFINITION OF COLLEGIATE PHONING

By this time, the telephone was playing a vital but transparent role in the college recruitment industry. Multiple telephones were appearing in every American household. Teenagers and telephones had become a part of Americana. Admissions officers began to recognize the opportunity and were already quietly deferring to the phone to reach prospective students. Directors of admissions, particularly from small, private colleges, were sensing the power and competitive edge of the phone, and were beginning to make it an integral part of the recruitment plan. The productivity and accountability of telephoning, compared to other media, was substantially impressive. By the mid to late 1970s, many private colleges were sponsoring frequent recruitment phone-a-thons using student volunteers.

With the public arrival of commercial telemarketing, colleges unfortunately began to frame collegiate phoning in the same context. Undoubtedly some innocent colleges used hard core telemarketing principles when communicating with prospective students. However, the old guard gatekeepers at larger schools and Ivy League campuses resisted the thought of using such perceived hard-sell tactics. Faculty acceptance of campus telemarketing was cool. Some colleges with declining departmental enrollments flirted with such options but encountered resistance from faculty, who refused to participate in phoning, claiming telemarketing degraded academia and phoning students was not in the faculty job description.

The eventual decision or concession to accept marketing strategies, including organized phoning to attract and retain satisfactory enrollments, likely justified collegiate telemarketing. However, the divestiture of the Bell Telephone System in the early 1980s ushered in a greater awareness of phone power and prepared the way for integrated functions.

As colleges began to explore the possibilities of recruitment phoning, it became apparent that retail telemarketing principles were not an appropriate model. Existing literature was centered around commercial phoning and collegiate concepts were not yet in place. Perhaps a major frustration was that collegiate phoning had not yet been defined nor distinguished from commercial telemarketing. Like many other techniques, this practice was developed much by trial and error among enterprising practitioners. Professional state, regional, and national associations offered forums to share experiences which further advanced the place earned by recruitment phoning. After two decades, collegiate phoning began to define itself differently than commercial telemarketing. As the definition was refined, more colleges and universities bought into the concept and saw broad applications.

Today, we define collegiate recruitment phoning as telecounseling. Telecounseling is similar to commercial telemarketing, but philosophically different. Telecounseling is an interval, outbound notification and advisement system. It functions as a live, ongoing, telephone enrollment outreach, designed to screen, qualify, and motivate eligible prospects through the initial entry or reentry admissions funnel.

Telecounseling is . . .	Telecounseling is not . . .
• a personal nurturing;	• conducted from cold calling lists;
• an "interest" qualification supported by tracking and sorting;	• driven by hard-core scripts;
• a revolving follow-up system that ushers prospects through the application and enrollment process.	• a one-shot deal intended to close a sale with a credit card.

Telecounseling is done by making interval phone contacts formatted as announcements, confirmations, and invitations. These courtesy calls are made to determine the level of interest, request necessary document collections, issue open house invitations, and set up standard interviews or testing and tuition/housing deposits, as required by the college. Interval format calling supports an invitational philosophy exclusive to collegiate telecounseling, which allows the telecounselor to conduct the call from a perspective that tells the prospect little or no sales attitude is intended.

Telecounseling is sweeping the college recruitment industry and is finding its way into almost every admissions operation. Many colleges are still depending deeply on the individual initiatives of persuasive counselors and recruiters to make enough phone calls to prospects within a given territory to produce sufficient enrollment. Other colleges are actively using the student phone-a-thon approach, a favorite college recruitment standard that directs a concentrated multi-phone blitz at a particular prospect population using campus volunteers over a short period of time. Usually this choice is designed to screen large volumes of leads for follow-up by counseling staff.

As an alternative to campus-based phone-a-thons, some colleges are outsourcing to commercial telemarketing vendors who specialize in lead qualification. As with every choice, there are positives and negatives. Commercial firms are typically fast, efficient, and experienced. However, they can be costly, lack timely knowledge of the college environment, deliver the message insincerely, and come across with a telemarketing edge.

Currently, the more competitive colleges are investing in telecenters. Telecenters are dedicated recruitment phoning operations housed in permanent quarters and typically managed by the office of admissions or the enrollment management division. The telecenter, the current standard in college phoning, offers high-impact results and can be rapidly redirected as priorities change. Maximum efficiency and success depend on how broadly the telecenter is used. If "call jobs" are defined too poorly, the entire office loses communication benefits that could be served by such an operation.

The telecenter is a natural fit for enrollment management. Call populations can range from first-time inquirers; applicants with incomplete application forms; former students; orientation, deposit, and survey lists; transfers; and honors students to endless classifications of potential students in the enrollment loop. Depending on the nature of the college, telecenters may focus on building the personal, "high-touch" relationship found in smaller schools or upon processing continuous high-volume applications typical of larger public institutions. These centers routinely operate during the evening and are supervised by a telecenter manager. The more advanced facilities are equipped with networked PCs, customized software, and telephone headsets.

Technology is now offering the progressive enrollment professional new opportunities to expand the role of telecounseling into automated telecommunication options. In particular, telecounseling can now be upgraded from the traditional outbound, one-way mode to an inbound, 24-hour electronic service. Prospective students and applicants can be coached to use a variety of interactive voice response systems linked to support recruitment activities. Students can access automated menus offering literature request selections, audio brochures, and application status-check features. Colleges with larger and diverse enrollments, particularly metropolitan commuter campuses, have already embraced remote telephone registration. Increasingly, innovative colleges such as Kennesaw State University in Marietta, Georgia, are using computerized calling or automated outdialing to successfully communicate with various student populations.

Telecounseling is a perfect partner in the media mix strategy. It is an ideal follow-up tool to any situation. Perceptive enrollment professionals do not consider designing recruitment literature without showcasing telecommunication options. A configuration might include a telephone icon, followed by toll-free 800 numbers; automated 24-hour, information request lines; and automated application status–check services. Office correspondence should be reviewed for opportunities to list phone services and a reminder that a counselor or representative will be calling, a personal touch that begins to educate the prospect or applicant that the college does much of its business by telephone.

The next evolution in telecounseling operations will likely expand to include an Internet role in "messaging services." It is foreseeable that the Internet will follow a similar acceptance to that of previous household communication and entertainment conveniences. One can reflect on how the radio and telephone gradually became necessary appliances in every American home. More contemporary examples arc the portable telephone, remote controlled color television, cellular phone, compact disc player, VCR, cable television, and home computer. It is only logical that the turn of the century will belong to residential Internet communication services.

Many college admissions offices are already on-line and equipping to gain access to the Internet. As Internet access is established, enrollment professionals will exploit such electronic avenues to enhance recruitment communications. Prospective students will be encouraged to contact colleges via E-mail options, request literature, download preformatted information, interact with selected material, and apply for admission directly from their home or office.

The future of telecounseling will likely surface to be a sophisticated messaging center with both outbound and inbound advantages. Enrollment officers will develop new communication strategies and likely centralize reply operations in the Telecenter. Common electronic messages will be initiated and transmitted to targeted populations similar to hardcopy search mailings. A bank of trained telecounselors will continue to make live outbound calls on a personal basis, while others will respond to queries via the Internet keyboard, reaching prospects around the world.

College admissions personnel have recognized the sophisticated nuances offered by collegiate telecounseling and alternative information delivery configurations. Collegiate phoning is already a fact of life in today's competitive market. Any college choosing not to use some form of telecounseling or related technology in their media mix is substantially less competitive and will be viewed as out-of-touch with today's reality.

STUDENT RECRUITMENT VIDEOS

The student recruitment video prototype innocently debuted on American television in the early 1980s. The National Collegiate Athletic Association, squeezed a 60-second vignette promoting each team's institution during football halftimes, among commercials, interviews, color commentary, and statistics. This innovation—a student recruitment video on national television—caught the attention of many colleges and suggested that the next step in the student recruitment industry would be video.

However, college athletic programming cannot be entirely credited with such a profound development. Already in place were requests from high school guidance counselors asking distant colleges to send 35mm slide shows or 16mm films to them for viewing by college-bound students and parents. In addition, federal government entitlement grants were requiring high schools to install ¾" Umatic videocassette recorder and Playback Units (industry-standard VCR units already in place for instructional purposes), but high schools and colleges had not yet recognized their recruitment potential.

As a first response, colleges began to struggle with how to afford, duplicate, package, and deliver existing audiovisual presentations to high school guidance offices using current media productions. In 1982 the University of Georgia's Office of Admissions surveyed all Georgia public high schools and learned that most had already installed a VCR. Once knowledge of the Umatic VCR surfaced, colleges quickly began to transfer existing slide shows and film to industry-standard ¾" video tape, and distributed reformatted productions to high schools on a loan arrangement. These tapes were often recovered and recirculated to other high schools upon request.

Simultaneously, the corporate world correctly envisioned the consumer demand for a home VCR and recognized the market potential. By 1983, the first home VCRs began to appear with companion video recording equipment. With equal pace the movie industry began to make movies available on videocassettes for purchase or rental. Again, innovative enrollment professionals recognized the recruitment potential of these unfolding media. Once questions of standardization, affordability, and inhome installations were resolved, college recruitment officials began to include video as part of the marketing mix. Timing was ripe for many reasons. Demographic information indicated that the college-bound market was reading less and watching more. Technology was ready. The baby boom TV generation was comfortable with video implementation. The Music Television Network (MTV)–"Sesame Street" generation became the target market.

EVOLUTION AND PRODUCTION OF THE ELECTRONIC VIEWBOOK

Colleges plunged into the video frenzy. This new medium was pioneered by instinctive trailblazers who developed first-generation recruitment videos by trial and error. In the beginning the technology and novelty were fresh. It was difficult not to mesmerize the audience. But with time, audiences became more difficult to impress. The sophistication of college video had to step up to the competitive challenge.

In many ways the recruitment video is an electronic extension of the college viewbook. The viewbook arrived on the college scene by the mid-1970s. It revolutionized the admissions literature package beyond a sterile catalog by presenting a pictorial collage of color photos, theme, facts, and depictions of attractive students. Perhaps the recruitment video was quickly embraced by college admissions because of the viewbook format. Viewbooks, which had already been tried and tested using a variety of approaches, were a familiar and convenient springboard from which to launch a video initiative. In comparison to telemarketing, with the exception of cost, video met little resistance from academe, perhaps because of its high profile, local celebrity appeal, instructional audiovisual nature, and claim to state-of-the-art technology.

Today, recruitment videos are commonplace. However, some colleges do a better job of producing videos than others. Videos should be aimed at a certain market niche, and should be carefully developed to communicate a distinctive (versus confused or empty) message about the institution (e.g., the institution is the only state or regional college with a corporate-oriented curriculum, single-sex enrollment, nontraditional commuter flavor, theological base, or military reputation). Because of its perceived cost and labor-intensive nature, however, generally a generic video is produced.

Viewbooks are designed to grab the prospect's attention. So, too, should the recruitment video stimulate the viewer's interest, build an image, and leave him or her with a single positive message about the campus. Fundamental to producing a recruitment video is knowing whom you want to influence. Historically, colleges do very little advance research before committing to such a project. Surveys indicate, however, that most viewers primarily want to see scenes of the community including nearby recreational facilities, sports action/facilities, classrooms, housing, and casual student life. Other popular requests include indications of faculty reputation, student body quality, gender ratio, minority percentage, cost, financial aid, and job placement.

While popular myth holds that any video should be less than ten minutes, video producers recommend a length of 12 to 15 minutes. Recent surveys suggest that 15- to 20-minute videos are well received if they are packed with good information. The trick is to offer just enough information to invite follow-up.

- Sample story lines have featured on-camera identical twins, a nontraditional/adult corporate theme, graduate emphasis, original rap music, and a wraparound format that follows a student through a typical day.

- Well-selected, spontaneous student testimonies inserted at the right places are tremendously popular and powerful, and they often give subconscious demographic cues about the student body (i.e., gender, race, geographical region, intellectual level).

- A subtle blend of still frame shots within the video action or slide sequence eliminates distraction by other movement captured in the video and gives the narrator time to describe a special feature in a dedicated sound bite. This strategic maneuver might best be used to stress a prized benefit.

- College recruitment videos with a subtle plot or realistic storyline are rated high by prospective students. Classic examples are those produced by Drake University.

Other questions to be asked when planning a video project include ways to distribute the video, action requested by the video, specific information the proposed audience wants to see/hear, the shelf life of the video, and the selected scenes vital to support the objective.

1. A good video begins with an objective and a rough script or brief storyboard outline that includes all vital information addressing the needs of the target audience. The script is accompanied by a shot sheet detailing scenes or locations supporting the on- and off-camera narration. This approach assumes that the office of admissions will play an associate producer role but will turn the project over to an outside video production company.

A turnkey arrangement may be handled very differently, with the production company assuming much more of the creative and scheduling responsibility. Colleges will be much happier with the final production if some initial homework is done to facilitate good communication with the production company. However, a word of caution. First, because client colleges typically want to put too much into a video, the advice of the video company in determining that point should carry a lot of weight. Second, it is advisable to use an off-camera narrator to establish authority and continuity, redefine the message, and provide transitions from one scene to another, especially if nonprofessionals (i.e., students) are delivering the message via speech or action. This combination can successfully balance the production and display a professional (not amateurish) image without relinquishing student appeal.

2. After a rough script outline when the objective is in place, a decision as to whether production is handled professionally or in-house (i.e., within the college) must be made. In-house production as a student class project or at an ill-equipped institutional resource center may be considerably less expensive but may also earn much less respect from an audience.

Prospective production companies should receive the tentative script outline and as much literature as possible. The production companies should then submit a written bid with whatever enhanced scripting and special features they may recommend. While they prepare a quote, the college representative should check references and review sample productions from each company invited to bid. As the old saying goes, "You get what you pay for."

3. Submitted bids should be evaluated. Colleges should consider the resources each company offers, the size of the crew, their experience, and the potential working relationship between the college and the production director. It is important to realize that the budget will dictate the quality of the final product. Often, to reduce the burden of cost, (1) related campus departments that can reach a satisfactory common ground will share the expense; (2) colleges may find an interested sponsor to underwrite the production in return for a recognition of the support at the close of the video; or (3) colleges may appeal to local merchants who consider the college market especially attractive.

4. Once the bid is awarded, a staff member should be assigned to shepherd the project and coordinate the entire "shoot." A project of this scope is unlikely to please all constituencies. A senior enrollment services official should take on the responsibility of handling on-campus political agendas. This individual's job is to keep the project focused and targeted on the audience for which it is being developed. This individual should be logistically helpful in gaining advance approval and access for difficult shots, and should remain flexible to accommodate unexpected dilemmas. Shooting will always take longer than planned. Equipment will fail, doors will be locked, lines forgotten, people will be late, or the weather will not cooperate.

5. In addition to production values, quality planning needs to focus on distinctive packaging and distribution. Too many videos are wrapped in humdrum white cardboard sleeves and labeled with black dot matrix adhesive labels. A small touch of color and logo design will entice people to view the video rather than ignore it. The video's arrival will generate even more excitement if it is packaged in a snappy tyvec or a U.S. Postal Service Priority envelope. Some institutions, such as Berry College, in Mount Berry, Georgia, and Vanderbilt University, have personalized videos (i.e., mentioned the prospect's name) in postproduction. Packaging and design must be matched with distribution media. Many colleges mail a video and (optional) postage paid reply card to highly qualified prospects or applicants to measure impressions. Others place videos in video rental stores, libraries, and, of course, high schools. These outlets may require four-color printed photos on the packaging to compete with other video selections or to stimulate immediate viewing.

6. Depending on the complexity of the script, shooting to capture sports action, aerial views, seasonal appeal, and graduation can take a few days or several weeks, if shot over multiple terms. Using on-camera personalities such as the college president, professional talent, faculty, or alumni celebrities can also extend shooting time. Once production is completed, the video moves to the studio for editing where music, voice-overs, fast cuts, and graphics bring it to life.

7. The first version should be field-tested in several locations (e.g., four to six high schools). If plans call for use with other audiences, then similar tests should be arranged. Following each viewing, a generic questionnaire or evalu-

ation should gather reactions to uncover problems and reinforce the video's message. Results should be compiled and compared for validation. If problem areas surface, reviews from multiple field tests can validate and suggest solutions. College and video production staff can discuss needed changes and decide on corrective edits. The completed video is ready for wide release according to the agreed-upon timetable and distribution plan. A comprehensive video production can take 12 to 16 months to complete and release to the prospective class. It is therefore recommended that funding be secured three years ahead of the enrolling class that viewed the video in its first showing.

The student recruitment video is entering its second decade of service. It is considered among the most glamorous of admissions marketing tools, but its current status will soon fall to the next evolution of integrated multimedia. Many colleges have yet to develop a video, and others are already looking to the next generation of video/computer partnerships. In the foreseeable future, more colleges will join the ranks. Marketing needs will guide other colleges to develop internal special niche productions to address narrow-interest populations. Some examples already appearing are specific videos for respective academic schools in nursing, engineering, graduate programs, and adult nontraditional features. With the explosion of affordable video camera equipment, more colleges will venture into campus-based productions. Such productions are already occurring in many colleges with well-equipped studios.

More colleges will likely move to alternative low-budget TV advertising and local cable industry to run current videos and commercials. Deliberate investments will be made to develop special productions to fit such formats, such as taping familiar faces and local events associated with the college. These low-budget videos may take the shape of ''informercials'' or testimonials that will work in the community cable industry. Cable will be especially attractive to institutions that draw heavily in a given area, and can also use cable to build awareness in a distant recruitment territory.

The current evolution in college recruitment is CD-ROM, which colleges may choose to use as a search piece or at college night programs. CD-ROM disks hold enormous amounts of audio text and associated photos. Data can be printed out at the user's discretion. Because they are menu formatted, students can immediately access what interests them first, without waiting, for example, for what the video reveals.

In order to remain on the cutting edge, colleges may choose to divert printing funds to support the new technology. However, the shelf life of a CD is really no greater than that of a video cassette or glossy brochure. After a short period of time, the information becomes stale and the photos out of date. CD-ROM is not retrievable to be updated.

Already on the scene is the reality of integrated multimedia technologies, such as the World Wide Web on the Internet. Even as this text is being written, many colleges are establishing their Web sites with home pages to promote the institution. Video recruitment will no longer be restricted to the magnetic tape cassette format chained to a VCR. As residential Internet subscriptions increase, so too will colleges and academic departments move to deliver generic and program specific images via the World Wide Web. Colleges already are blazing trails once again as they learn to transfer existing video onto mainframe hard drives so prospective students can directly access on-line images and text. New technology will be superior in that it will function much like the movies on a demand basis. Colleges will contract with outsource vendor services or install equipment that will permit students to directly access audio, text, and imagining/video files in the comfort of their own homes using integrated cable TV and/or telecommunication services. The advantage of this technology will be that it will furnish current information and will offer students interactive options using primary databases supported by the host institution. This will be a significant advancement beyond CD-ROM because students will have direct daily access to fresh information maintained by the institution and will not be dependent on an intermediate delivery vehicle.

SUMMARY

The information highway is upon us. Enrollment professionals must better learn to use the electronic tools already in place and anticipate those that will come. Institutions of higher education are notoriously slow to accept innovations. Old stereotypical attitudes must be frequently reexamined and, if found obsolete, must be abandoned or ordered differently to permit other paradigms to prevail.

The expanding roles of telecommunications and video are perfect vehicles for the future of college admissions and recruitment. How to effectively reach each new generation is a question with which all enrollment professionals are destined to struggle. The electronic future is before us, and the way is clear for those pioneers who have the passion to put new electronic methodology in place.

REFERENCES

Hartnagel, Douglas. 1990. Telephone service as a marketing strategy. *College and University* 65(4): 328–34.

Head, Joe F. 1994. *Phone power for college admissions and the communications explosion.* 4th ed. Acworth, GA: Star Printing for Collegiate Telemarketing Institute.

Roehr, Robert J., ed. 1991. *Student recruitment—Electronic advancement.* Washington, DC: Council for the Advancement and Support of Education.

Young, Lee. 1991. Telemarketing as a vital part of enrollment management. *The Journal of the National Association of College Admission Counselors* (130) (Winter).

17

Admissions Partners on Campus

Kathleen G. Plante

HELPING STUDENTS SUCCEED

Teamwork is the essential element that enables faculty, students, staff, and administrators of a college or university to reach their desired goal—success. Success in higher education today is often measured by the number of student applications received, the number of students enrolled, the diversity of the student population, the number of students returning semester after semester, the number of graduates, and the number of degrees/certificates awarded. No unit within a college or university can succeed without interaction with other units, and all must recognize that the most important commodity is the student or prospective student. In today's highly competitive market, attracting and retaining the brightest, most talented students to meet the mission of an institution requires the coordinated efforts of the entire college or university community. This effort must begin with a well-orchestrated, multifaceted marketing and recruitment plan, which includes on-campus functions. Such campus visitations can include both one-on-one opportunities and group activities, along with preview and orientation programs.

While academic quality should be the primary reason why students select an institution, the support activities and services help entice students to attend and remain in school. This chapter addresses the student services areas and programs that contribute to the academic, social, and physical well-being of students and help them succeed.

ORIENTATION PROGRAMS

Orientation programs contribute to student success. Research results prove that students who participate in an orientation program are more likely to remain in school, attain higher overall grade point averages, and earn degrees than those who do not attend orientation. For these reasons orientation programs are no longer limited to the traditional population of 18-year-old, entering freshmen. An array of orientation programs designed to meet the needs of a diverse group of entering students is generally offered.

Rather than offering the same agenda under a different title, orientation programs should establish specific goals for each group targeted. Objectives should be established after determining the needs of the audience (Dannells 1993). The techniques—for example, focus groups, questionnaires, program evaluations, and telephone surveys—used to identify the needs can be as diverse as the complexity of any given campus (Plante, Smith, and Bracklin 1993). (See the sample orientation checklist in Appendix 18.1 at the end of this chapter.)

Orientation is different from preview programs that allow prospective students to visit the campus during their junior or senior year. Preview is one step removed from an orientation program; it is itself a form of orientation or introduction to campus life and should be planned accordingly. Some preview programs are tied to an athletic event and may include overnight on-campus accommodations, classroom visits, and other forms of student activities. Publicizing the availability of these visits early in the recruitment year and allocating limited dates and space for participation make programs of this type more appealing and provide a controlled view of the best the institution has to offer. The selection of program dates may be tied to prominent campus events, but consideration should be given to activities in the feeder school areas. A time of year when the campus looks its best should be selected. If skiing in winter is a feature of the area or if the azaleas add to the beauty of the campus, those features should be emphasized in planning. Spring programs scheduled during high school spring breaks may serve as an entree for rising juniors. The program should not be conducted during the university or college's break period because activity on campus helps sell the institution.

In general, the primary purpose of an orientation program that includes placement testing, campus tours, information sessions, and get-acquainted activities is to provide students with information to help them understand the university and its expectations. The complexity of each segment depends upon the college or university's predetermined assessment. The best enticement to get prospective students to participate in such a program is to include an opportunity for early academic advisement and registration (Strumpf and Sharer 1993).

Depending on institutional demographics, selected groups may require special orientation programs geared to their needs. Special programs may be developed for first-time international students, older-than-average students, and graduate students, as well as other special groups (Strumpf and Sharer 1993).

- Programming for international students should address legal and visa matters, hygiene, student rights, American customs, an orientation to the area, and information on shopping. Community support groups and, if possible, an on-campus mentor should be provided.

• Older entering students often have doubts. They wonder if they can be competitive, can handle the stress, or can communicate with fellow classmates. Providing role models from among the peers of this group helps alleviate anxiety. A successful semester is a proven confidence booster. An on-campus organization can also provide the support that many of these people need. Some campuses have provided lounges or offices specifically designated for older or international students.

Students have proven to be more effective orientation leaders than faculty or administrators because entering students find them nonjudgmental and less intimidating. Incoming students also identify better with student leaders. Being selected to serve as a peer orientation leader and/or student ambassador is an honor. While opportunities to receive leadership training and the ability to interact with prospective students or other visitors to the campus may be incentive enough for students to seek these positions, monetary inducements in the form of scholarships or hourly pay may help attract a more diverse and qualified group of applicants from which to select orientation leaders.

As representatives of their institutions, orientation leaders leave an impression on students and others they encounter. Therefore, these leaders should be involved in an intense training program that includes all the information leaders need either to instruct or to respond to questions. The development of presentation skills and situational role playing is necessary to ensure a quality program. A well-received, up-beat, accurate program provides a positive image; one that is poorly prepared and presented does an institution more harm than good as attendees share their experiences. Word of mouth can be an institution's most successful recruitment aid or its most damaging. Throughout any program, evaluation must be an on-going process among program leaders, coordinators, and directors to identify problems, review attendee concerns, and find solutions. Additionally, a reevaluation of the focus of the program and its content should be part of program assessment (Miles 1988).

Follow-up work with orientation attendees through telephone calls, group sessions, or fun activities that reconnect the students with each other and/or their group leaders provides opportunities for the former to seek help or to ask questions. Such contacts also provide reminder information in a nonjudgmental environment. The goal of any orientation program is to get students off to a good start and keep them on their intended track. (For additional information on the National Orientation Directors Association, see the listing in Appendix 18.2 at the end of this chapter.)

FINANCIAL AID

While orientation and preview programs are effective ways to build student enthusiasm, some attention must be given to finances, which is a primary concern for many entering students. The majority of today's students cannot afford to pay all of the costs related to attending college. For this reason, campus-based financial aid services and offices are expanding to meet the growing number of students seeking assistance. (For additional information on financial aid, see the listing in Appendix 18.2 at the end of this chapter.)

An institution's financial aid programs can also contribute to helping students succeed. One of the greatest concerns of college or precollege-age students and their parents or guardians is how to make college affordable. While the U.S. government may promote the monthly purchase of U.S. savings bonds to ensure available funds to pay for a child's postsecondary education, the reality is that very few parents have formulated and followed an 18-year savings plan of any kind. Through the use of state and regionally sponsored financial aid workshops, interested persons can begin to learn about the options available to them. Additionally, every college or university should provide information on the types of aid (scholarships, loans, and grants) available through their institution.

Deadlines often limit the accessibility of particular forms of aid, so the sponsorship of workshops or participation in parent orientation programs by the financial aid office can be helpful. For institutions with a regional draw, providing assistance in completing aid application forms through workshops or individual conferences will help alleviate parental concerns, even though the assisting office can make no guarantees of financial award.

Many aid offices have a low public relations quotient because of the information forms required, the processing time required once forms are completed, the ever-increasing volume of applicants each year, and the need to meet governmental regulations. The office's overall image may be improved by providing help sessions early in the process and making parents, guardians, spouses, or independent students aware of the processing timeline and pitfalls. Too often, the printed word is not as understandable as the spoken word. For this reason, promoting opportunities for interface helps all parties concerned.

As a recruiting tool, financial assistance can make a difference in whether or not a student enrolls at a particular school. The larger the aid package and the smaller the loan factor, the greater the appeal of an institution. How the aid is packaged can also make a difference. It is important that potential recipients understand the ramifications of all forms of aid and what, if any, repayment factors may be involved. Often aid can be tied to academic standing, a particular major, or student classification. Students and their families, therefore, need to have a clear understanding of all requirements.

Just as financial aid may have been the reason for a student to attend a particular school, the withdrawal of that aid may cause the student to leave. The availability of counselors knowledgeable about a school's financial aid policies is important to help identify financial options and thereby assist the student to remain in school or return.

ACADEMIC ADVISING

Advising is multifaceted in today's academic environment. Advising not only encompasses the traditional academic role of guidance toward degree completion, but focuses on the whole student—his or her career aspirations and physical, and mental well-being. Advisors need not be expected to provide counsel in all areas, but they should know the availability of services and the process for referral. They should also employ a follow-up process to encourage student interaction and to show their concern. Such interest may play an important part in the academic success and retention of the student.

Campus academic advising models have evolved with the change in student demographics. Factors such as location and institutional mission may impact the extent of required advising. The reduction in the number of traditional students has caused institutions to reassess the differences between the needs of this group and adult learners. Many institutions have developed advising centers that are housed within academic divisions to ensure quality guidance. Some institutions have centralized freshman or entry advising within a junior division or university college for much the same reason. The success of these programs is determined by the accessibility of advisors, institutionally supported and funded training for advisors, and mandated, ongoing support for personnel associated with the programs.

Too often, academic advising has been directly tied to the registration process and becomes a scheduling activity rather than a discussion of goals, progress, problems, and assessment. Many institutions have moved away from mandatory advising under the assumption that advising should be an ongoing institutional activity that can occur in formal or informal settings. At-risk students who enter with below-average qualifications, who encounter academic difficulty, who are on academic probation, or who are returning to school after a period of academic suspension or extended absence need special services. Extra attention also should be given to all first-time entering students, regardless of whether they are freshmen or transfer students, and also to those who change majors, to ensure they have some form of guidance. All advising sessions need not be one-on-one encounters. Small group sessions, led by professional or peer counselors, can be very effective, particularly for delivering general information and encouraging academic exploration and career planning. Regardless of the method chosen for information sharing, those providing the guidance should be versed in identifying students with problems who require referral to professionals.

Computer-assisted advising can work effectively for the student who is well on the way toward degree completion (Tanner 1985). Using computer-maintained academic records, the university can provide a checklist of completed requirements coupled with a list of those still needed. Institutions with computer programs projecting course offerings over an extended period of time (including prerequisites and corequisites), and institutional/program requirements can also provide an on-track student with information concerning when courses should be taken. A computer-based system can be more accurate than a manual system, but one key to success is the accessibility of the information. Terminals located throughout the campus and in university housing facilities or ports available for modem connectivity can serve as points of query. Providing an advising sheet does not ensure that the student will follow the guidelines provided; therefore, students should be informed that they assume personal responsibility for meeting degree requirements when they choose self advising. Computer-generated advising sheets or degree audits are not necessarily intended for student use only. They can also be used effectively by faculty or other advisors. These documents can serve as points of discussion from which other areas of interest or concern can be identified.

Computer-generated, degree-audit evaluations, advising forms, and advising centers do not replace one-on-one advising sessions (Ray, Moore, and Oliver 1991). They release faculty from working with first- and second-year students on general issues, thus freeing them to work with individual student needs. These advising aids increase faculty accessibility on an ongoing basis, so that they are not just advising on class schedules during restricted designated times that simply meet the college or university's advising requirement but may not necessarily meet the students' needs. Too often, faculty are considered unapproachable and uninterested. It is incumbent on faculty to encourage student access by maintaining posted office hours; becoming involved in academic-related activities such as departmental clubs, field trips, or sponsorship; and participating in other school-related activities where students have opportunities to interact with them outside the formal classroom.

More students than an institution would like to admit enter a college or university with no specific career goals or intended majors. That is acceptable up to a point, for students should be encouraged to investigate a variety of educational avenues in developing goals. Often, however, faculty members cannot help a student explore career and educational options outside their areas of expertise. In such cases, career and counseling centers are the ideal offices to which to refer students for assistance.

CAREER AND COUNSELING SERVICES

Career centers and counseling services offer more than psychological evaluation and job placement. Both can help students identify career interests and explore possible employment opportunities without the student feeling faculty pressure to pursue options in the instructor's area of expertise. Planning for the future should include more than just knowing the degree requirements. Upon entering a college or university, students need to begin exploring academic and career options so that they can set both short- and long-range, postgraduation goals. Making the services known to both faculty and staff is imperative, since they are the source of referral. Students also are good referral agents. If these students have had success working with one or both of these services, they will share their experiences with other students.

Counseling services play an important role in retention as both a proactive and reactive aid to students. The inclusion of counselors in orientation, new student, residence hall, and special needs programming can help prevent problems that might lead to student failure. This is in addition to any preventive or personal development initiatives that counseling centers might offer under their own auspices. Counseling also assists with retention through intervention with students already having problems or even in crisis. Often a counselor can work with a troubled student to solve, or at least ameliorate, problems. A byproduct of this can be a student who is able to remain in school.

The key to success in either instance is an informed faculty and staff. They are the ones who need to include a comment concerning counseling services in their lectures and programs. Faculty are the ones who need to alert a counselor about a student in trouble, even to the point of walking with that student over to the counseling center (Allen and Trimble 1993). For more information, contact the American College Counselors Association through the American Counseling Association (see Appendix 18.2 at the end of this chapter).

Career centers also play a role throughout a student's college or university enrollment and help with the retention of those students.

- As freshmen, students should be exploring occupations to which specific majors might lead.

- Sophomores should be working toward narrowing down the number of occupational choices and exploring exactly what occupation is right for them. Career services professionals can help students with their decision-making process through workshops, self-help materials, computer-assisted guidance programs, and counseling sessions.

- During the junior year, students should be researching the occupation they have chosen to pursue upon graduation. Their investigation should include learning about the necessary job qualifications and potential employers, making networking contacts, and looking into ways to gain experience in their chosen field. Internships often will help students with on-the-job learning opportunities in their chosen profession.

- Seniors anxiously pursue the job search. Those students who have availed themselves of the services of a career center will have attended career preparation workshops. These workshops provide information on how to write a resume, how to dress for an interview, and how to participate fully in the interview process. The intent of the services of both career and counseling centers is to help students learn more about themselves and their goals, both key elements in student success and completion of their degrees. While the student is exploring occupational opportunities, other support offices can help with the general well-being of the student. Together, the support areas help build a well-rounded student, and ultimately, a well-rounded graduate.

OTHER SUPPORT SERVICES

Reference has already been made to the need to inform prospective and enrolled students and families of offices and services available for their use. These, like the career and counseling centers, are often the same areas with which advisors and faculty must be knowledgeable in order to make referrals. Whether they are used to assist a student encountering adjustment problems to college or help a student become more involved and well rounded, most of these support services are available on a college or university campus. Student services, student development, student activities, student affairs, health services, international student services, minority student services, wellness centers, intercollegiate, co-curricular, or intramural athletics, and student organizations (such as social and honorary fraternities, student government, departmental, and special interests clubs) all play an integral part in the growth of the student and, therefore, should be incorporated into the academic experience. (See the publications of the American Association of Collegiate Registrars and Admissions Officers.)

RECORDS

To provide the best possible information to a student—whether advisement is coming from a financial aid, career, or academic advisor—the ability to have access to records is imperative. Increasingly, persons with need-to-know access to specific data have the needed information available at their desks through terminals and personal computers. Records offices serve as an interface in the release of that data and help determine who has the right to know.

Technology has increased the efficiency of institutional records operations and the accessibility of the data within those records. The days of typed transfer credit evaluations, advanced placement and departmental credit awards, along with gummed grade labels affixed to hard copy records, are becoming remembrances for most records management offices. Automation using SPEEDE/ ExPRESS (Standardization of Postsecondary Education Electronic Data Exchange/Exchanging Permanent Records Electronically for Students and Schools) to receive and send academic records, transfer equivalency tables, and degree evaluation has ensured greater accuracy and timely advising for entering and continuing students.

The records office, while maintaining and ensuring accurate records, also performs related functions to better serve the student and the agencies that support his or her attendance. Personnel in the records office often have more contact with students on a continuing basis than other campus offices because of the variety of services provided. These functions may include, depending upon the charge of the particular office, any or all of the following: enrollment verification; veterans counseling and processing; transcripts; record maintenance; enrollment functions; maintenance of the master course, class schedule, and related files; graduation processing; and commencement.

While a list of available services provided by a records office may be included in an institution's schedule of classes, some institutions have developed campus directories or handbooks. These list available services with cross listings depending on the variety of the services; the appropriate telephone extension; location; office hours; processing time, if applicable; and any related costs. However the message of "where's what" is delivered, the important point is that the entire university community, including students, knows where to get needed service or information.

Access to information can also be provided through the use of electronic bulletin boards. Service requests can be initiated electronically, eliminating the need for students to come into a records office. The use of Automatic Teller Machine (ATM)–type machines along with terminal and telephone access to the computer for requesting grades, changing enrollment, ordering transcripts, and other such services normally provided by a records office has improved response and service. Even when costs are associated with the requests, these machines normally can handle debit or credit card functions.

REGISTRATION

Most records offices operate as a primary service office of the institution, and bear responsibility for registration and enrollment-related record keeping. As records storage, retrieval, and dissemination have evolved through the use of improved technology, so have registration processes. Historically, registration was something students had to endure, regardless of the multitude of steps or the time involved. As electronic capabilities changed and computers became smaller, faster, and easier to program, the process by which students registered followed a similar pattern. In the past 20 years, most institutions have moved from prepunched class cards to entry processes such as scan forms, terminals, bar codes, and telephones. The process has also moved from institution-controlled to student-controlled. Overall, the intent has been to simplify the process for the student. In many cases, the time allocated for registration has been extended from a day to several months because of direct access to the process.

Voice response systems and student-operated terminal access allow for increased availability since the student has input control. Most institutions using one of these forms extend access up to 24 hours a day, except when their computer centers need time for processing and system backup operations. Accessibility translates into sensitivity to student needs:

- availability when students want access;
- relative freedom in course selection;
- review of class schedules and grades;
- prerequisite and co-requisite checking by more sophisticated systems;
- verification of student class placement eligibility manually through class announcements, printed statements included on course syllabi, or advisor review; and
- periodically running a computer program that compares students' academic records with registrations and produces a list of students with insufficient preparation. Notifi-

cation of ineligible enrollment in a class can take the form of computer-generated mailings or personal telephone calls.

Regardless of the registration process used, students will ''shop'' courses, seeking preferred times and faculty. Some automated systems allow wait listing or provide either voice-activated or printed alternate times, days, and sections for filled courses. In their favor, the latter includes information on sections added after the printing of the schedule of classes. Added sections are a reflection of academic review to meet student demand. Academic units sensitive to this issue are constantly monitoring course enrollment during a registration period. Classes added after the schedule has gone to press will have a difficult time meeting enrollment minimums, unless special publicity is provided for the late additions or sections already listed are duplicated.

Key to the efficiency and effectiveness of a registration system is the clarity of instruction and the interaction with the advising system. Any process should be designed with a limited number of easy-to-follow steps. At the same time, the process should not reward or excuse students who have not adhered to university policies and procedures. However, when a flowchart of the registration system yields a tangle of boxes and lines that overlap and backtrack, the system needs reassessment. Using focus groups comprised of a cross-section of the student body to reevaluate the system is useful, as are meetings with peers in the profession to discuss new approaches and technologies.

A common question on campuses is the proper balance between required procedures and student convenience. A few major factors impacting on this student friendliness are providing timely service regardless of the office function; exhibiting a willingness to listen to students, and involve them in developing university projects and programs that may affect them; offering a smile and generally trying to be helpful; reflecting genuine concern for each student's needs; and eliminating bureaucracy whenever possible. Since records personnel represent a major point of contact between students and the institution, the school will also receive high marks for friendliness with students and a concerned and convenient records operation.

RETENTION

Retention—like recruitment—is a major focal point in universities today. The enrolled student is increasingly valuable as the pool of traditional-aged students declines. According to Frank Spicuzza, ''Retention is a by-product of student satisfaction'' (Spicuzza 1992). The student who cannot find him- or herself; who is not meeting personal and/or family expectations; who is not meeting faculty expectations; who lacks the financial means to remain in school; or who faces increasing family responsibilities may be among the first to drop out of school. Colleges and universities should provide programs and services to help those students avoid or overcome obstacles. Administrators and faculty must be willing to listen and advise the student and then make good referrals as necessary. Faculty must be aware of students who are frequently absent and must make an effort to contact them individually. Students with problems that may lead to absenteeism and poor academic performance will seldom come forward on their own accord. The zealous student who wants to know more should be encouraged and challenged to do more.

National research has shown that attrition is greatest between the freshman and sophomore years of college. Students who attend some form of orientation program have a greater retention rate than those who do not, regardless of whether or not the program is required. Institutions looking at ways to improve retention must make orientation a high campus priority along with a commitment to structured academic advising.

Intervention programs that focus on first-semester and first-year students increase the likelihood of retaining those students. Intervention can take several forms.

1. Credit courses can focus on skills that will assist learning and academic success, such as study skills, note taking, test taking, and test anxiety. Such classes also include mentoring opportunities initiated by faculty or staff, and interaction with peers in group activities. Most public institutions provide these courses only on a voluntary basis or as a requirement for at-risk students.

2. Faculty and administrators volunteer to adopt and mentor a number of students for a semester, thus communicating their genuine concern for individual students. Often, the key element in the success of these programs is that the advisor is not from the student's intended major or one of the student's current instructors. Faculty can maintain contact by telephoning students when they miss class, provide and keep flexible office hours and genuinely welcome the visit and express it both verbally and non-verbally, and encourage students to contact them when needed. Some institutions provide funds for faculty to entertain small groups of students. These techniques may need to be taught and refreshed regularly in faculty or staff development sessions.

3. Telemarketing, often considered a recruitment tool, also can be used for retention, particularly with the increasing numbers of adult, commuter, night, weekend, or part-time enrollees who do not have time for on-campus activities, counseling, and advising. Proactive, general follow-up by faculty, staff, orientation or peer counselors; contacts with students who frequently miss class; and advising can all be done by telephone, thus allowing the school to reach out to the student rather than wait for the student to initiate all contact. Unless the impetus to seek assistance is instilled from the onset, many students will drop or stop out because they do not know whom to contact, do not have the time, or are not assertive enough to impose on university personnel.

In 1991 the National Collegiate Athletic Association (NCAA) began requiring member institutions to report athlete graduation rates as compared to those of nonathletes. As a result of these annual studies, the U.S. Department of Education initially proposed legislation known as the Student Right-to-Know and

Campus Security Act (Public Law 101–542, signed into law on November 8, 1990, and, as amended by Public Law 102–26, the Higher Education Technical Amendments of 1991), requiring institutions to report retention and completion data. The American Association of Collegiate Registrars and Admissions Officers monitored the legislation, providing commentary in support of the diversity of their member institutions and student populations, and sought equitable definition and reporting methodology, given the nontraditional road so many students follow today. The final rule was released in the *Federal Register* (60, no. 231, December 1, 1995, with an effective date of July 1, 1996).

Retention is not just a student issue. Satisfaction and the drive for student success must consume the entire campus, from maintenance personnel through the faculty and staff ranks and up to the top administrators. Persons unhappy with their work environment will portray that feeling in their interaction with students. There must be an ongoing, campus-wide effort to promote a positive attitude which leads to high motivation. College is a growth experience, and institutions must provide the support to move students toward goal completion, satisfaction, and success.

SUMMARY

Students enter and leave the college environment as individuals. During the intervening time, they become part of the greater university community and participants in the educational growth cycle. As they work through the rigors of attaining a college education, many student support areas must work together to help them meet their individual goals and find success.

APPENDIX 17.1: ORIENTATION CHECKLIST

The following is a listing of possible topics that could be incorporated into an orientation program. Time and audience should be the primary consideration in determining specific content.

Topics	Potential Audiences				
	Entering Freshmen	Transfer	International	Parents	Graduate Students
The Campus					
Emergency Services					
Office Hours					
Physical Plant—Facilities					
Safety					
Tours					
University College/Junior Division					
University Organization (colleges, school, departments)					
Other:					
Academics					
Academic Advisors/Advising					
Academic Calendar					
Academic Status					
Class Attendance					
Class Schedule					
Class Times					

Topics	Potential Audiences				
	Entering Freshmen	Transfer	International	Parents	Graduate Students
Computers					
Course Numbering					
Degree Audit					
Departmental Credit					
Evaluation of Advanced Placement (AP) Credit					
Evaluation of Military Service Schools					
Evaluation of Transfer Credit					
Experiential Education					
Faculty Office Hours					
Final Examinations/Schedule					
General Education Requirements					
Grades					
Graduation Checkout					
Graduation, Requirements for					
Grievances/Appeals					
Internships/Co-op Programs					
Library					
Majors/Minors					
Placement Tests					

Topics	Potential Audiences				
	Entering Freshmen	Transfer	International	Parents	Graduate Students
Proficiency Tests					
Other:					
Records/Registration					
Deadlines/Academic Calendar					
Enrollment Verification					
Holds on Records					
Registration					
Resignation/Withdrawal Policy					
Schedule/Course Changes					
Transcripts					
Other:					
Fiscal Matters					
Campus					

Topics	Potential Audiences				
	Entering Freshmen	Transfer	International	Parents	Graduate Students
Campus Employment Debit Accounts					
Debit Accounts					
Deferred Payments					
Financial Aid					
Grants					
Loans					
Scholarships					
Work Study Program					
Parking Policy					
Tuition/Fees					
Tutoring/Academic Assistance					
Use of Credit Cards					
Other:					
Personal Development					
Athletics					
Campus Clubs					

Topics	Potential Audiences				
	Entering Freshmen	Transfer	International	Parents	Graduate Students
Concerts, Lectures					
Drugs, Alcohol, Firearms					
Greek Life					
Intramurals					
Performing Arts					
Recreation Facilities					
Student Activities					
Student Organizations					
Other:					
Services					
Bookstore					
Campus Employment					
Career/Placement					
Counseling					
Daycare					
External Employment Listings					

	Potential Audiences				
Topics	**Entering Freshmen**	**Transfer**	**International**	**Parents**	**Graduate Students**
Food					
Health					
Health Insurance					
Housing					
I.D. Cards					
Immunization					
Residence Life					
Security					
Student Affairs					
Student Handbook					
Support Groups					
Testing					
Vending					
Volunteer Services					
Wellness Center					
Other:					

	Potential Audiences				
Topics	Entering Freshmen	Transfer	International	Parents	Graduate Students
Publications					
Catalog					
Class Schedule					
Student Handbook					
Student Newspaper					
Other:					
Community					
Banks					
Churches					
Museums					
Parks					
Recreational Opportunities					
Other:					

APPENDIX 17.2: PROFESSIONAL ASSOCIATION SUPPORT

American Association of Collegiate Registrars and Admissions Officers
One Dupont Circle, Suite 330
Washington, DC 20036–1171

American College Counselors Association
c/o American Counseling Association
5999 Stevens Avenue
Alexandria, VA 22305–3300

National Academic Advising Association
Kansas State University
2323 Anderson Avenue, Suite 225
Manhattan, KS 66502
(*NACADA Journal* is published by NAAA)

National Association of Colleges and Employers/NACE
College Placement Council
62 Highland Avenue
Bethlehem, PA 18017–9085

National Association of Student Financial Aid Advisors/NASFAA
1920 L Street NW, Suite 200
Washington, DC 20036–5020

National Orientation Directors Association
University of Tennessee–Knoxville
42 Student Services Building
Knoxville, TN 37996

REFERENCES

Allen, Deborah R., and Ralph W. Trimble. 1993. Identifying and referring troubled students: A primer for academic advisors. *NACADA Journal* 13 (Fall): 34–41.

Beal, Philip E., and Lee Noel. 1980. *What works in student retention: The report of a joint project of the American College Testing Program and the National Center for Higher Education Management Systems.* The American College Testing Program and the National Center for Higher Education Management Systems.

Dannells, Michael. 1993. Theoretical perspectives on orientation. Designing successful transitions: A guide for orienting students to college. Paper delivered at the AACRAO Annual Meeting, April, Orlando, Florida.

Delworth, Ursula, Gary R. Hanson, et al. 1989. *Student services: A handbook for the profession.* San Francisco: Jossey-Bass.

Fidler, Paul P. 1991. Relationship of freshman orientation seminars to sophomore return rates. *Journal of the Freshman Year Experience* 3(1): 7–38.

Gordon, Virginia N., and George E. Steele. 1992. Advising major-changers: Students in transition. *NACADA Journal* 12 (Spring): 22–27.

Jacoby, Barbara. 1989. *The student as commuter: Developing a comprehensive institu-*

tional response. ASHE-ERIC Higher Education Report No. 7. Washington, DC: George Washington University, School of Education and Human Development.

Kinloch, Graham C., Geraldine A. Frost, and Charles MacKay. 1993. Academic dismissal, readmission conditions and retention: Study of social science majors. *NACADA Journal* 13 (Spring): 18–22.

Kramer, Gary L. 1992. Using student focus groups to evaluate academic support services. *NACADA Journal* 12 (Fall): 38–41.

Miles, Lorna. 1988. Learn from experience. *Currents* (September): 27–30.

Noel, Lee, Randi Levitz, Diana Saluri, et al. 1985. *Increasing student retention*. San Francisco: Jossey-Bass.

Plante, Kathleen, Becky F. Smith, and Richard Bracklin. 1993. Components of a comprehensive orientation program. Designing successful transitions: A guide for orienting students to college. Paper delivered at the AACRAO Annual Meeting, April, Orlando, Florida.

Ray, Howard N., W. Kent Moore, and John E. Oliver. 1991. Evaluation of a computer-assisted advising system. *NACADA Journal* 11 (Fall): 21–27.

Spicuzza, Frank J. 1992. A customer service approach to advising: Theory and application. *NACADA Journal* 12 (Fall): 49–58.

Strumpf, Gerry, and Greg Sharer. 1993. Trends and issues in orientation programs. Designing successful transitions: A guide for orienting students to college. Paper delivered at the AACRAO Annual Meeting, April, Orlando, Florida.

Tanner, Jeffrey M. 1985. Paper delivered at the AACRAO Annual Meeting, April, Cincinnati, Ohio.

Upcraft, M. Lee, Richard H. Mullendore, Betsy O. Barefoot, and Dorothy S. Fidler (eds.). 1993. *Designing successful transitions: A guide for orienting students to college*. Columbia: University of South Carolina.

18

Admissions Partners off Campus

Tim Washburn

Effective external relations are important for every successful university or college. One only has to look at the increased emphasis placed on public relations within businesses, social agencies, and educational institutions to understand that public perception is a powerful influence for success or failure.

Most postsecondary educational institutions have a university relations office specifically charged with managing the university's public image. Increasingly, however, institutions are becoming aware that admissions and school and college relations offices play a significant role in external relations. These related offices are not in the business of managing crises or putting a positive spin on soaring college grade point averages, but instead are responsible for educating the public about academic and student life on their campuses and for representing the institution to other sectors of the educational community. Successful admissions officers understand the importance of external relations and ensure that adequate attention is directed toward this activity.

The primary responsibility of an admissions office is the admission of new, transfer, and returning students. To some degree every aspect of the admissions process affects external relations. An inaccurate and unresponsive application processing system negatively affects both enrollment yields and the public's opinion of the entire institution. Similarly, a poorly prepared or disheveled admissions counselor negatively affects the number and quality of applicants and represents the entire institution as disorganized and lacking standards. As the eye is the window to the soul, the admissions office is the window to the collegiate institution.

Most admissions activities influence external relations in one way or another. This section will focus on activities that (1) provide the general public, parents, alumni, and local and state governmental agencies and legislators with a better and more complete understanding of the institution's educational and student life programs; (2) improve articulation between educational sectors; and (3) promote improved intercollegiate institutional understanding.

External relations activities may indirectly influence student recruiting, but recruiting is not the primary objective. It is sometimes initially difficult to see how certain activities will benefit either the admissions office or the college, but, as in personal life, selfless contribution is never without its reward.

COMMUNICATIONS

Clear and consistent communication is a necessary element in any successful external relations program. As the complexity of admissions requirements increases, so does the need for publications designed to meet the needs of different audiences. Time is a scarce resource, and publications should focus on information that will be relevant and interesting to the reader. Bulk is no substitute for content.

For an admissions office the primary publications directed to external constituents will normally take the form of a newsletter published at regular intervals throughout the year and distributed to high schools and community colleges in primary service areas. In some cases, a single publication may not meet an institution's information needs, and separate newsletters—one designed to meet high school informational needs and one for community colleges—may be more effective. Information in newsletters typically includes:

- A profile of the most recent entering class (number of students, gender and ethnic distribution, grade point averages, rank-in-class, test score ranges, state and country distribution, and most popular majors) and any information that will give the public a picture of the institution.

- Names of incoming students receiving scholarships and their high schools or community colleges in order to recognize outstanding students and to acknowledge their schools for a job well done.

- Descriptions of new academic programs or majors, new general education requirements, grading issues, reports on foreign study programs, domestic exchange programs, financial aid availability, public safety issues, retention, and graduation rate information.

- Information about distinguished faculty, their academic awards, community service activities, and special interests.

- Stories and personal quotes from undergraduates describing their experiences at the university or college.

- A directory of campus contacts and admissions office staff likely to be of assistance.

- Explanations of admission or transfer credit policies such as the necessity for college preparatory core courses, English as a Second Language courses for immigrants, and the transferability of vocational or technical courses when included in Associate of Arts degrees.

Special newsletters to parents of undergraduates can be particularly useful in describing the undergraduate experience. A newsletter to parents early in the fall describing campus happenings can allay parents' apprehensions about their children leaving home for the first time and provide parents with inside information to discuss with their children when the family gathers for the holidays. A spring newsletter can provide information about new academic programs, foreign study opportunities, the hazards of working while attending school, and the need for parents to remain financially helpful to students throughout their undergraduate years.

The Internet is fast becoming available as a communication link between schools and colleges. Institutions should consider developing electronic mailing lists to deliver information quickly. Significant publication cost savings can result from electronic mail use as well as more frequent and timely communications. Whatever communication medium is utilized, mailing lists should always direct information to the primary reader. Newsletters sent to a school principal will frequently not find their way to the college guidance office. Important information for the guidance counselor should be sent to the guidance office.

Some universities find it helpful to contact parents of freshmen by telephone early in the first semester to determine how things are going. The call helps identify institutional shortcomings and lets parents know the institution cares about their children. Admissions offices can help make the calls if time permits, or can call parents back if admissions problems are identified by the caller.

FORMAL ORGANIZATIONAL STRUCTURES TO FACILITATE COMMUNICATION

National Organizations

Although written and telephonic communication are the most efficient ways to communicate, it is useful to meet periodically in person to discuss items of mutual interest. An admissions officer should, when possible, participate in the annual meetings of the American Association of Collegiate Registrars and Admissions Officers, the National Association for College Admission Counseling, The College Board, and NAFSA: Association of International Educators. Each of these organizations also has state or regional meetings that provide opportunities for participation. While these organizations are designed primarily for professional development, they also allow participants to showcase their institutions' accomplishments in a useful way to influence external relations.

A Model State Organization. Since 1957 the Washington Council for High School and College Relations (WCHSCR) has successfully facilitated communication between the various educational sectors. Washington is one of a number of states with voluntary nonprofit organizations, such as WCHSCR, whose members represent public and private four-year colleges, community colleges, the state Higher Education Coordinating Board, the State Board for Community and

Technical Colleges, the Office of the Superintendent of Public Instruction, the Washington State High School Senior Principals' Association, the Washington State Junior High/Middle School Principals' Association, the Washington State Association for Counseling and Development, and the Washington State Association of Financial Aid Officers.

Governance and administration of the council is provided by an elected board of directors with representatives from each of the member sectors. Commissions manage activities associated with college conferences, publications, admissions, intercollege relations, and minority affairs.

- The Commission on College Conferences is responsible for coordinating statewide tours that provide admissions information to 90 percent of the state's high schools, and an annual tour that offers admissions and academic planning information to each of the state's 27 community colleges.

- The Commission on Publications coordinates publication of the *Four-Year Book*, a guide for high school counselors and students which includes academic planning and admission information for each of the state's public and private colleges and universities; a quarterly *Bulletin*, which is distributed to secondary and postsecondary audiences; and an annual *Education Directory*, which includes names and telephone numbers of individuals important to admissions, guidance, and counseling at each high school and college in the state.

- The Commission on Admissions coordinates publication and distribution of a common application form that can be used to apply to any of the state's public and private colleges. It sponsors and coordinates meetings for high school guidance counselors and admissions personnel, and it reviews issues affecting admission to the state's postsecondary education institutions.

- The Intercollege Relations Commission (ICRC) deals with transfer articulation issues between two- and four-year state institutions, including the specification of minimum general education requirements for community college transfer degrees. ICRC has adopted guidelines affecting transfer credit policies that have subsequently been adopted by the Higher Education Coordinating Board as state policy. ICRC also sponsors workshops for two- and four-year college administrators to discuss transfer articulation issues. Students or colleges may request that the Commission review an institution's transfer credit acceptance policy or the content of a transfer degree if they feel the need for arbitration. Member colleges may request a visit from the Commission's transfer team to review their office policies and procedures and to make suggestions for improved transfer services.

- The Commission on Minority Affairs works to increase the enrollment of underrepresented student populations by arranging special recruiting tours, early outreach programs, and the publication of special recruiting publications. This voluntary council has been responsible for creating and sustaining goodwill between educational sectors and has developed policies that have benefited students for four decades. Time invested in council activities contributes to all educational constituencies and represents a highly effective model for a statewide external relations program.

Curriculum Articulation

During the nineteenth century, transportation and commerce relied on major rivers for the movement of goods and services. Businesses located on the edge of the river in the middle of a trade route were in a better position to know what went on upstream and downstream than those at either end. Similarly, admissions officers live on the edge of a river, halfway between high school and college. Admissions personnel, therefore, have the advantage of knowing more about high schools than other college administrators and more about college than most high school personnel. This knowledge makes the admissions officer one of the most critical links connecting secondary and postsecondary education. High schools need to know how their students perform in college, and colleges need to understand the preparation students have received in high school if college courses are to meet student needs without repetition.

Articulation between high schools and colleges has always been an important responsibility of admissions officers, but as school restructuring and school reform initiatives are explored, it is even more critical for admissions professionals to become involved in discussions that will shape the preparation of future college students. Across the nation, school districts are struggling to find ways to make K-12 education more effective. Traditional curricula are being reviewed and repackaged in an attempt to improve student retention, to improve learning, and to make teaching and learning more relevant to business and commerce in the twenty-first century. Admission core courses defined in terms of Carnegie units, the traditional measure of college preparation, are likely to disappear as schools look toward integrated curricula, outcomes-based assessment, and portfolios of representative student work to improve learning and describe student accomplishment. How these changes will affect the preparation of college-bound students is uncertain, but college admissions officers should become involved in these discussions if they are to be knowledgeable about emerging changes and if they hope to design fair and equitable admission strategies in response to these educational innovations. Universities and colleges not participating in the restructuring discussion will be perceived as disinterested and will lose the opportunity for shared leadership.

Admissions officers should identify local leaders in the educational arena, determine which schools are considering restructuring and which state commissions or councils are working on curriculum affairs. They should follow these groups' discussions and attend their meetings. Similarly, involvement in community college articulation issues is of extreme importance, and admissions officers must find effective ways to interact and communicate with community college representatives.

High school counselor advisory boards offer another strategy for linking a college or university to its external constituents. An admissions officer interested in appointing an advisory board should first determine which high schools to invite—those that send them the most or the best students or those that are geographically representative or, perhaps, underrepresented. After the schools have been selected, the admissions officer should contact the principals and invite them to name a counselor for membership on the board who can provide direction to the admissions office and to the college. Most high school counselors want to be better informed about college activities and will gladly serve on an advisory board.

State Legislation

As educational leaders, admissions officers should be aware of issues under consideration by their state legislatures and educational boards and commissions. Proactive admissions officers know, and are known by, chairs of state legislative education committees and attend hearings on issues affecting and influencing postsecondary education in their state. State legislatures are increasingly interested in access, tuition rates, financial aid, retention, graduation rates, assessment, and secondary school preparation issues. Admissions officers are in a position to have detailed knowledge about these and other educational issues and should be involved to ensure institutional representation. In all such cases it is critically important that involved admissions officers communicate frequently with colleagues within their institution to ensure complete understanding of the issues within the college or university and gain institutional approval of policies to be recommended.

Alumni Programs

Many colleges operate successful alumni admission recruitment programs. Such programs have significant overhead costs and, if improperly supported, can lead to confusion and dissatisfaction among both alumni and applicants. Colleges choosing not to develop alumni recruiting programs may still use their alumni officers and boards to communicate information about admissions and undergraduate education programs to other alumni and the broader community. Admissions criteria are continually changing, and parents of college-age children are frequently misinformed about admissions information, relying instead on past personal experiences for guidance. Admissions officers can overcome many of these misunderstandings by speaking at regional alumni meetings and periodically attending alumni board meetings. They can also use alumni newsletters to communicate admissions information to parents and other public constituents. It is especially important to communicate with alumni when admission selection criteria are modified; alumni can be advocates for change if they are kept fully informed.

Visitation Programs for Parents and the Community

Many universities and colleges offer opportunities for prospective students and the community to visit their campuses during open houses designed to showcase teaching, research, and residential life programs. These events may focus on a particular academic department or college through programs such as a computer or science fair, or they may involve the entire campus. Freshman convocations and commencement exercises provide traditional opportunities for the university or college to extend itself to its public.

Special weekends, designed to bring parents to the campus, provide an opportunity for them to share in the college experience and meet faculty and administrators. Special opportunities are typically arranged for the president, academic vice president, and dean of students to greet parents, to express their interest in undergraduate education, and to explain how the institution contributes to the educational development of the student.

Washington State University, located in a rural part of the state, has long featured exemplary Mom's and Dad's Day programs. A typical Dad's Day might begin Friday evening with a dinner featuring wine tasting, a vocal extravaganza, and a presentation by a choir singing historical fight songs. Saturday activities might include breakfast at the student union or athletic events such as a football game, soccer, or volley ball. Saturday night might offer a food fest of Washington cuisine and entertainment by a comedian. A typical Mom's Day might include a Friday night dinner with songs by a choir, and on Saturday an on-campus rodeo, a craft fair in the coliseum, and a mother and daughter look-alike contest, followed by a Sunday brunch.

All of these events are designed to extend the university beyond its geographic boundaries and to bring the campus closer to extended constituency. A little brainstorming among colleagues is all that is required to design a successful campus visitation program.

Part VI

Perspectives on the Twenty-First Century

Part VI looks at the challenges to education from the perspective of the enrollment manager.

19

Students of the Future

Greta S. Mack

ESCALATING DIVERSITY

During the past two decades, colleges and universities in the United States witnessed an increasing diversity of college applicants. The applicant pool changed from what might be described as a batch of plain vanilla cookies to something more resembling a trail mix. More change is inevitable. By the year 2020, the U.S. Bureau of the Census projects that the nation's population will be older and will include fewer persons of European heritage. Future college students will represent diverse ethnic and cultural groups with diverse backgrounds, values, and precollegiate educational experiences. Paralleling population changes, an energized school reform movement is challenging traditional learning methods and proposing alternate methods of reporting the results of various learning experiences. Despite distinct institutional missions that temper the ability to mirror precisely all the evolving changes, U.S. colleges and universities are intent on incorporating America's increasingly diverse population into the halls of ivy.

POPULATION CHANGES

The population of the United States is projected to increase from 249 million in 1990 to 326 million by the year 2020. Most of the population growth will stem from large numbers of immigrants expected to enter the United States in the remaining years of the twentieth century. The representation of various ethnic groups will shift considerably, with the white population expected to shrink from 83 percent in 1993 to 78 percent in 2020. Slow population growth is anticipated for African-Americans (from 12 to 14 percent). In contrast, Hispanics will become the nation's largest minority, up from 10 to 16 percent of the population by 2020. The fastest growing group, Asians and Pacific Islanders, will more than double their representation, increasing from 3 to 7 percent (Campbell 1994).

Over the long term, the proportion of persons under age 20 will decline. However, the Western Interstate Commission on Higher Education (WICHE) estimates that the number of high school graduates will increase from 2.5 million in 1993 to 3.3 million in 2008. That encouraging prediction is based on anticipated improvements in high school retention rates. Postsecondary institutions can expect larger pools of potential applicants. To prepare for the larger pool of high school graduates expected to stem from the nation's changing demographics, a reevaluation of existing college outreach and admission policies is essential to ensure the representation of all ethnic and cultural groups.

African-Americans

The desegregation movement of the 1960s resulted in a national realization that major sectors of society were disenfranchised and that special efforts were needed to remedy inequities. Upward Bound; Step-to-College; the Mathematics, Engineering, Science Achievement (MESA); and similar programs were initiated to recruit, support, and provide remediation for promising students with poor preparation. Reaching out to students in elementary through high school, affirmative action programs successfully helped minority students prepare for postsecondary study. High school dropout rates decreased, and African-American enrollments in colleges and universities tripled between 1966 and 1978. Since then, the representation of African-Americans has remained fairly stagnant while other minority group representation has continued to grow (Snyder and Hoffman 1994).

Early affirmative action efforts were rooted in an understanding that minority access to higher education is directly related to the quality of education in grades K–12. Little has changed. The nation's rural areas and inner cities, which are generally recognized as having poor educational environments, continue to be home to most African-American families. To these economically and educationally disadvantaged families, a college education often is not considered feasible. Early outreach strategies are absolutely essential to nurture academic achievement and to counter the low self-esteem that festers in low socioeconomic environments.

Designed to increase African-American enrollment in Georgia's institutions of higher education, Kennesaw State College (Marietta, Georgia) offers a Career/ Education Opportunities for Black Youth program, which targets first-generation high school juniors and seniors. The two-week workshop motivates students for success, provides an opportunity to run mock businesses, arranges visits with successful black professionals and entrepreneurs, and presents an overview of higher education opportunities. Kennesaw's program, as with other effective programs reaching out to disadvantaged students, emphasizes the importance of each individual, the ability of each to succeed, and the availability of resources to help.

Hispanics

In 1993, three-fourths of the nation's Hispanics lived in five states: California, Texas, New York, Florida, and Illinois (Campbell 1994). California, with the largest Hispanic population, provides a preview of the future. Immerwahr and Farkas (1993) conducted a series of focus groups and public opinion surveys to determine the attitudes of Californians toward higher education. Although the results parallel national findings, the priorities of California's Hispanic population differed from the general population in several important areas. A full 73 percent of California Hispanics, compared to 43 percent of the non-Hispanic population, singled out "giving minorities such as Blacks and Hispanics opportunities to succeed" as the most important goal of a college education.

Opinions also diverged about college access, with 68 percent of Hispanics, compared to 48 percent of the non-Hispanic population, feeling that many qualified people do not have the opportunity to attend college. With Spanish as the language of the home and the community among Hispanics, English fluency is sometimes inhibited and results in required enrollment in intensive English programs. When enrollment in college preparatory courses is delayed because of limited English proficiency, the dream of a college education fades. Hispanics also perceived government grants and loans to be the most appropriate sources of support for needy students.

Such attitudes toward education can become embedded and reinforced in communities where Hispanic families cluster and the Hispanic culture dominates. Recognizing that educational expectations are shaped by both individual and community attitudes, postsecondary institutions have developed programs responsive to the expressed concerns of prospective Hispanic students. Early outreach materials emphasize institutional commitment to diversity, educational opportunities that provide solid foundations for future employment, financial aid resources that ensure access to postsecondary study, and campus support services to help students achieve their educational goals. Chapter 15 describes efforts of the University of Texas at El Paso to nurture first-generation Hispanic students by sponsoring a college awareness program that begins in the first grade. Yearly activities, appropriate to the educational level, familiarize students and their parents with the university, build and reinforce positive self-images, develop community skills, and encourage university attendance.

Asian–Pacific Islanders

Asian–Pacific Islanders are the fastest growing sector of the U.S. population. They have become a significant presence on college campuses, almost doubling in number, from 351,000 in 1982 to 635,000 in 1991 (Eck 1993). In the 1980s, the popular press touted the extraordinary educational and economic accomplishments of Asian–Pacific Islanders, but the model minority image did not take into consideration the vast socioeconomic variations within the group. According to the 1990 census, 35 percent of Vietnamese, 47 percent of Cambodian, and 67 percent of Laotian families live below the poverty line, compared to the national population average of 10 percent (Campbell 1994).

In the 1990s, Asian–Pacific Islanders rallied against what they perceived to be neglect and mistreatment by higher education. Charges were leveled at many colleges and universities (the Los Angeles and Berkeley campuses of the University of California, among them) that the admission of Asian–Pacific Americans was being limited (Nakanishi 1989). Two complaints were voiced. First, by not differentiating among the various subgroups within the population of Asian–Pacific Islanders, colleges were arbitrarily limiting access to large numbers of prospective students who do not fit the stereotypical perception of having achieved phenomenal academic success. Second, Asian–Pacific Islanders in needy subgroups often were excluded from affirmative action opportunities available to other minority groups. Also, once admitted, many Asian–Pacific Islander students were in the unenviable position of having to live up to expectations based on the accomplishments of a few.

While the concerns raised by Asian–Pacific Islanders were being addressed, there arose a broader national debate over the use of nonacademic criteria in the admission process. The Board of Regents of the University of California issued new admissions guidelines in December 1995, which ended the explicit use of race, religion, sex, color, ethnicity, and national origin as criteria for admission (University of California Board of Regents 1995). The new admissions guidelines constituted an important step toward resolving Asian–Pacific Islander issues; still, the challenge remains to achieve diversity and equity on campus.

Few university programs specifically serve Asian–Pacific Islander students. Other than providing for campus-based affinity groups and campus-sponsored cultural events, categorical programs—similar to those established in earlier years to serve black and Hispanic students—have not been developed to serve Asian–Pacific Island students. Establishing mobile outreach efforts to Asian–Pacific Island communities can underscore an institution's commitment to diversity and open communication channels to prospective students and their parents. Community temples and churches, major indoor market malls, and recreational facilities may be more appropriate sites than the campus for introducing Asian–Pacific Islanders to higher education opportunities. Presentations deftly combining campus highlights with financial aid information can target the specific concerns of an Asian–Pacific Island subgroup.

Just as there are differences among Asian–Pacific Island subgroups, there are differences among the subgroups of other ethnic and cultural categories. A continuing reevaluation of university services is required to ensure responsiveness both to existing and to newly spotlighted minority groups. Most students approach the college years with an awareness of group identity. Students face conflicting pressures to adopt either more ethnic or less ethnic identities and behaviors. As they adjust to the college environment and search for identity, students want to be included in the greater campus community, yet want reassurance that they have the support of other students and faculty members like themselves. (See also Chapter 15.) Colleges have responded to these needs by planning special orientation sessions for minority students, by sponsoring campus-based identity groups, by offering ethnic studies, and by adding to the diversity of the college faculty. Although care must be taken to avoid generalizations, attitudes fostered by identity groups must be taken into consideration if colleges are to attract and adequately serve students from underrepresented groups.

Older Americans

By the year 2000, Americans over the age of 30 will make up close to 60 percent of the population (Day 1993). Current college outreach efforts tend to be predicated on the assumption that high school and community college students must be courted, while out-of-school, older, part-time students seek out educational opportunities. Because older, part-time students constitute an increasingly significant pool of potential students, at least as much attention should be given to developing outreach materials appropriate to older, part-time students as has been invested in preparing attractive materials for high school students. Targeted outreach strategies should reach out to these prospective students in their own environment. Work sites, restaurants, malls, community organizations, convention centers, and other areas frequented by adults can serve as staging areas for outreach efforts. To be conveniently accessible for adults, information sessions and other activities should be scheduled during evening, lunchtime, or weekend periods rather than during normal working hours.

Adult students often do not meet admissions requirements that are based largely on college preparatory courses completed in high school. They are usually admitted to college under vaguely defined admissions categories that recognize adult experiences but do not measure them. Although mechanisms to adequately assess the richer, more diverse experiences of adults are not well defined, adults can demonstrate previous learning through campus challenge examinations and standardized achievement tests such as the College Level Examination Program (CLEP). Awarding credit for military and industry training and courses, based on American Council on Education (ACE) guidelines, further recognizes broad life experiences that may not be adequately demonstrated through testing or course completion.

As the average age of the American workforce climbs toward 40, postsecondary institutions are actively reaching out to prospective adult students whose ranks include women wishing to reenter the workforce, professionals requiring in-service training, college dropouts who only recently have realized the value of a college degree, underemployed workers needing to upgrade skills, unemployed persons who want to acquire salable skills, and well-educated employees from downsized industries who need new skills in order to find positions in other industries.

WORKPLACE 2000

Astin's survey (1994) of the aspirations, activities, and attitudes of fall 1993 first-time freshmen demonstrated that today's students view the college experience in very pragmatic terms. The opportunity to gain a general education and appreciation of ideas (65 percent) took second place to being able to get a better job (82 percent). This student priority is warranted in view of the skill levels projected to be essential in the future workplace. Between now and the year 2000, the American economy is expected to grow, but the number of jobs available in manufacturing industries will decline. High-paying production jobs requiring unskilled labor to perform simple repetitive tasks are being decimated. Growth will occur in the professional, technical, sales, and service industries, all of which are increasingly dependent on high technology.

Americans expect to work at six or seven different jobs during their lifetimes. This number undoubtedly will increase as technological advancements continue to shape the world of work. Many people are in jobs that will soon be modified or eliminated. Whether precipitated by individuals choosing to seek new employment or by technological changes realigning employment patterns, retraining the workforce has become a significant responsibility of postsecondary institutions. By working together, representatives of industry and education can avoid unnecessary job displacements by providing employee retraining prior to anticipated changes in the workplace. Colleges and universities must respond to the need for retraining, not by requiring all persons to complete baccalaureate degrees, but by offering compact programs designed to give individuals needed marketable skills. Without losing sight of the importance of a general education, the three Rs must be reemphasized. The reorganized marketplace requires greater skills in reading, mathematics, and communication.

Students need help in understanding how a college degree prepares them for jobs to which they aspire. Although the match between degree earned and occupation is not precise, data from the U.S. Bureau of the Census's January 1991 current population survey reaffirm popular wisdom that educational attainment is directly related to earnings (Eck 1993). Unfortunately, education by itself does not guarantee high earnings. There are more college graduates than can be placed in appropriate jobs, and tales of college graduates working in fast-food establishments are all too common. American education strategies must ensure that students are prepared to meet the more sophisticated skill levels required to qualify for the jobs of tomorrow. Without such intervention, the result will be more joblessness among the economically and educationally disadvantaged (Johnston and Packer 1987).

PREPARATION FOR COLLEGE

Educators have been highly critical of high school graduates who are not prepared for rigorous collegiate study and require compensatory coursework. Astin's (1994) survey of fall 1993 freshman students reinforces that concern. Entering freshman students are aware of shortfalls in their secondary preparation; approximately 12 percent identify a need for additional help in science, and 29 percent need remedial work in mathematics.

Questions about the adequacy of the American educational experience raised by the publication *A Nation at Risk* (Harvey 1984) provided momentum to the movement to raise high school graduation requirements. Believing that higher college admission standards would help secondary schools strengthen the curriculum, colleges and universities have systematically increased admissions requirements.

Traditional College Preparation

Twenty-seven states have formal statewide requirements for admission to all public postsecondary institutions (Flanagan 1992). Since 1986, 20 of the 27 states have modified standards. Some states implemented minimum admission requirements for the first time. Other states increased existing minimums. College preparatory course requirements across the nation, as might be expected, are similar. A typical high school preparatory course pattern includes four years of English and three years each of mathematics, science, and social science. Although this may be perceived as a measure of mandated equivalence of exposure to learning, it does not ensure that students completing the prescribed curriculum will be similarly prepared for college-level study.

In 1989, the Center for Policy Research in Education evaluated the effects of increased high school graduation requirements. Interviews with individuals closely involved in educational policy making and in the educational process revealed that affluent school districts and college-bound students were not significantly affected by increasing the number of courses required for high school graduation. College-bound students already were taking more college preparatory courses than the required minimum. The courses that had been added to the curriculum tended to be at the remedial, basic, and general levels and geared to average and low-achieving students. The short-term impact on high school education was considered minimal, but the expectation was that eventually, higher standards for all students would result in a gradual upgrading of courses and in increased achievement levels for all students (Clune, White, and Patterson 1989).

Enrichment Opportunities

Concurrent Enrollment. At least 22 states have attempted to enrich the high school educational experience by allowing high school students to enroll in vocational and academic courses offered by colleges and universities. Minnesota's concurrent enrollment program allows all public high school juniors and seniors to enroll in nonsectarian courses at any of Minnesota's public or private postsecondary institutions, subject to their meeting admission requirements. There is no cost if the course is taken only for high school credit, but the student must pay tuition if baccalaureate credit is sought. Under Florida's early admission program, high school seniors may enroll full-time in postsecondary institutions without paying fees. Enrollment in college preparatory courses offered by postsecondary institutions is not permitted because the intent of the program is to supplement, and not to supplant, high school offerings. In New Jersey, freshman-level college credit courses are offered in the high school setting with qualified high school faculty as teachers (CPEC 1992).

Utah has taken a more comprehensive view by calling for high school curriculum modifications enabling students to graduate at the conclusion of grade 11 or to enroll concurrently in college credit courses in grades 11 and 12. Courses are available at state higher education institutions and at high schools, where they may be taught by college, university, or high school faculty. Utah's public postsecondary institutions are required to award transfer credit for the satisfactory completion of college-level courses.

Most states with concurrent enrollment programs allow students to apply earned baccalaureate credit toward high school graduation requirements, college transfer credit, or both, although funding differs for the two kinds of credit. Predating the state-sponsored concurrent enrollment programs are the special summer programs offered by individual colleges and universities where high school students earn college-level credit and participate in enrichment experiences.

Special Programs. Prior to the clarion call for educational reform in 1984, many high schools already had embraced the College Board's Advanced Placement (AP) program, which is designed to provide an enriched educational environment. Participation in the AP programs provides opportunities for stimulating college-level study to high school students who are willing and able to apply themselves. AP programs provide richer high school experiences and permit students to speed progress toward a baccalaureate degree, thereby gaining additional time for additional meaningful activities such as study abroad, internships, or work.

The College Board provides curricular outlines, teaching guides, and professional development opportunities to help interested teachers teach AP courses effectively. AP examinations, available for 29 courses in 16 subject areas, validate the classroom experience. Almost half of all secondary schools in the United States offer AP courses and examinations. In 1994, the Educational Testing Service (ETS) reported that 450,000 students took more than 700,000 examinations (College Entrance Examination Board 1992). Approximately 1,200 postsecondary institutions, including 22 international universities, grant baccalaureate credit or advanced placement for satisfactory performance on AP examinations (College Entrance Examination Board 1992).

The International Baccalaureate (IB) program provides another option for highly motivated and academically gifted students to engage in rigorous preuniversity studies and to earn baccalaureate credit while in high school. It is a compromise between the specialization required by some national education systems and the breadth preferred by others.

The IB program includes an integrated program similar to the AP curriculum with the addition of a research paper or essay, and a "creative or aesthetic expression or social service activity" (International Baccalaureate 1990). Higher-level IB courses are considered on a par with the AP courses of the College Board. Institutions in 75 countries, including 300 U.S. colleges and universities, recognize the IB experience. Credit practices range from acknowledgment of the rigorous quality of the IB program to well-defined policies for awarding credit for the higher-level examinations.

Credit by Examination. Advanced Placement (AP) tests are generally recognized as a reliable basis for the award of baccalaureate credit. However, AP tests were developed to evaluate learning received in a traditional classroom setting. To evaluate nontraditional learning experiences, the College Level Examination Program (CLEP) offers an alternative to students wishing to earn college credit for learning that occurs outside the classroom and is comparable in substance and achievement to that expected of students regularly enrolled in college classes. Campus-challenge examinations are still another avenue for earning credit for courses without having to enroll in them. Entirely the prerogative of the institution and the academic departments, challenge examinations relieve competent students of the tedium of completing repetitive courses and expedite their progress toward the degree.

Tests, when used as a method of assessing students' learning, assume that students have been exposed to a common body of knowledge. The increasing diversity of the student population exacerbates differences in learning and test performance. Myriad sociological, economic, and cultural factors impacting on students' experiences combine exponentially, so that it can no longer be assumed that students have had similar educational experiences. Students must be acknowledged as having a potpourri of knowledge rather than a common core that can be evaluated easily. A single test, single scores, or a few subscores are not adequate measures of past learning. Rather than attempting to measure what has been learned, tomorrow's students will be able to engage in individualized learning programs that identify, and are responsive to, their particular deficiencies or efficiencies in knowledge. An education, tailored to fit, will provide students with learning experiences that expand with students' increased competencies, needs, and interests.

Electronic Frontier

Off-campus instruction programs historically offered courses taught in the traditional lecture format by faculty members at off-campus centers or transmitted lectures to remote sites. Emerging delivery systems expand the horizon by making access to instruction and information available anytime and anywhere. Telecommunication technology, by harnessing the capabilities of videoconferencing and computers, offers the possibility of combining lectures with other teaching techniques. Electronic education is particularly useful for offering postsecondary opportunities to high school students and adults in remote areas. For example, the California Young Scholars Project telecommunicates beginning college-level courses to high school students in small rural schools throughout California.

Older part-time students are especially receptive to the flexible education opportunities afforded by interactive television. Mind Extension University, a 24-hour cable-television education network based in Colorado, offers 10 degree programs to students across the nation who, because of time, lifestyle, or geographic constraints, have been unable to pursue a degree in the traditional on-campus manner.

Using electronic media to reach expanded student audiences is a metamorphosis of the off-campus center model. Old concerns over the quality of teaching and learning achieved in traditional off-campus settings are now directed at the electronic model. However, the excitement of being able to reach vast audiences should propel development of appropriate assessment models. How student learning is assessed is the real issue rather than the format of the learning situation.

SCHOOL REFORM MOVEMENT

The trend toward raising admission standards by requiring more college preparatory courses is encountering a crosscurrent that was set in motion by the school reform movement. Educational initiatives such as school restructuring, charter schools, and competency-based curricula are being embraced by K–12 programs. While these initiatives are motivated by the desire to improve the quality of learning, the potpourri of new educational experiences will challenge the ingenuity of higher education professionals. Not only will students have been prepared in different classrooms and in different high schools, using a variety of teaching techniques, but high school graduates will offer documentation that they are prepared for baccalaureate study in widely differing ways.

Outcome Measurement

Minnesota plans to implement procedures to measure high school graduation on the basis of demonstrated achievement outcomes rather than completion of courses based on clock hours. Assessment will measure content and exit outcomes. Content outcome is defined as the knowledge, concepts, principles, and processes needed to deal with new information and complex situations, while the exit outcome encompasses generic abilities related to thinking, organization, and communication (Houghton 1993). Educational initiatives in Oklahoma and Wyoming also represent moves away from using Carnegie units to measure learning. Oklahoma has identified 7,000 learner competencies for grades 1–12, to be assessed by criterion-referenced testing (Houghton 1993).

Proponents of the educational reform movement perceive portfolios as a means of enhancing information traditionally gathered by classroom testing. Focused collections of materials associated with the classroom experience and supplemented by out-of-class activities supportive of the learning experience are expected to provide a far richer picture of students' true abilities than can be obtained from traditional grading practices.

School Restructuring

School restructuring requires a redefinition of how the school community does business, how resources are used, how people interact within the community, and how the high school relates to the outside world. Restructuring advocates see a shift from today's lockstep academic model to a more holistic one. In determining how best to meet the educational needs of the community, schools may elect to embrace flexible scheduling, variable teaming of teachers, and student clustering in programs that support personalized learning. New courses and course sequences will be created within and among academic disciplines (Intersegmental Coordinating Council 1993).

A California law enacted in 1992 made provision for 100 charter schools. Unlike other public schools, which operate under a myriad of state laws and local rules and regulations, a charter school operates under the terms and conditions defined by its charter. Charter schools provide opportunities for teachers, parents, students, and communities to establish and maintain schools that are responsive to local needs. Such efforts are expected to result in improved student learning, increased learning opportunities for all students with special emphasis on those identified as academically low achieving, the use of different and innovative teaching methods, new professional opportunities for teachers, teacher responsibility for the learning program at the school site, expanded educational choices for students and parents, and accountability for meeting measurable student outcomes (Intersegmental Coordinating Council 1993). In Wyoming, accreditation standards for elementary and secondary schools are not based on a statewide curriculum but rather give school districts latitude to implement more integrative approaches to education, such as team teaching and interdisciplinary instruction (Houghton 1993).

It will be difficult to formalize the understanding of restructured high school experiences since each school will establish individual learning outcomes, which may or may not be related to postsecondary admissions criteria. Integrated learning blocks consolidating mathematics sequences or combining biology, chemistry, and physics may not be easily equatable with traditional college preparatory course requirements.

College and university professionals are carefully watching, evaluating, and cooperating with the school reform movement. In addition to simply recognizing changes that are occurring in grades K–12, higher education itself must enter into a self-evaluation process to ensure that future high school graduates are able to make an orderly transition into postsecondary institutions. Anticipating the changes that will follow from school restructuring, the University of Wisconsin is piloting a competency-based admissions policy as a supplement to the University of Wisconsin System Freshman Admission Policy (SHEEO/NCES 1994).

Home Schooling

Increasing numbers of American parents are choosing to educate their children at home. Parents may cooperate with local school districts to establish curriculum and assessment procedures or opt to follow more structured programs offered through nationally accredited home-study schools. Home-study schools provide lesson materials and correct, grade, and comment on work assignments. Evaluating home study is difficult since there are no standardized criteria on which to evaluate the educational experience of home-schooled students. ACT, SAT, and CLEP test results give some insight into how these students learn. Unless validated by nationally standardized tests or by completion of community college courses, it is not likely that home-schooled students will be able to provide sufficient documentation of the completion of a college-preparatory course pattern. In response to this dilemma, colleges and universities may elect to conditionally enroll home-schooled students and students who have attended small, unaccredited high schools, with the provision that they satisfactorily complete freshman-level courses within a specified time period. Other colleges and universities may resort to required percentile scoring on national standardized tests for enrollment prerequisites.

SUMMARY

As the nation moves toward the year 2000, colleges and universities are gearing up to respond to the educational demands of students representing various ethnic, cultural, socioeconomic, and age groups. Meeting those needs requires the development of outreach programs and support services that foster educational success and incorporate features sensitive to specific group needs.

Periodic reviews of enrollment strategies will ensure continuing responsiveness to the everchanging population of the United States. The time-honored method of targeting prospective students based on class rank is too narrow to ensure the inclusion of underrepresented groups. A modified prospective student pool must recognize and accommodate the special attributes and specific concerns of various ethnic and cultural populations. Outreach to older Americans, both as first-time students and as participants in retraining programs, will take on greater significance as the American population ages.

At the same time, colleges and universities must be active participants in the school reform movement, which is currently centered in the K–12 sector, to ensure that changes made in that segment will be accommodated and supported by postsecondary institutions. Changes in K–12 settings that enhance the educational experience are welcome and necessary, but educational changes do not occur in a vacuum. As high schools implement new ways of teaching and assessing student achievement, higher education institutions will be challenged to develop admission standards sufficiently flexible to respond to the new formats. Interdisciplinary courses, new course sequences, competency-based assessment, and portfolio assessment do not fit neatly into an admission formula that depends on the completion of traditional college preparatory courses, A–F grading patterns, and Carnegie units.

The assumption is no longer valid that having completed a college preparatory curriculum, however configured, is equivalent to the traditional classroom lecture model. Tomorrow's students will have been seated in different classrooms and in different high schools. Their educational experience will include traditional lectures, computer-assisted learning, television courses, individual study, and other techniques that will emerge out of school reforms. They also will demonstrate that they have met college preparatory requirements in widely differing ways.

The school reform movement, coupled with changing demographics, provides an unparalleled opportunity for higher education to examine its goals, objectives, practices, and procedures. Postsecondary institutions will be expected to build on the disparate high school experiences of students and to provide at least comparable support for the students' educational goals. New sensitivities and flexibilities will be required to adequately serve the students of tomorrow.

REFERENCES

Astin, Alexander, 1994. *The American freshman: National norms for fall 1992.* Los Angeles: Higher Education Research Institute.
California Postsecondary Education Commission (CPEC). 1992. *Postsecondary enrollment opportunities for high school students.* Sacramento: CPEC.
Campbell, Paul R. 1994. *Population projections for states, by age, race and sex: 1993 to 2020.* Washington, DC: U.S. Government Printing Office.
Clune, William H., Paula White, and Janice Patterson. 1989. *The implementation and effects of high school graduation requirements.* New Brunswick, NJ: Center for Policy Research in Education.
College Entrance Examination Board (CEEB). 1992. *1992–93 AP yearbook.* New York: CEEB.
Day, Jenifer. 1993. *Population projections for states by age, race, sex, and Hispanic origin: 1993–2050.* Washington, DC: U.S. Government Printing Office.

Eck, Alan. 1993. Job-related education and training: Their impact on earning. *Monthly Labor Review* 116: 21–38.

Flanagan, Patricia A. 1992. *Raising standards—State policies to improve academic preparation for college.* Washington, DC: U.S. Department of Education.

Harvey, James. 1984. *A nation at risk: The implications for educational reform.* Washington, DC: U.S. Department of Education.

Houghton, Mary J. 1993. *College admission standards and school reform.* Washington, DC: National Governors' Association.

Immerwahr, John, and Steve Farkas. 1993. *The closing gateway: Californians consider their higher education system.* San Jose: California Higher Education Policy Center.

International Baccalaureate. 1990. *Recognition policies of North American universities.* New York: International Baccalaureate.

Intersegmental Coordinating Council (ICC). 1993. *K–12 school reform: Implications and responsibilities for higher education.* Sacramento, CA: ICC.

Johnston, William B., and Arnold H. Packer. 1987. *Workforce 2000: Work and workers for the twenty-first century.* Indianapolis, IN: Hudson Institute.

Nakanishi, Don T. 1989. A quota on excellence? *Change* (November/December): 39–47.

SHEEO/NCES [communication network]. 1994. Alternate approaches to college admission. *Network News* 13 (October): 13–14.

Snyder, Thomas D., and Charlene M. Hoffman. 1994. *Digest of education statistics 1994.* Washington, DC: U.S. Department of Education.

University of California Board of Regents. 1995. *Policy on undergraduate admission.* Oakland: University of California.

Appendix A: Professional Practices and Ethical Standards

The American Association of Collegiate Registrars and Admissions Officers (AACRAO) is concerned with the advancement of postsecondary education and the standards and conduct of those professionals who are involved at all levels. To provide guidance to these professionals, AACRAO has adopted the following principles, which exemplify those qualities and attributes that distinguish members of the Association both past and present.

AACRAO members shall:

Believe in and be loyal to the philosophy and goals of the profession and the institutions we serve.

Understand and respect the civil and human rights and responsibilities of all individuals while supporting and protecting the principles of due process and confidentiality.

Adhere to the principles of nondiscrimination and equality without regard to race, color, creed, gender, sexual orientation, age, disability, religion, or national origin.

Represent an institutional or Association perspective without vested interests or personal bias.

Initiate policies that support the goals of our profession.

Assert ourselves when policies or practices are proposed that seem to be contrary to the philosophy and goals of our professions and our institutions.

Participate in and contribute to professional activities and their development to ensure effective and efficient management of resources, data, and personnel.

Communicate an accurate interpretation of our institutions' admissions criteria, educational costs, financial aid availability, and major offerings to assist prospective students and their parents in making an informed decision.

Assist in improving educational standards and methods of evaluation at the institutional, state, and federal level so that grading is meaningful in reflecting the academic achievement of students.

Understand and appreciate the dynamics of interpersonal relationships when dealing with students, parents, faculty, administration, associates, and the public.

Develop and implement effective management systems that will ensure integrity, confidentiality, security of institutional records, and provide an accurate interpretation of such information.

Dedicate ourselves to the ideals and principles that will enable students to develop their talents and interests to become responsible citizens and contributors to the improvement of society.Practice honesty and integrity in our professions and in our lives.

Appendix B: Statement of Principles of Good Practice

Revised October 1997

Ethics in recruiting students and awarding scholarships provided the impetus for creating NACAC in 1937. As a reflection of that major purpose, one of the first actions taken by the founders was the creation of a Code of Ethics. After many years of reviewing, updating, and rewriting, this Code is today's *Statement of Principles of Good Practice.*

While the Code originally applied only to NACAC members, the importance of ethical practices in the admission process for all institutions was recognized by those in the profession. As a result, a joint statement utilizing the basic philosophy of NACAC's Code of Ethics was developed in tandem with the American Association of Collegiate Registrars and Admission Officers and The College Board, and was endorsed by the American Council on Education, the National Association of Secondary School Principals, the National Student Association, and the American School Counselor Association.

The *Statement of Principles of Good Practice* is reviewed annually and revised to reflect new concerns for ethical admission practices and policies.

High schools, colleges, universities, other institutions and organizations, and individuals dedicated to the promotion of formal education believe in the dignity, the worth, and the potentialities of every human being. They cooperate in the development of programs and services in postsecondary counseling, admission, and financial aid to eliminate bias related to race, creed, gender, sexual orientation, age, political affiliation, national origin, and disabling conditions. Believing that institutions of learning are only as strong ultimately as their human resources, they look upon counseling individual students about their educational plans as a fundamental aspect of their responsibilities.

They support, therefore, the following *Statement of Principles of Good Practice* for members of the National Association for College Admission Counseling:

I. ADMISSION PROMOTION AND RECRUITMENT

A. *College and University Members agree that they*

1. will ensure that admission counselors are viewed as professional members of their institutions' staffs. As professionals, their compensation shall take the form of a fixed salary rather than commissions or bonuses based on the number of students recruited.

2. will be responsible for the development of publications, written communications, and presentations, i.e., college nights, college days, and college fairs, used for their institution's promotional and recruitment activity. They

   a) will state clearly and precisely the requirements for secondary school preparation, admission tests, and transfer student admission.

   b) will include a current and accurate admission calendar. If the institution offers special admission options such as early admission, early action, early decision, or waiting list, the publication should define these programs and state deadline dates, notification dates, required deposits, refund policies, and the date when the candidates must reply. If students are placed on wait lists or alternate lists, the letter which notifies the students of the placement should provide a history that describes the number of students placed on the wait lists, the number offered admission, and the availability of financial aid and housing. Finally, if summer admission or mid-year admission is available, students should be made aware of the possibility in official communication from the institutions.

   c) will not falsely advertise or misrepresent their academic offerings. Rather, members will provide precise information about their academic majors and degree programs. Such information should include a factual and accurate description of majors, minors, concentrations and/or interdisciplinary offerings that apply toward the completion of the undergraduate degree.

   d) will provide students, families and secondary schools with the most comprehensive information about costs of attendance and opportunities and requirements for all types of financial aid, and state the specific relationship between admission practices and policies and financial aid practices and policies.

   e) will describe in detail any special programs, including overseas study,

256

credit by examination, or advanced placement.

f) will include pictures and descriptions of the campus and community which are current and realistic.

g) will provide accurate information about the opportunities/selection for institutional housing, deadline dates for housing deposits, housing deposit refunds, and describe policies for renewal availability of such institutional housing.

h) will provide accurate and specific descriptions of any special programs or support services available to students with handicapping conditions, learning disabilities, and/or other special needs.

i) will identify the source and year of study when institutional publications and/or media communications cite published ratings of academic programs, academic rigor or reputations, or athletic rankings.

j) should indicate that the institution is a NACAC member and has endorsed the principles contained in this *Statement*.

3. will exercise appropriate responsibility for all people whom the institution involves in admission, promotional, and recruitment activities (including their alumni, coaches, students, faculty, and other institutional representatives), and educate them about the principles outlined in this *Statement*. Colleges and universities which engage the services of admission management or consulting firms shall be responsible for assuring that such firms adhere to this *Statement*.

4. will speak forthrightly, accurately, and comprehensively in presenting their institutions to counseling personnel, prospective students, and their families. They

a) will state clearly the admission requirements of their institutions, and inform students and counselors about changed admission requirements so that candidates will not be adversely affected in the admission process.

b) will state clearly all deadlines for application, notification, housing, and candidates' reply requirements for both admission and financial aid.

c) will furnish data describing the currently enrolled freshman class and will describe in published profiles all members of the enrolling freshman class. Subgroups within the profile may be presented separately because of their unique character or special circumstances.

d) will not use disparaging comparisons of secondary or postsecondary institutions.

e) will provide accurate information about the use/role of standardized testing in their institutions' admission process.

5. will not use unprofessional promotional tactics by admission counselors and other institutional representatives. They

a) will not contract with secondary school personnel for remuneration for referred students.

b) will not offer or pay a per capita premium to any individual or agency for the recruitment or enrollment of students, international as well as domestic.

c) will not encourage students to transfer if they have shown no interest in doing so.

d) will not compromise the goals and principles of this *Statement*.

6. will refrain from recruiting students who are enrolled, registered, or have declared their intent or submitted contractual deposit with other institutions unless the students initiate inquiries themselves or unless cooperation is sought from institutions which provide transfer programs.

7. will understand the nature and intent of all admission referral services utilized by their institutions (including their alumni, coaches, students, faculty, and other institutional representatives) and seek to ensure the validity and professional competency of such services.

257

B. Secondary School Members agree that they

1. will provide a program of counseling which introduces a broad range of postsecondary opportunities to students.

2. will encourage students and their families to take the initiative in learning about colleges and universities.

3. will not use disparaging comparisons of secondary or postsecondary institutions.

4. will establish a policy with respect to secondary school representatives for the release of students' names. Any policy which authorizes the release of students' names should provide that the release be made only with the students' permission consistent with applicable laws and regulations. That permission may be a general consent to any release of the students' names. Secondary school representatives shall, in releasing students' names, be sensitive to the students' academic, athletic, or other abilities.

5. will refuse any reward or remuneration from a college, university, or private counseling service for placement of their school's students.

6. will be responsible for all personnel who may become involved in counseling students on postsecondary options available and educate them about the principles in this *Statement*.

7. will be responsible for compliance with applicable laws and regulations with respect to the students' rights to privacy.

8. will not guarantee specific college placement.

9. should provide information about opportunities and requirements for financial aid.

10. should indicate that the institution is a NACAC member and has endorsed the principles in this *Statement*.

C. Independent Counselor Members agree that they

1. will provide a program of counseling which introduces a broad range of postsecondary opportunities to students.

2. will encourage students and their families to take initiative in learning about colleges and universities.

3. will not use disparaging comparisons of secondary or postsecondary institutions.

4. will refuse unethical or unprofessional requests (e.g., for names of top students, names of athletes) from college or university representatives (e.g., alumni, coaches, or other agencies or organizations).

5. will refuse any reward or remuneration from a college, university, agency, or organization for placement of their clients.

6. will be responsible for all personnel who may become involved in counseling students on postsecondary options and educate them about the principles in this *Statement*.

7. will be responsible for compliance with applicable laws and regulations with respect to the students' rights to privacy.

8. will not guarantee specific college placement.

9. will provide advertisements or promotional materials which are truthful and do not include any false, misleading, or exaggerated claims with respect to services offered.

10. will communicate with the secondary school counselor about the college admission process, after obtaining student and parental consent.

11. should provide information about opportunities and requirements for financial aid.

12. should consider donating time to students who need the services of an independent counselor but who are unable to pay.

13. should indicate that the NACAC member has endorsed the principles in this *Statement*.

D. All other members providing college admission counseling services to students agree to adhere to the principles in this *Statement*.

E. College fairs, clearinghouses, and matching services that provide liaison between colleges and universities and students shall be consid-

ered a positive part of the admission process if they effectively supplement other secondary school guidance activities and adhere to this Statement.

II. ADMISSION PROCEDURES

A. *College and University Members agree that they*

1. will accept full responsibility for admission decisions and for proper notification of those decisions to candidates and, when possible, to their secondary schools.

2. will receive information about candidates in confidence and respect completely, consistent with applicable laws and regulations, the confidential nature of such data.

3. will not apply newly-revised requirements to the disadvantage of a candidate whose secondary school courses were established in accordance with earlier requirements.

4. will not require candidates or the secondary schools to indicate the order of the candidates' college or university preferences, except under early decision plans.

5. will not make offers of admission to students who have not submitted admission applications.

6. will permit first-year candidates for fall admission to choose, without penalty, among offers of admission and financial aid until May 1. Colleges that solicit commitments to offers of admission and/or financial assistance prior to May 1 may do so provided those offers include a clear statement that written requests for extensions until May 1 will be granted, and that such requests will not jeopardize a student's status for admission or financial aid. Candidates admitted under an early decision program are a recognized exception to this provision.

7. will work with their institution's administration to ensure that financial aid and scholarship offers and housing options are not used to manipulate commitments prior to May 1.

8. will, if necessary, establish a wait list that:

   a) is of reasonable length.

   b) is maintained for the shortest possible period and in no case later than August 1.

9. will establish wait list procedures that ensure that no student on any wait list is asked for a deposit in order to remain on the wait list or for a commitment to enroll prior to receiving an official written offer of admission.

10. will state clearly the admission procedures for transfer students by informing candidates of deadlines, documents required, courses accepted, and course equivalency and other relevant policies.

11. will inform students and counselors about new or changed requirements which may adversely affect candidates who have met all required deadlines, deposits, and commitments according to the students' original notification from the institution.

12. will accept, for the purposes of documenting student academic records, only official transcripts in the admission or registration process which come directly from the counseling, guidance, or registrar's offices of the institution(s) the candidate attends or has attended or from other appropriate agencies.

13. will, in the development and administration of their application policies and procedures for early decision programs, abide by the NACAC Guidelines for Admission Decision Options.

14. should admit candidates on the basis of academic and personal criteria rather than financial need. This provision shall not apply to foreign nationals ineligible for federal student assistance.

15. should notify high school personnel when the institution's admission selection committee includes students.

16. should notify candidates as soon as possible if they are clearly inadmissible.

17. should make every effort to provide candidates for financial aid with financial aid decisions as soon as possible following an offer of admission.

B. Secondary School Members agree that they

1. will provide, in a timely manner, for colleges and universities accurate, legible, and complete official transcripts for the school's candidates.

2. will provide colleges and universities with a description of the school's marking system which may include the rank in class and/or grade point average.

3. will in their profiles and other publications provide true and accurate information with regard to test scores for all students in the represented class cohort group who participated in college admission testing.

4. will provide accurate descriptions of the candidates' personal qualities which are relevant to the admission process.

5. will urge candidates to understand and discharge their responsibilities in the admission process. Candidates will be instructed to

   a) comply with requests for additional information in a timely manner.

   b) respond to institutional deadlines and refrain from stockpiling acceptances.

   c) refrain from submitting multiple deposits or making multiple commitments.

   d) refrain from submitting more than one application under any early decision plan and, if admitted under such a plan, comply with all institutional guidelines including those regarding the obligations to: enroll, withdraw all other applications, and refrain from submitting subsequent applications.

   e) respond to institutional deadlines on housing reservations, financial aid, health records, and course prescheduling, where all or any of these are applicable.

6. will not reveal, unless authorized, candidates' college or university preferences.

7. will sign only one early decision agreement for any student.

8. will counsel students and their families to notify other institutions when they have accepted an admission offer.

9. will encourage students to be the sole authors of their applications and essays and will counsel against inappropriate assistance on the part of others.

10. should report any significant change in candidates' academic status or qualifications, including *personal conduct record,* between the time of recommendation and graduation, where permitted by applicable laws and regulations and if requested by an institution's application.

11. should provide a school profile which clearly describes special curricular opportunities (e.g., honors, Advanced Placement courses, seminars) and a comprehensive listing of all courses with an explanation of unusual abbreviations and any information required for proper understanding.

12. should advise students and their families not to sign any contractual agreement with an institution without examining the provisions of the contract.

13. should counsel students and their families to file a reasonable number of applications.

C. Independent Counselor Members agree that they

1. will urge candidates to recognize and discharge their responsibilities in the admission process. Candidates will be instructed to

   a) comply with requests for additional information in a timely manner.

   b) respond to institutional deadlines and refrain from stockpiling acceptances.

   c) refrain from submitting multiple deposits or making multiple commitments.

   d) refrain from submitting more than one application under any early decision

260

plan and, if admitted under such a plan, comply with all institutional guidelines including those regarding the obligations to: enroll, withdraw all other applications, and refrain from submitting subsequent applications.

e) respond to institutional deadlines on housing reservations, financial aid, health records, and course prescheduling, where all or any of these are applicable.

2. will not reveal, unless authorized, candidates' college or university preferences.

3. will follow the process recommended by the candidates' high school for filing college applications.

4. will encourage students to be the sole authors of their applications and essays, and counsel against inappropriate assistance on the part of others.

5. should advise students and their families not to sign any contractual agreement with an institution without examining the provisions of the contract.

6. should counsel students and their families to file a reasonable number of applications.

D. All other members providing college admission counseling services to students agree to adhere to the principles in this Statement.

III. STANDARDIZED COLLEGE ADMISSION TESTING

Members accept the principle that fairness in testing practices should govern all institutional policies. Because test results can never be a precise measurement of human potential, members commit themselves to practices that eliminate bias of any kind, provide equal access, and consider tests as only one measure in admission/counseling practices.

A. College and University Members agree that they

1. will use test scores and related data discretely and for purposes that are appropriate and validated.

2. will provide prospective students with accurate and complete information about the use of test scores in the admission process.

3. will refrain from using minimum test scores as the sole criterion for admission, thereby denying certain students because of small differences in scores.

4. will use test scores in conjunction with other data such as school record, recommendations, and other relevant information in making decisions.

5. will educate staff in understanding the concepts of test measurement, test interpretation, and test use so they may make informed admission decisions from the test data.

6. will maintain the confidentiality of test scores.

7. will publicize clearly policies relating to placement by tests, awarding of credit, and other policies based on test results.

8. will, in the reporting of test scores, report first on all first-year admitted or enrolled students, or both, including special subgroups (e.g., athletes, nonnative speakers) and then, if they wish, may present separately the score characteristics of special subgroup populations. Universities with more than one undergraduate division may report first by division and then by special subgroups within divisions. Clear explanations of who is included in the subgroup population should be made. Those institutions that do not require tests or for which tests are optional will only report scores if the institution clearly and emphatically states the limits of the group being reported.

9. should conduct institutional research to inquire into the most appropriate use of tests for admission decisions.

10. should counsel students to take only a reasonable number of tests and only those necessary for their postsecondary plans.

11. should refrain from the public reporting of mean and median admission test scores and instead, depending upon the requested information, report scores by any or all of the following methods

a) middle 50 percent of the scores of all first-year applicants.

b) middle 50 percent of the scores of all first-year students admitted.

261

c) middle 50 percent of the scores of all first-year students enrolled.

d) appropriate score bands for all first year students applied, admitted, and enrolled.

B. Secondary School Members agree that they

1. will release and report test scores only with students' consent.

2. will avoid comparing colleges and universities solely on the basis of test scores.

3. will work with other school officials and other groups to keep test results confidential and in perspective.

4. will, in the reporting of test scores, report on *all* students within a discrete class (e.g., freshman, sophomore, junior, senior) who participated in college admisson testing.

5. should avoid undue emphasis on test scores as a measure of students' potential and ability when representing students to colleges and universities.

6. should inform students about what tests they need for admission, where they may take them, and how to interpret the results in their own contexts.

7. should be knowledgeable about the limitations of standardized tests and counsel students with these limitations in mind.

8. should inform students about the use and validity of test scores, both for admission and as measures of potential and ability.

9. should counsel students and families on how test scores may be used in the admission process by colleges and universities.

10. should counsel students to take only a reasonable number of those tests necessary for their postsecondary plans, without regard to the impact the test results may have on the school profile report.

11. should counsel students and families about data, other than test results, that may be submitted as part of the application process.

12. should counsel students about test preparation programs and inform them about alternative programs and/or approaches.

13. should refrain from the public reporting of mean and median admission test scores and instead, report scores by either or both of the following:

a) middle 50 percent of *all* students tested by discrete grade level.

b) appropriate score bands of *all* students tested by discrete grade level.

C. Independent Counselor Members agree that they

1. will release and report test scores only with students' consent.

2. will avoid comparing colleges and universities solely on the basis of test scores.

3. will avoid undue emphasis on test scores as a measure of students' potential and ability when representing students to colleges and universities.

4. will work with other school officials and other groups to keep test results confidential and in perspective.

5. should inform students about what tests they need for admission, where they may take them, and how to interpret the results in their own contexts.

6. should be knowledgeable about the limitations of standardized tests and counsel students with these limitations in mind.

7. should inform students about the use and validity of test scores, both for admission and as measures of potential and ability.

8. should counsel students and families on how test scores may be used in the admission process by colleges and universities.

9. should counsel students to take only a reasonable number of tests and only those necessaryfor their postsecondary plans.

10. should counsel students and families about data, other than test results, that may be submitted as part of the application process.

11. should counsel students about test preparation programs and inform them about alternative programs and/or approaches.

D. All other members providing college admission counseling and/or testing services to students agree to adhere to the principles in this *Statement*.

IV. FINANCIAL AID

This section was revised through a collaborative effort among representatives from the American Association of Collegiate Registrars and Admissions Officers (AACRAO), National Association for Student Financial Aid Administrators (NASFAA), the College Scholarship Service (CSS) and NACAC. Member institutions of NACAC are encouraged to support the principle of distributing financial aid funds on the basis of proven financial need. Financial need is defined as the difference between a student's total annual educational expenses and the amount the student and his or her family is expected to pay. In other words, the equation for determining financial need is "cost of attendance" minus the "expected family contribution" equals "financial need." Members agree that financial aid should be offered to candidates in the forms of grants, scholarships, loans, or employment, either alone or in combination. Members agree that financial aid should be viewed as supplementary to the efforts of students' families when students are not self-supporting.

A. College and University Members agree that they

1. will, to the extent possible, through their publications and communications, provide students, families, and schools with the most current, clear, factual and comprehensive information about their institutions' total costs of attendance (both direct and indirect), when referencing institutions' financial aid opportunities, and practices including practices for foreign nationals.

2. will utilize a consistent and equitable needs analysis methodology in determining the expected financial contribution of candidates' families and in making the expected estimates or awards of the amount of financial aid which may be available to them after documentation.

3. will notify accepted aid applicants of institutional financial aid decisions before

the date by which a reply must be made to the offer of admission, assuming all requested application forms are in on time.

4. will state clearly policies on renewal of financial aid which will typically include a review of their current financial circumstances.

5. will permit first-year candidates for fall admission to choose, without penalty, among offers of financial aid until May 1. Colleges that solicit commitments to offers of need-based and/or merit-based financial aid prior to May 1 may do so provided those offers include a clear statement that written requests for extensions until May 1 will be granted, and that such requests will not jeopardize a student's status for housing and/or financial aid. Candidates admitted under an early decision program are a recognized exception to this provision.

6. will not publicly announce the amount of need-based aid awarded to individuals; however, amounts of no-need scholarship awards to individuals may be a matter of public record.

7. will not knowingly offer financial aid packages to students who have committed to attend other institutions unless the students initiate such inquiries.

8. will not award grants, including scholarships, or final financial aid packages to students who have not submitted admission applications. Institutions may provide estimated aid packages and information regarding scholarship programs prior to the time an application is filed. Athletic scholarships, which adhere to nationally established signing periods, are a recognized exception to this provision and are viewed in the same light as an early decision agreement.

9. should refrain from using financial need as a consideration in selecting students. This provision shall not apply to internationals who are ineligible for United States federal student assistance.

10. should, to the extent possible, within the institutions' capabilities, meet the full need of accepted students.

B. *Secondary School Members agree that they*

1. will refrain, in public announcements, from giving the amounts of financial aid received by individual students; however, amounts of no-need scholarship awards may be a matter of public record.

2. will not make guarantees of any financial aid or scholarship awards.

3. should not encourage students to apply to particular colleges and universities to enhance their high schools' statistical records regarding the number or amount of scholarship awards received.

4. should advise students who have been awarded financial aid by non-collegiate sources that they have the responsibility to notify the college of the type and amount of such outside aid.

C. *Independent Counselor Members agree that they*

1. will refrain, in public announcements, from giving the amounts of financial aid received by individual students; however, amounts of no-need scholarship awards may be a matter of public record.

2. will not make guarantees of any financial aid or scholarship awards.

3. should advise students who have been awarded financial aid by non-collegiate sources that they have the responsibility to notify the college of the type and amount of such outside aid.

D. *All other members providing college admission and financial counseling services to students agree to adhere to the principles in this Statement.*

V. ADVANCED STANDING STUDENTS AND THE AWARDING OF CREDIT

A. *College and University Members agree that they*

1. will design placement, credit, and exemption policies to augment educational placement opportunities, not to recruit students.

2. will evaluate student competency through the use of validated methods and techniques.

3. will define and publish in the institutions' pre-admission information the policies and procedures for granting credit.

4. will evaluate previously earned credit, published by the admitting college or university, in a manner which ensures the integrity of academic standards as well as the principle of fairness to the students.

B. *Secondary School Members agree that they*

1. will alert students to the full implications of college and university placement, credit, and exemption policies with regard to their educational planning and goals.

2. will make students aware of the importance of accreditation.

3. will make students aware of the possibilities of earning credit through both nontraditional educational experiences and examinations and alternative methods of instruction.

C. *Independent Counselor Members agree that they*

1. will alert students to the full implications of college and university placement, credit, and exemption policies with regard to their educational planning and goals.

2. will make students aware of the importance of accreditation.

3. will make students aware of the possibilities of earning credit through both nontraditional educational experiences and examinations and alternative methods of instruction.

D. *All other members providing admission counseling services to students agree to adhere to the principles in this Statement.*

Appendix C: Admission Decision Options in Higher Education

Approved by NACAC Assembly, October 1991

In response to member concerns about the plethora of special admission plans, the National Association of College Admission Counselors (NACAC) has studied the various admission decision options in an attempt to develop standard definitions. Member colleges and universities should strive to utilize these definitions to eliminate the confusion and lack of clarity regarding nomenclature that are currently being experienced by students, parents, and in some instances, by counselors and other educators. In particular, NACAC believes there is a need for:

- Institutions to clearly describe all admission and financial aid policies and deadlines including all institutional and student obligations.
- Institutions to recognize the stressful nature of the admission process for students and families and to be attentive to timely communication through out the admission cycle.
- Institutions not to use various admission policies as positioning tools at the expense of the student.
- Final notification of students to occur early enough to allow them to participate in and benefit from the full range of student enrollment services.
- Institutions to be aware that to require a commitment, in the absence of a specific aid award, compromises the student's right to make a well-informed decision.

Because the primary goal of NACAC is to assist students in their transition from secondary school to college, all NACAC members should strive to adhere to the following definitions and guidelines.

Early Decision

Early Decision is the term used to describe the application process in which a commitment is made by the student to the institution, that, if admitted, the student will enroll. Only a student who can make a deliberate and well-reasoned first choice decision should apply under an Early Decision plan because the institution will require a nonrefundable deposit well before May 1.

- Student may apply to other colleges but may have only one Early Decision application pending at any time.
- Institution will notify the applicant of the decision within a reasonable and clearly stated period of time after the Early Decision deadline.
- Student applying for aid will adhere to institutional Early Decision aid application deadlines.
- Institution will respond to application for financial aid at or near the time an offer of admission is extended.
- If admitted, student will enroll unless aid award is inadequate.
- Immediately upon acceptance of offer, student will withdraw all other applications and make no subsequent applications.

- Institution will not offer special incentives (such as scholarships, special aid awards, or special housing opportunities) to encourage students to apply under an Early Decision plan.

NACAC recommends that the application and/or acceptance form include a request for parents and/or counselor signature in addition to the student's signature indicating an understanding of the Early Decision commitment.

Early Action

Early Action is the term used to describe the application process which permits a student to make application to an institution of preference and receive a decision during the senior year, well in advance of the normal response dates in the spring. The candidate is not committed to enroll at that particular institution.

- Student may apply to other colleges.
- Institution will notify the applicant of the decision within a reasonable and clearly stated period of time after the Early Action deadline.
- Institution will not offer more than one Early Action deadline date or cycle.
- Student applying for aid will adhere to institutional aid application deadlines.
- Student will not be required to make a commitment prior to May 1 but is encouraged to do so as soon as a final college choice is made.

Regular Decision

Regular Decision is a term used to describe the application process in which an institution reviews most of its applications prior to notifying the majority of its candidates.

- Student may apply to other colleges.
- Institution will state a deadline for completion of applications and will respond to completed applications by a specified date.
- Student applying for aid will adhere to institutional aid application deadlines.
- Student will not be required to make a commitment prior to May 1 but is encouraged to do so as soon as a final college choice is made.

Rolling Admission

Rolling Admission is a term used to describe the application process in which an institution reviews applications as they are received and offers decisions to students as applications are reviewed.

- Student may apply to other colleges.
- After a stated date each year, the institution will notify candidates of decisions within a reasonable and clearly stated period of time after completion of the application.
- Institution may have a stated or recommended application deadline.

- Student will not be required to make a commitment prior to May 1 but is encouraged to do so as soon as a final college choice is made.
- Student applying for aid will adhere to institutional aid application deadlines.

Wait List

Wait List is a term used by institutions to describe a process in which the institution does not initially offer or deny admission, but extends to a candidate the possibility of admission in the future.

- Institution should use a wait list to protect against shortfalls in enrollment rather than to manipulate yield.
- Institution should ensure that a wait list, if necessary, be of reasonable length and be maintained for a reasonable period of time, but never later than August 1.

- In the letter offering a wait list position, institution should provide a past wait list history which describes the number of students placed on a wait list(s), the number offered admission from the wait list, and the availability of financial aid. Whenever possible, students should be given an indication of when they can expect to be notified of final admission decision.
- Institution is encouraged to resolve final status and notify wait list candidates as soon after May 1 as possible.
- Institution should not require students to submit deposits to remain on a wait list or pressure students for a commitment to enroll prior to sending an official offer of admission in writing.

Appendix D: Students' and Transfer Students' Rights and Responsibilities in the College Admission Process

WHEN YOU APPLY TO COLLEGES AND UNIVERSITIES YOU HAVE RIGHTS

Before You Apply:

- You have the right to receive factual and comprehensive information from colleges and universities about their admission, financial costs, aid opportunities, practices and packaging policies, and housing policies. If you consider applying under an early decision plan you have a right to complete information from the college about its process and policy.

When You Are Offered Admission:

- You have the right to wait to respond to an offer of admission and/or financial aid until May 1.

- Colleges that request commitments to offers of admission and/or financial assistance prior to May 1, must clearly offer you the opportunity to request (in writing) an extension until May 1. They must grant you this extension and your request may not jeopardize your status for admission and/or financial aid. (This right does not apply to candidates admitted under an early decision program.)

If You Are Placed on A Wait List or Alternate List:

- The letter that notifies you of that placement should provide a history that describes the number of students on the wait list, the number offered admission, and the availability of financial aid and housing.

- Colleges may require neither a deposit nor a written commitment as a condition of remaining on a wait list.

- Colleges are expected to notify you of the resolution of your wait list status by August 1 at the latest.

WHEN YOU APPLY TO COLLEGES AND UNIVERSITIES YOU HAVE RESPONSIBILITIES

Before You Apply:

- You have a responsibility to research and understand the policies and procedures of each college or university regarding application fees, financial aid, scholarships, and housing. You should also be sure that you understand the policies of each college or university regarding deposits that you may be required to make before you enroll.

As You Apply:

- You must complete all material that is required for application, and submit your application on or before the published deadlines. You should be the sole author of your applications.

- You should seek the assistance of your high school counselor early and throughout the application period. Follow the process recommended by your high school for filing college applications.

- It is your responsibility to arrange, if appropriate, for visits to and/or interviews at colleges of your choice.

After You Receive Your Admission Decisions:

- You must notify each college or university which accepts you whether you are accepting or rejecting its offer. You should make these notifications as soon as you have made a final decision as to the college that you wish to attend, but no later than May 1.

- You may confirm your intention to enroll and, if required, submit a deposit to only one college or university. The exception to this arises if you are put on a wait list by a college or university and are later admitted to that institution. You may accept the offer and send a deposit. However, you must immediately notify a college or university at which you previously indicated your intention to enroll.

- If you are accepted under an early decision plan, you must promptly withdraw the applications submitted to other colleges and universities and make no additional applications. If you are an early decision candidate and are seeking financial aid, the previously mentioned withdrawal of other applications presumes that you have received notification about financial aid.

If you think that your rights have been denied, you should contact the college or university immediately to request additional information or the extension of a reply date. In addition, you should ask your counselor to notify the president of the state or regional affiliate of the National Association of College Admission Counselors. If you need further assistance, send a copy of any correspondence you have had with the college or university and a copy of your letter of admission to: **Executive Director, NACAC, 1631 Prince Street, Alexandria, VA 22314-2818.**

The information presented here is consistent with changes to the NACAC Statement of Principles of Good Practice, approved in September 1994.

WHEN YOU APPLY TO TRANSFER FROM ONE COLLEGE OR UNIVERSITY TO ANOTHER YOU HAVE RIGHTS

Before You Apply:

- You have the right to receive information from colleges and universities about their transfer admission requirements, including all documents required for admission, financial aid, scholarship and housing.

- You have the right to receive information about transfer of courses, credit hours, quality points, and degree requirements. This includes information about transferring courses with grades below a "C," courses you may have repeated, and credit previously granted by examination or advance placement.

- You should know that admission officers at NACAC member institutions will not recruit students who are currently enrolled at other institutions unless those students initiate the inquiries, or unless institutions that provide transfer programs seek such cooperation.

When You Are Offered Admission:

- You have the right to receive an official notification of acceptance and at least one month prior to enrollment:

  a) Written evaluation of courses and credits accepted for transfer credit and their course equivalences;

  b) An outline of transfer courses and requirements which these courses and requirements will satisfy for the degree you are seeking;

  c) A statement about your previous grade-point average/quality points and how they will affect or not affect (your new index);

  d) A written analysis of the number of semesters/quarter-hours and credits required to complete a degree in your currently stated major field of study (if applicable).

- You have the right to wait to respond to an offer of admission and/or financial aid until May 1.

- Colleges that request commitments to offers of admission and/or financial assistance prior to May 1, must clearly offer you the opportunity to request (in writing) an extension until May 1. They must grant you this extension and your request may not jeopardize your status for admission and/or financial aid.

WHEN YOU APPLY TO TRANSFER FROM ONE COLLEGE OR UNIVERSITY TO ANOTHER, YOU HAVE RESPONSIBILITIES

Before You Apply:

- You have the responsibility to research and understand the transfer policies and procedures of each college and university to which you plan to apply, including admission, financial aid, scholarships and housing. This includes being aware of any deadlines, restrictions and other transfer criteria. You also have to be sure that you understand the policies of each college or university regarding deposits that you may be required to make before you enroll.

As You Apply:

- You must complete all materials that are required for application and submit your application materials on or before the published deadlines. You should be the sole author of your applications.

After You Receive Your Admission Decisions:

- You must notify each college or university which accepts you whether you are accepting or rejecting its offer. You should make these notifications as soon as you have made a final decision as to the college you wish to attend.

- You may confirm your intention to enroll and, if required, submit a deposit to only one college or university. The exception to this arises if you are placed on a wait-list by a college or university and are later admitted to that institution. You may accept the offer and send a deposit. However, you must immediately notify a college or university at which you previously indicated your intention to enroll.

If you think that your rights as a transfer applicant have been denied, you should contact the college or university immediately to request additional information. In addition, you should notify the Executive Director of the National Association of College Admission Counselors, 1631 Prince Street, Alexandria, Virginia 22314-2818. This individual will notify the president of the NACAC state or regional affiliate who will initiate an investigation of your complaint.

The information ;presented here is consistent with the changes to the NACAC Statement of Principles of Good Practice approved in October 1993.

Appendix E: IACAC Statement of Practices and Courtesies

The Illinois Association of College Admission Counselors recommends the following standard practices and common courtesies be extended to and from hosts and participants in visits to high school or college campuses, college day/night programs, and other events which are arranged to assist the transition from secondary to higher education through the exchange of information.

A. Practices and courtesies which should be extended by representatives to high school counselors and other hosts:

1. Representatives should request appointments a minimum of one month in advance.

   a. If a request is made by telephone, written confirmation of the request and arrangements should follow.

   b. A request should include the telephone number and address of the representative.

   c. A request should be accompanied by self-addressed, return card or envelope.

2. If a representative cannot meet a scheduled appointment, the school counselor or host should be notified as soon as possible.

3. It is expected that representatives will be prepared to meet with all students without regard to race, nationality, creed, gender, or sexual orientation.

4. A representative should be well informed and should not misrepresent his or her institution or any other. If the representative is to be a student or alumnus rather than a paid employee of the institution, the high school counselor should be informed. The high school counselor or host should also be informed if a student or alumnus is to accompany the representative.

5. Institutions of higher education should assure that high school counselors receive the following information.

   a. A clear statement of admission policies, including transfer.

   b. The admission decisions on students from the high school.

   c. A listing of the students from the high school who attend the institution.

B. Practices and courtesies which should be extended by high school counselors and other hosts to representatives:

1. Secondary schools should make a serious effort to allow representatives of higher education to visit on a reasonable schedule, and should notify a representative of any change affecting an established appointment.

2. During a visit, a representative should have accommodations which allow for an adequate vocal interchange with a student or students. Arrangements in cafeterias or other general purpose areas in use at the time for other purposes should be avoided.

3. A representative should have the opportunity to meet a professional staff member of the host institution or, at a minimum, a trained volunteer who can collect college information about the representative's institution.

4. Secondary school personnel should, within legal limits, notify an institution of higher education of special information which would bear on a student's adjustment to, or development at, the institution of higher education.

5. If the high school counselor or other invited guest accepts an invitation to attend an institution's event, he or she should attend or arrange for a suitable replacement. If complete cancellation is necessary, it should be in time to allow the college or other institution to arrange for a replacement.

C. Practices and courtesies involving college programs:

1. Representatives should not attend a program unless officially invited and have the responsibility of accepting or refusing an invitation as soon as possible.

274

2. In selecting institutions for participation in college programs which are coordinated by the IACAC College Day/Night Calendar Committee, space limitations being the exceptional circumstance, all accredited, not-for-profit, two- and four-year colleges and universities should receive consideration for inclusion.

3. Representatives should arrive on time for a program and remain until the end.

4. Promotional and informational materials should be in good taste. Gifts, trinkets (i.e. pencils, keychains, candy, etc.), and monetary incentives are prohibited.

5. The use of audio-visual equipment or display materials should be left to the discretion of the host and stated in the invitation. When audio-visual or display materials are permitted, and shared facilities are used, they should not intrude upon another institution's presentation.

6. Conversations with students and parents are to be conducted in a professional manner. Representatives are asked to remain behind or on the side of tables, not in the aisles.

7. Institutions will be expected to notify the program sponsor if a representative other than a professional staff member or a faculty member will be attending the scheduled program.

8. Participation fees should be levied only to cover documented expenses other than institution facility costs, which should be borne by the high school or other host institution.

9. Programs should be scheduled through the IACAC College Day/Night Calendar Committee.

D. Methods for supporting this statement of practices and courtesies:

1. It is the responsibility of hosts and representatives to be cognizant of both the "IACAC Statement of Practices and Courtesies" and "Statement of Principles of Good Practice for Members of the National Association of College Admission Counselors."

2. Violations of this statement or the NACAC statement should be brought to the attention of the offending party. Negotiations based on the above mentioned statements should attempt to resolve the problem.

3. If a negotiated resolution cannot be reached between the offended party and the violator, the assistance of IACAC should be requested through the President, who will typically assign this task to the Admission Practices Committee.

Glossary

Accreditation. The process whereby a nationally recognized agency or organization grants public recognition to a unit of an educational organization (such as a school, institute, college, university, or specialized program of study) indicating that it meets established standards of quality, as determined through initial and periodic self-study and evaluation by peers. Accreditation provides professional judgment on the quality of the educational institution or programs offered and thus encourages continual improvement.

Admission, Conditional. Admission granted a candidate who lacks the minimum preparation prescribed by the admitting institution. Conditional admission may place the student on probation for a specified period of time or, in the case of an older student, until such time as the ability to do acceptable work has been demonstrated.

Admission, Rolling. A procedure by which decisions are made and applicants notified about their request for admission. Under this procedure, admission decisions are made continuously throughout the year, as opposed to applications being pooled during the year and all decisions being made within a limited time.

Admission, to Graduate Standing. For admission to graduate standing, an accredited baccalaureate degree and a specified grade average are generally required. Examinations may also be required. Frequently, the graduate dean or dean of the student's major department and/or a committee must approve the applicant, and personal recommendations may be required. Admission to a graduate school gives the privilege of taking coursework; it does not imply that the student will later be admitted to candidacy for a degree.

Admission, Transient. Admission, for a limited period of time, of a student who is regularly enrolled at another institution.

Admissions Committee. The group of individuals involved in reviewing applicant credentials or formulating admissions policy. In some cases, the committee is made up of all faculty or a number of faculty members elected by their peers.

Admissions Counseling. Guidance offered to prospective students to acquaint them with such matters as the choice of an institution, factors considered for admission, nature of studies at various levels, and preparation necessary for various occupational or professional goals.

Admissions Counselor. A professional staff member in the admissions office who provides information and advice for prospective applicants, parents, school counselors, and other interested persons. Usual duties will include participating in college fairs held days and nights, making individual visits to high schools, conducting interviews with applicants, assisting in admissions decisions, and answering correspondence.

Admissions Criteria. The clearly defined, institutionally approved, and systematically validated elements used to select students (e.g., high school record, letters of recommendation, course requirements, test scores).

Admissions Funnel. A graphic form of depicting (in an upside-down triangle) the number of admissions inquiries, applications, admitted, and enrolled, plus any additional segments of interest.

Admissions Information System. The procedures, methodologies, organization, software, and hardware elements needed to collect and retrieve selected data for an admissions operation.

Admissions Policy. Guidelines for establishing appropriate criteria for making student selection decisions.

Advanced Placement. Progressing beyond the normal academic level. A common illustration for secondary and college students is the exemption of basic-level coursework through the achievement of strong scores on subject matter examinations such as The College Board's Advanced Placement tests.

Advising. The process of assisting the student in planning and executing an educational program, with emphasis on meeting departmental and institutional requirements for graduation.

Aptitude/Achievement Tests. Various tests that may be used to indicate the general academic ability and levels of individual academic accomplishment. The two major postsecondary education entrance tests are the American College Testing (ACT) and Scholastic Aptitude Test (SAT).

Articulation. The process of coordinating enrollment patterns among colleges/universities. Traditionally referred to the transfer of students from two-year to four-year colleges; more recently it has come to involve double-degree programs and summer internships. May also refer to arrangements between high schools and colleges or exchanges of faculty among schools and colleges.

Attrition. A term referring to the portion of a class of students that failed to reenroll for a subsequent term, voluntarily or involuntarily, without completing the degree requirements. The term may also refer to the loss of those accepted applicants who failed to enroll.

Baccalaureate. A term referring to the bachelor's degree.

Basic Educational Opportunity Grants (BEOG). A federal grant (P.L. 92–381, Higher Education Act of 1965, Title IV-A, Section 411) to help qualified undergraduate students finance their postsecondary education.

Candidate's Common Reply Date. A generally accepted practice that allows candidates to respond to offers of admission until May. Refunds of tuition deposits submitted before May 1 should be refundable until May 1, if requested by that date.

Carnegie Unit. A unit for measuring the amount of secondary school work. One unit normally represents a year's study of one subject in a class meeting, comprising not less than 120 sixty-minute recitation hours or the equivalent.

Certificate, High School Equivalency. Issued by state departments of education upon evidence that a person has completed the equivalent of a high school course. Accepted by some colleges in lieu of the regular high school diploma. See also *GED.*

Chief Admissions Officer. The dean of admissions, director of admissions, or that person designated as primarily responsible for admissions functions.

Class Profile. A demographic and academic description of the characteristics of a selected class (or of a graduating high school or college class), including such data as numbers of applicants (graduates), acceptances, and enrollees; description of academic qualifications (distributions by rank, grade point average, test scores); and geographic origins.

Deferred Admission. The practice of allowing a student to begin studies one or more semesters later than originally intended. Students applying for early decision may also be deferred for later consideration with the full applicant pool.

Demographic Data. Scientific and social statistics based upon population statistics, socioeconomic and educational characteristics, and behavioral patterns. Demographic data reflect ethnic and racial proportions and patterns of participation, that is, historical rates of attendance.

Direct Access. The ability to obtain data from, or to enter data into, a storage device in such a way that the process does not depend on a reference to data previously accessed.

Distance Education. Begun in the 1980s, an educational methodology developed to permit students to take coursework away from the central site through electronic instruction.

Early Action. The practice of notifying students of their acceptance earlier than usual; commitment required at a later date.

Early Admissions. Practice followed by some colleges/universities allowing students to enter college prior to high school graduation.

Early Decision. The practice by which a student applies early to his or her first-choice college/university and, upon acceptance, commits to attend that college and withdraws applications at other colleges or else to notify the first-choice college of the intent not to enroll.

Electronic Data Interchange. The exchange, by electronic means, of educational records elements among official users.

Enrollment Management. The practice of coordinating activities related to the successful recruitment, enrollment, and retention of students.

Family Contribution. The amount determined by the needs analysis process that colleges will expect a family to be able to pay toward college/university.

Family Educational Rights and Privacy Act of 1974 (FERPA; formerly known as the Buckley Amendment). A federal law designed to protect the privacy of education records, to establish the right of students to inspect and review their education records, and to provide guidelines for the correction of inaccurate and misleading data through informal and formal hearings. Students and parents must have access to records and are protected against the dissemination of records without authorization. Students (and parents of minors) have the right to view all documents, including letters of recommendation, that students have not waived the right to view.

Feeder School. The schools (secondary and two- or four-year colleges) from which students enroll in a college or university.

Financial Aid Package. The combination of grants, loans, work, and the family contribution assigned to a student to use for attendance.

GED. General Education Development test. Issued by state departments of education upon evidence that a person has completed the equivalent of high school coursework. Accepted by some colleges in lieu of the regular high school diploma.

Goal. A major variable that the colleges/university will emphasize, such as profitability, enrollment, reputation, or market share.

Governing Board of Control. The decision-making body (e.g., board of trustees, college council, county executive board) that directs college/university operations through authorizations of revenue collection and expenditures broken down by program.

GPA. Grade point average, or high school or college academic average.

Inquiry System (Tracking System). The process through which prospective students are identified and communicated with during the recruitment process.

Internet. A collection of networks and gateways that use the TCP/IP protocol suite and function as a cooperative virtual network.

Kiosk. An arrangement, usually in an octagonal design, of computer stations whereby users (students, faculty, workers, customers, etc.) can access pertinent information.

Management Information System. A formal or rational plan whereby administrators receive and transmit vital information. It is an attempt to match information needs with information sources.

Marketing Plan. The administrative activities designed to promote a college/university to specific constituencies. A marketing plan for students might include a combination of elements such as publications, a video, one-on-one contacts, alumni visits, direct mail, advertising, and on-campus visitation programs.

Merit-Based Aid. Campus-based aid awarded to students based upon merit criteria, such as academic achievement or special talent.

Need-Based Aid. Aid awarded to students to meet their demonstrated financial need.

Need-Blind Admission. The acceptance of applicants to an institution without regard to the family or student's ability to pay.

Needs Analysis. The determination of the amount of financial aid needed by a student to balance his or her budget after taking into consideration money available from personal and parental resources and all sources outside the institution. The amount of financial need is the difference between these resources and a calculation of the student's expenses for the academic year.

Noncontinuous Enrollment. Those students who do not enroll in consecutive terms. This pattern affects retention. Often, special services are planned to avoid large numbers in a noncontinuous enrollment category. In institutions where noncontinuous enrolling is the rule rather than the exception, unique services are offered to these special students.

Nondiscrimination Statement. A statement defining compliance of the college/university with legal statutes against discrimination. Most college/university (all those receiving federal aid) are required to publish such a statement in official publications.

Nontraditional Students. Generally students who have been out of high school for some time and are beginning (or returning) to college/university study; occasionally, groups of students historically bypassed in higher education such as members of racial/ethnic groups, women in male-dominated disciplines (e.g., engineering), and men in female-dominated disciplines (e.g., nursing).

Objective. A goal of the college/university that is set with specific requirements relating to magnitude, time, and the persons or positions responsible.

Open Admission. The policy of a college/university to accept all students, regardless of level of performance, who have met certain prerequisites, such as high school graduation.

Operating System. Software that controls the execution of computer programs, which may provide scheduling, debugging, input/output control, accounting, compilation, storage assignment, data management, or other related services.

Optical Reader. A device that reads hand- or machine-written printed symbols into a computing system. Also called an optical scanner.

Orientation. A program through which entering undergraduates are made familiar with the aims of higher education, the principles governing the wise use of time and effort, methods of study, and the ideals and traditions of the college/university. It is also a period for tests and examinations that provide the faculty with a basis for advising and assisting students in planning their programs.

Output. The results produced by a computer program's execution.

Performance-based (Outcomes-based, Proficiency-based) Education. An educational system defining predetermined results of learning modules or curriculum plans.

Performance Program. A written document describing job responsibilities and defining the basis upon which job performance will be measured.

Portfolios. Admissions files and policies that include a wider array of credentials than simply academic records and standardized test results.

Positioning. The assignment or the posture of the institution or of a particular office or officer in the total enrollment management plan.

Precipice Admission. This processing methodology involves the establishment of a notification date before which only the most qualified applicants are accepted, after which applicants are ordered sequentially and admitted as long as space is available.

Professional Development. Formal and informal training and education, both on and off campus; involvement in professional associations and other activities that further an individual's professional knowledge and experience.

Random Access. To obtain data directly from any storage location, regardless of its position with respect to previously referenced information.

Random Access Storage. A storage technique in which the time required to obtain information is independent of the location of the information most recently obtained. This strict definition must be qualified by the observation that access is usually only relatively random. Thus, magnetic disks are relatively nonrandom when compared to magnetic core memory but relatively random when compared to magnetic tape.

Rank. The position of a student in his or her graduating class; weighted ranks refer to ranks that are computed by giving extra points for honors, Advanced Placement, or other advanced programs.

Readmission. The practice of admitting students to a college/university that they previously attended.

Records, Confidentiality of. The right of the student not to have his or her official educational record or other records released except through personal consent or another, legal process. See also *Family Education Rights and Privacy Act of 1974.*

Records, Permanent Academic (Educational). The official institutional document listing the student's courses, grades, and credits.

Recruitment. The act of providing information and service to prospective applicants and encouraging them to apply for admission.

Registration. The procedure by which students are assigned to classes. This process includes approval of courses to be taken by the student, organization of class sections, and the assessment and collection of fees.

Retention. The ability to keep students enrolled at a particular college/university.

Retention Programming. Activities that are intended to keep students enrolled, generally including tutoring, counseling, and other support services. Particular attention is paid to monitoring academic progress, campus climate, and financial aid issues. Retention, similar to enrollment management, is a campus-wide concern.

Retention Rate. The rate at which students persist in their educational program at an institution, often expressed as the percentage of an entering class that enrolls for each succeeding academic year and graduates within the normal time period.

Rolling Admissions. Sending status or decision notification issued when the applicant's file is complete (i.e., all required items and credentials have been received).

Satisfactory Academic Progress. The acceptable status of a student; specifically, he or she is in good academic standing, based upon grade point average and courses completed.

Scholarship. The quality of achievement of a student in his or her studies; financial or honorary award made to a student in recognition of superior scholastic ability or achievement and, possibly, his or her contribution to student life or scholarship. In many instances stipends or waivers are adjusted to the scholarship holder's financial need.

Scholarship, Endowed/Restricted. Endowed scholarships are provided through funds established by individuals or organizations. Restricted scholarships are limited to applicants who meet particular requirements in such matters as geographical or family origins, religious affiliation, or choice of curriculum.

Section 504. A section of education law referring to protection of the rights of disabled students with respect to the attainment of educational services. It states that colleges and universities must provide reasonable accommodation and access to all educational programs and facilities to all individuals capable of benefiting from such service.

Segmentation. Division among data that allows for special focus and planned action.

Selective Institutions. Institutions that have more qualified applicants than can be admitted and that generally accept only a small percentage of these candidates. Other categories include competitive institutions whose application processing allows acceptance of the best qualified applicants.

Special Talent Admission. The selection of candidates for admission based upon criteria related to extraordinary achievement or capability in a certain area (e.g., music performance, athletics, community service, leadership). Conformity with regularly defined admission criteria is not usually required.

SPEEDE/ExPRESS. The electronic exchange/transfer of student records information.

SPRE. The State Postsecondary Education Review Entities. A government provision to examine financial records of higher education institutions within states. Deleted from the 1996 congressional budget.

Standardized Test. Often included as a criterion for the selection of candidates, a standardized test is a widely administered exam intended to measure a specific achievement, competency, or aptitude. Common undergraduate admissions tests include the Scholastic Aptitude Test (SAT), Achievement Tests (ACH), the ACT, and the Test of English as a Foreign Language (TOEFL).

Strategic Planning. The process of defining the mission of a college/university.

Student, Transfer. A student who has withdrawn from one institution and been admitted to another.

Student, Transient. A student in good standing in any recognized institution who is taking work in another institution with the intent to transfer back to the first institution.

Student Budget. Total costs for attending a college/university used as the basis for awarding financial aid.

Target Population (or Audience). A specific group to which a communication or marketing program is directed (e.g., parents, counselors, multicultural students).

Title IV Programs. Those programs that were enacted under the 1965 Higher Education Amendments: NDSE, CWS, SEOG, BEOG, SSIG, GSL, and TRIO Programs.

Title IX. Refers to Title IX of the Educational Amendments of 1972.

TOEFL. The Test of English as a Foreign Language, which is administered by the Educational Testing Service and is an English language proficiency exam required of foreign student applicants for many universities. (Also administered by the College Board, TOEFL, Box 899, Princeton, NJ 08540.)

Transcript. A copy of the permanent academic (educational) record at an institution of higher education. The transcript becomes official when the seal of the institution is affixed and the signature of an authorized person is appended.

Transcript Evaluation. The appraisal of a transcript of the student's record from another institution to determine eligibility for admission and the advanced placement and credit to be granted.

Transfer Credit Evaluation. Determination of the amount of credit earned at one college/university that will be credited toward work at another college. For the optimum recruitment results, this information should be mailed to the applicant at the time of acceptance.

Transfer Student. A student who has earned college-level credit after high school at one college/university that will be credited toward work at another.

Tuition Deposit. A fee paid by an admitted student to reserve a space in the class at a college or university.

Viewbook. A publication produced to offer general information and pictures to the prospective student constituency.

Wait List. Student applicants awaiting notification about available space in the class.

Work-Study Program. A federally funded financial aid program that pays the college/university to give the student work at the institution.

Yield Rate. The percentage of students who accept a college/university's offer of admission; can also refer to the percentage of student prospects who file an application.

Suggested Readings

Allen, Deborah R., and Ralph W. Trimble. 1993. Identifying and referring troubled students: A primer for academic advisors. *NACADA Journal* 13 (Fall): 34–41.

American Association of Collegiate Registrars and Admissions Officers (AACRAO).
1988. *Emerging issues, expectations and tasks for the '90s: Report of the task
force on the '90s*. Washington, DC: AACRAO.

———. 1995. *Guidelines for postsecondary institutions for implementation of the Family
Educational Rights and Privacy Act of 1974 as amended*. Rev. ed. Washington,
DC: AACRAO.

American Association of Collegiate Registrars and Admissions Officers (AACRAO),
The College Entrance Examination Board (CEEB), the Educational Testing Ser-
vice (ETS), and the National Association for College Admission Counseling
(NACAC). 1986. *Standards and equity: Challenges in college admissions: Re-
port of a survey of undergraduate admission policies, practices and procedures*.
Washington, DC: AACRAO, CEEB, ACT, ETS, and NACAC.

———. 1995. *Challenges in college admissions: A report of a survey of undergraduate
admissions policies, practices, and procedures*. Washington, DC: AACRAO, The
College Board, ETS, and NACAC.

American Council on Education. 1988. *One-third of a nation: A report of the Commission
on Minority Participation in Education and American Life*. Washington, DC:
American Council on Education.

Astin, Alexander. 1994. *The American freshman: National norms for fall 1992*. Los
Angeles: Higher Education Research Institute.

Beal, Philip E., and Lee Noel. 1980. *What works in student retention: The report of a
joint project of the American College Testing Program and the National Center
for Higher Education Management Systems*. American College Testing Program
and National Center for Higher Education Management Systems.

Blackburn, J. C. 1979. Marketing techniques used by admissions officers. Unpublished
doctoral thesis, Indiana University.

California Postsecondary Education Commission (CPEC). 1992. *Postsecondary enroll-ment opportunities for high school students.* Sacramento: CPEC.

Campbell, Paul R. 1994. *Population projections for states, by age, race and sex: 1993 to 2020.* Washington, DC: U.S. Government Printing Office.

Canchola-Flores, Anthony. 1987. Target Hispanic students: A growing potential college market. *Admissions Strategist* 9: 17–22.

Carter, Deborah J., and Reginald Wilson. 1992. *1991 Minorities in higher education: Tenth annual status report.* Washington, DC: American Council on Education.

Clune, William H., Paula White, and Janice Patterson. 1989. *The implementation and effects of high school graduation requirements.* New Brunswick, NJ: Center for Policy Research in Education.

College Entrance Examination Board (CEEB). 1992. *1992–93 AP yearbook.* New York: CEEB.

Dannells, Michael. 1993. Theoretical perspectives on orientation. Designing success-ful transitions: A guide for orienting students to college. Paper delivered at the AACRAO Annual Meeting, April, Orlando, Florida.

Day, Jenifer. 1993. *Population projections for states by age, race, sex, and Hispanic origin: 1993–2050.* Washington, DC: U.S. Government Printing Office.

Deering, Ellen, ed. 1954. *Professional training recommended for the registrar and ad-missions officer.* Washington, DC: American Association of Collegiate Registrars and Admissions Officers.

Delworth, Ursula, Gary R. Hanson, et al. 1989. *Student services: A handbook for the profession.* San Francisco: Jossey-Bass.

Eaton, Judith S. 1989. Foreword to *Minorities on campus: A handbook for enhancing diversity,* ed. Madeleine F. Green. Washington, DC: American Council on Edu-cation.

Eck, Alan. 1993. Job-related education and training: Their impact on earning. *Monthly Labor Review* 116: 21–38.

Fidler, Paul P. 1991. Relationship of freshman orientation seminars to sophomore return rates. *Journal of the Freshman Year Experience* 3(1): 7–38.

Flanagan, Patricia A. 1992. *Raising standards—State policies to improve academic prep-aration for college.* Washington, DC: U.S. Department of Education.

Gillis, Ezra L. 1936. A graduate program suggested by registrars. *Proceedings.* Wash-ington, DC: American Association of Collegiate Registrars and Admissions Of-ficers.

Goldgehn, L. A. 1988. The interpretation of marketing in colleges and universities in the United States. Unpublished paper, University of San Francisco.

Gollnick, William A. 1990. The reappearance of the vanishing American. *College Board Review* 155 (Spring): 1–36.

Gordon, Virginia N., and George E. Steele. 1992. Advising major-changers: Students in transition. *NACADA Journal* 12 (Spring): 22–27.

Graff, A. S. 1986. Mobilizing for institutional change. In D. Hossler, ed., *Managing college enrollments.* New Directions for Higher Education No. 53. San Francisco: Jossey-Bass.

Hartnagel, Douglas. 1990. Telephone service as a marketing strategy. *College and University* 65(4): 328–34.

Harvey, James. 1984. *A nation at risk: The implications for educational reform.* Wash-ington, DC: U.S. Department of Education.

Hauser, J., and P. Lazarsfeld. 1964. *The admissions officer.* Washington, DC: American Association of Collegiate Registrars and Admissions Officers.

Head, Joe F. 1994. *Phone power for college admissions and the communications explosion.* 4th ed. Acworth, GA: Star Printing for Collegiate Telemarketing Institute.

Henderson, Stanley E. 1990. Competencies for admissions and records professionals: An AACRAO guide to entry and advancement in the profession. *College and University* (Spring): 243–59.

Hikes, Zenobia Lawrence. 1993. Decoding college admission for first-generation families. *Admissions Strategist* 19 (Fall): 9–13.

Hodgkinson, Harold. 1992. *A demographic view of tomorrow.* Washington, DC: Center for Demographic Policy, Institute for Educational Leadership.

Hossler, Don, John P. Bean, et al. 1990. *The strategic management of college enrollments.* San Francisco: Jossey-Bass.

Houghton, Mary J. 1993. *College admission standards and school reform.* Washington, DC: National Governors' Association.

Immerwahr, John, and Steve Farkas. 1993. *The closing gateway: Californians consider their higher education system.* San Jose: California Higher Education Policy Center.

International Baccalaureate. 1990. *Recognition policies of North American universities.* New York: International Baccalaureate.

Intersegmental Coordinating Council (ICC). 1993. *K–12 school reform: Implications and responsibilities for higher education.* Sacramento, CA: ICC.

Jackson, Marshall. 1987. Effective strategies for recruiting minority students. *Admissions Strategist* 9: 11–16.

Jacoby, Barbara. 1989. *The student as commuter: Developing a comprehensive institutional response.* ASHE-ERIC Higher Education Report No. 7. Washington, DC: School of Education and Human Development, George Washington University.

Johnston, William B., and Arnold H. Packer. 1987. *Workforce 2000: Work and workers for the twenty-first century.* Indianapolis, IN: Hudson Institute.

Judd, Charles H. 1924. Lines of study suitable for college registrars. *Proceedings.* Washington, DC: American Association of Collegiate Registrars and Admissions Officers.

Kally, Robert L. 1919. *Proceedings.* Washington, DC: American Association of Collegiate Registrars and Admissions Officers.

Kemerer, F., J. V. Baldridge, and K. Green. 1982. *Strategies for effective enrollment management.* Washington, DC: American Association of State Colleges and Universities.

Kinloch, Graham C., Geraldine A. Frost, and Charles MacKay. 1993. Academic dismissal, readmission conditions and retention: Study of social science majors. *NACADA Journal* 13 (Spring): 18–22.

Kramer, Gary L. 1992. Using student focus groups to evaluate academic support services. *NACADA Journal* 12 (Fall): 38–41.

Ladson-Billings, Gloria. 1990. Culturally relevant teaching: Effective instruction for black students. *College Board Review* 155 (Spring): 20–25.

Lehn, Mary B. J. 1931. Training administrative assistants. *Proceedings.* Washington, DC: American Association of Collegiate Registrars and Admissions Officers.

Lowery, William R., et al. 1982. *College admissions counseling: A handbook for the professional.* San Francisco: Jossey-Bass.

Lynch, R. G. 1969. Marketing the small college. *College Management* 4 (September): 56–58.

Magner, Denise K. 1993. Colleges faulted for not considering differences in Asian American groups. *Chronicle of Higher Education* (10 February): A32, A34.

Matthay, Eileen R., et al. 1991. *Counseling for college: A professional's guide to motivating, advising, and preparing students for higher education.* Princeton, NJ: Peterson's Guides.

Miles, Lorna. 1988. Learn from experience. *Currents* 14 (September): 27–30.

Morgan, R. 1994. *Effects of scale choice on prediction validity.* Princeton, NJ: Educational Testing Service.

Nakanishi, Don T. 1989. A quota on excellence? *Change* (November/December): 39–47.

National Association for College Admission Counseling. 1993. *Achieving diversity: Strategies for the recruitment and retention of traditionally underrepresented students.* Washington, DC: NACAC.

———. 1995. *The admission practitioner.* Alexandria, VA: NACAC.

———. 1998. *Membership directory and association policies.* Alexandria, VA: NACAC.

National Association of College Admission Counselors (NACAC). 1937. Minutes of a meeting of college representatives at the LaSalle Hotel, Chicago, in May. Washington, DC: NACAC Archives.

National Association of College and University Business Officers (NACUBO). 1989. *Assessing the cost of student recruitment at smaller independent colleges and universities.* Washington, DC: NACUBO.

Noel, Lee, Randi Levitz, Diana Saluri, et al. 1985. *Increasing student retention.* San Francisco: Jossey-Bass.

O'Brien, Eileen. 1990. Indian students' needs not the same as those of other minorities, advocates say. *Black Issues in Higher Education* (6 December): 22–23.

O'Connor, Patrick J. 1994. The needs of adult university students: A case study. *College and University* 69 (Winter): 84–86.

O'Hare, William. 1990. A new look at Asian Americans. *American Demographics* (October): 26–31.

Plante, Kathleen, Becky F. Smith, and Richard Bracklin. 1993. Components of a comprehensive orientation program. Designing successful transitions: A guide for orienting students to college. Paper presented at the AACRAO Annual Meeting, April, Orlando, Florida.

Pope, Loren. 1990. *Looking beyond the Ivy League: Finding the college that's right for you.* New York: Penguin Books.

Quann, C. James, et al. 1979. *Admissions, academic records, and registrar services: A handbook of policies and procedures.* San Francisco: Jossey-Bass.

Ray, Howard N., W. Kent Moore, and John E. Oliver. 1991. Evaluation of a computer-assisted advising system. *NACADA Journal* 11 (Fall): 21–27.

Richardson, Charles. 1993. A baker's dozen: What a president should know about recruiting and retaining students of color. *ACCESS: The newsletter for recruiting and retaining students of color* 1 (July): 4–5.

Roehr, Robert J., ed. 1991. *Student recruitment—Electronic advancement.* Washington, DC: Council for the Advancement and Support of Education.

Scannell, James J. 1992. *The effect of financial aid policies on admission and enrollment.* New York: College Entrance Examination Board.

SHEEO/NCES Communication Network. 1994. Alternate approaches to college admission. *Network News* 13 (October): 4.

Snyder, Thomas D., and Charlene M. Hoffman. 1994. *Digest of education statistics 1994*. Washington, DC: U.S. Department of Education.

Spicuzza, Frank J. 1992. A customer service approach to advising: Theory and application. *NACADA Journal* 12 (Fall): 49–58.

Strumpf, Gerry, and Greg Sharer. 1993. Trends and issues in orientation programs. Designing successful transitions: A guide for orienting students to college. Paper presented at the AACRAO Annual Meeting, April, Orlando, Florida.

Suzuki, Bob H. 1989. Asian Americans as the "model minority": Outdoing whites? or media hype? *Change* (November/December): 12–19.

Tanner, Jeffrey M. 1985. Paper presented to the American Association of Collegiate Registrars and Admissions Officers, Cincinnati, Ohio.

Thresher, B. Alden. 1966. *College admissions and the public interest*. New York: College Entrance Examination Board.

Tinto, V. 1987. *Leaving college: Rethinking the causes and cures of student attrition*. Chicago: University of Chicago Press.

Treadwell, D. R., Jr. 1977. In admissions, the ideal director boasts the speech of Demosthenes and the patience of Job. *Chronicle of Higher Education* 14(7): 18.

University of California Board of Regents. 1995. *Policy on undergraduate admission*. Oakland: University of California.

Upcraft, M. Lee, Richard H. Mullendore, Betsy O. Barefoot, and Dorothy S. Fidler, eds. 1993. *Designing successful transitions: A guide for orienting students to college*. Columbia: University of South Carolina.

U.S. Bureau of the Census. 1993. *School enrollment—Social and economic characteristics of students: October 1992*. Current Population Reports, Series P-20, No. 474. Washington, DC: U.S. Government Printing Office.

Vinson, D. E. 1976. *The admissions officer: A decade of change*. Dissertation copy 77-08, 122. Ann Arbor, MI: University Microfilms.

Index

About the Contributors

WAYNE E. BECRAFT has been Executive Director of the American Association of Collegiate Registrars and Admissions Officers (AACRAO) since 1989, following brief terms as Associate Executive Director and Interim Executive Director (1987–1989). Prior to that he was Director of Admission and Registration Services at The University of Maryland University College, a position he held for fifteen years. During his term as Executive Director, he has worked closely with the AACRAO Board of Directors to implement a Strategic Plan for the Association and to expand the programs and services available to the membership.

JAMES C. BLACKBURN is Director of Admissions and Records at California State University–Fullerton, a position he has held since 1986. Previously, he served as Director of Admissions at the University of Northern Colorado and at campuses of the University of North Carolina and the University of Tennessee. Dr. Blackburn holds graduate degrees from the University of Tennessee and Indiana University. He has completed the Management Development Program at the Harvard Graduate School of Education. His work has appeared in *College and University*, *The College Board Review*, and elsewhere.

JOHN CASTEEN was named the University of Virginia's seventh president in 1990. He served as Dean of Admissions at Virginia from 1975 to 1982. In 1982, he was appointed Secretary of Education for the Commonwealth of Virginia. He served as President of the University of Connecticut from 1985 to 1990. A medievalist, Mr. Casteen has taught in the English departments of the universities of California (Berkeley), Connecticut, and Virginia.

LINDA M. CLEMENT is Assistant Vice President and Director of Undergraduate Admissions at the University of Maryland, where she has worked in undergraduate admissions for the past fifteen years. She has also held positions in other student service areas (e.g., residence halls and orientation). She has been active in College Board activities, has served as chair of the Middle States Regional Council, and is currently a Trustee of The College Board. She has been a frequent presenter at College Board Regional and National meetings, and with coauthor Teresa M. Flannery has been leading workshops on marketing research for NACAC.

MICHAEL G. DOLENCE is President of Michael G. Dolence and Associates. He consults with educational institutions, government agencies, and corporations on strategic management and organizational transformation. He is a leading presenter at AACRAO's annual Strategic Enrollment Management Conferences and Annual Meetings. Mr. Dolence has written extensively in the areas of strategic planning, information resource management, and organizational decision processes. Among his latest titles are *Strategic Enrollment Management: Cases from the Field* (editor), *Transforming Higher Education: A Vision for Learning in the 21st Century* (co-author), and *Strategic Change in Colleges and Universities: Planning to Survive and Prosper* (co-author), all available from AACRAO. Forthcoming is a SEM Primer for Community Colleges.

TERESA M. FLANNERY is the Executive Director of University Communications and Director of University Marketing at the University of Maryland. From 1986 to 1997 she worked in Maryland's Office of Undergraduate Admissions as an admission counselor, Assistant Director for Marketing and Research, and most recently as Associate Director for Marketing. Flannery has served as a member of NACAC's Professional Development Committee and has consulted with many admission officers on the development and application of market research in college admissions. A contributing author to NACAC's *The Admission Practitioner*, Flannery and co-author Linda M. Clement were also commissioned by NACAC to conduct a national study of admission practices in 1996 that culminated in the *NACAC Early Decision and Early Action Report.*

DIANA GUERRERO is Director of Admissions at The University of Texas at El Paso, has been a member of the American Association of Collegiate Registrars and Admissions Officers (AACRAO) for over twenty-five years, and is the 1995–1999 AACRAO Vice President for Enrollment Management, Admissions, and Financial Aid. She is a contributing author to AACRAO's *Becoming a Leader in Enrollment Services: A Development Guide for the Higher Education Professional* (1987) and *The Admissions Profession: A Guide to Staff Development and Program Management* (1991).

JOE F. HEAD is a senior-level collegiate administrator with more than two decades of experience, including positions as Dean of Admissions, Director of Admissions, and Director of Recruitment in public and private institutions. He is currently Dean of Enrollment Services at Kennesaw State University. He has written several telecounseling articles for national and regional publications including The College Board's *Admissions Strategist* and CASE *Currents* magazines. He is currently chair of the AACRAO Task Force on Certification and Credentialing Standards for Enrollment Officers.

STANLEY E. HENDERSON is Associate Vice President for Enrollment Management at the University of Cincinnati. Prior to this, he was Director of Admissions and Orientation at Western Michigan University. He has co-edited *The Admissions Profession: A Guide for Staff Development and Program Management* (1991) and wrote "Competencies for Admissions and Records Professionals: An AACRAO Guide to Entry and Advancement in the Profession" (1990). His professional interests in staff development have made him a frequent presenter at the regional and national levels on innovative methods to enhance productivity and encourage professional development. His involvement in the emerging enrollment management field led him to chair the first AACRAO Strategic Enrollment Management national conference in 1991. He has been active in the American College Testing Program's state councils and in AACRAO's regional and national programs. He served as President of AACRAO in 1996–1997.

MARY LEE HOGANSON has been the College Counselor at the University of Chicago Laboratory School since 1982. She served as Vice-President for Admission Practices of the National Association for College Admission Counseling from 1990 to 1994. She has also served as an officer for the Illinois Association for College Admission Counseling (IACAC). She is a member and Chair-Elect of the Midwest Regional College Board Council. Her articles have appeared in the *Journal of College Admissions*, the IACAC newsletter, and she is author of an article on selecting a college which appears in The College Board's *College Times* and *The College Handbook*. She is a frequent presenter on ethics in college admissions.

TIMOTHY D. LETZRING is Associate Professor of Higher Education at the University of South Carolina. His research focus revolves around law and higher education. He has made numerous presentations to national audiences and published in this area. Tim is also the coeditor for *The College Student and the Courts*, a quarterly publication for practitioners on the various court decisions affecting colleges and students.

GRETA S. MACK has over 25 years of experience in higher education as a teacher and administrator. She has been active in AACRAO throughout that period. From 1988 to 1996 she was Associate Director of Admission Services for the California State University System. Prior to that she was Director of Admission and Records at Arkansas State University. Her special interest in the educational needs of diverse student groups is currently being utilized at Al Akhawayn University in Ifrane, Morocco, where she serves as Director of Enrollment Services.

M. OVERTON PHELPS is Director of Admissions Emeritus, University of Georgia. He is currently serving as a travel and educational consultant in the Athens, Georgia area.

KATHLEEN G. PLANTE is Registrar and Director of Admissions at Louisiana State University (LSU) in Shreveport, where she oversees all admissions, recruitment, records, and registration-related activities for the university. Prior to joining LSU in 1987, she served for fourteen years in a number of related positions at the University of Arkansas at Little Rock. Currently, she serves as Past President of AACRAO, having served as President in 1996–1997, and as Vice President for Professional Development, Research and Publications from 1991 to 1994.

CLIFFORD SJOGREN served as Director of Admission at The University of Michigan from 1972 to 1988 and as Dean of Admission and Financial Aid at the University of Southern California from 1989 to 1993. He continued as a board member and school visit representative for the International Baccalaureate of North America and chair of the National Collegiate Athletic Association committee. He has been a consultant on foreign student educational records. Now retired, he is seriously engaged in volunteer work out of his Traverse City, Michigan home.

JOYCE E. SMITH has served in both public and private college admissions counseling positions at Kansas State University, Amherst College (MA), and Queens College, CUNY, where she worked as the Executive Director of Admissions, Marketing and Scholarship Services for undergraduate and graduate admissions. In the area of association management, she was the Program Service Officer of the Student Search Service of The College Board for seven years. She is now executive director of the National Association for College Admission Counseling.

DONALD STEWART is President of The College Board, a post he has held since 1987. Before coming to The College Board, Dr. Stewart served for ten years as the sixth president of Spelman College. Dr. Stewart is an advisor to, trustee, or director of the Martin Luther King, Jr. Center for Nonviolent Social Change; Center for National Policy, Grinnell College; Teachers College, Columbia University; and the Committee for Economic Development. He is a member of the Council on Foreign Relations and former chairman of the National Advisory Committee on Accreditation and Institutional Eligibility of the U.S. Department of Education. Dr. Stewart also served as trustee and board chairman of the Educational Testing Service and as director and vice-chairman of the American Council on Education.

DAVID H. STONES has been at the University of Texas at Austin since 1965 as a student and staff member. He has managed the Student Information Systems since 1979. He has been active in TACRAO, SACRAO, and AACRAO, and served as President of SACRAO. He has been active with the EDI and the SPEEDE movement since it began in 1988.

CLAIRE C. SWANN has had a long tenure of responsibility for recruitment, enrollment planning and strategy, operations, and orientation programs and services. A student personnel administrator whose professional career began 35 years ago, she has held counseling positions, college housing positions, and various admissions assignments at a small private college and at a large public research university. She is now an educational consultant for the Southern Association of Colleges and Schools and is an educational consultant and chairperson of secondary school five-and ten-year studies, renewal and improvement planning. She is the University of Georgia's Emerita Director of Admissions.

STEVEN T. SYVERSON has been Dean of Admissions and Financial Aid at Lawrence University in Appleton, Wisconsin, since 1983. Prior to that he served as Director of Admissions at Pomona College in Claremont, California. His activity with professional organizations includes service as Vice President for Admissions Practices (Ethics) of the National Association for College Admission Counseling (NACAC); as President of the Wisconsin Association for College Admissions Counseling (WACAC); as a member of the Wisconsin ACT Council, and the Wisconsin Advanced Placement Advisory Council.

TIM WASHBURN has served as Executive Director of Admissions and Records at the University of Washington since 1975. He served as University Registrar from 1969 to 1975. He has served in many professional capacities including Vice President and President of the Pacific Association of Collegiate Registrars and Admissions Officers, Vice Chair of The College Board Council on Entrance Services, member of the Governor's Council on School to Work, and many task forces dealing with curriculum articulation between educational sectors. Presently, he serves on the Washington Higher Education Board's Admissions Standards Action Committee, the State Board for Community and Technical Colleges' Articulation Committee, and is Vice-Chair of the Washington ACT Advisory Council.

D. PARKER YOUNG is Professor of Higher Education in the Institute of Higher Education at the University of Georgia. He has received the Outstanding Contribution to Literature or Research Award by the National Association of Student Personnel Administrators. The Association for Student Judicial Affairs has created the D. Parker Young Award, to be given annually to recognize the outstanding scholarly achievement of an individual in the area of higher education, law, and judicial affairs.